THE
CANCEL
CULTURE
CURSE

THE
CANCEL
CULTURE
CURSE

FROM RAGE TO REDEMPTION IN A WORLD GONE MAD

EVAN NIERMAN
MARK SACHS

Skyhorse Publishing

Skyhorse Publishing books may be purchased in bulk at special discounts for sales promotion, corporate gifts, fund-raising, or educational purposes. Special editions can also be created to specifications. For details, contact the Special Sales Department, Skyhorse Publishing, 307 West 36th Street, 11th Floor, New York, NY 10018 or info@skyhorsepublishing.com.

Skyhorse® and Skyhorse Publishing® are registered trademarks of Skyhorse Publishing, Inc.®, a Delaware corporation.

Visit our website at www.skyhorsepublishing.com.

10 9 8 7 6 5 4 3 2 1

Library of Congress Cataloging-in-Publication Data is available on file.

Hardcover ISBN: 978-1-5107-7719-4
eBook ISBN: 978-1-5107-7755-2

Cover design by Evan Nierman

Printed in the United States of America

Contents

Foreword

Anyone reading this book might inadvertently find themselves in the eye of a cancel culture-related storm, facing great risk to their reputation and livelihood.

Evan Nierman and Mark Sachs are strategic communications professionals who operate in the eye of that storm every day, so nobody is better positioned to write the definitive account of how to avoid and mitigate the scourge of cancel culture.

The "post-first, think-later" nature of social media has fundamentally changed the tempo of our lives—of *your* life—and this is nowhere more evident than in the way information, true and untrue, spreads virally. Too often, innocent people and organizations have their lives disrupted and sometimes ruined.

To once again be perfectly blunt: *it could happen to you*. You need a guide to help you prevent yourself from becoming the victim of a cancel culture attack, and you need to know what to do if the worst happens. *The Cancel Culture Curse* is that guide.

This book weaves insights drawn from academia, politics, business, and culture, to discuss how the profoundly illiberal phenomenon of cancel culture was able to spring from America's classically liberal tradition. It also breaks new ground by amending and enhancing previous academic research by introducing an actionable new definition of cancel culture that will help individuals, companies, and professionals from all industries maneuver with confidence through the minefield.

On that note: the title of this book is not subtle, but its value lies in the fact that it is not a tunnel-visioned polemic. It is a handbook for smart and sober decision making, drawing on many case studies and solid research and data to back up its assertions. Importantly, *The Cancel Culture Curse* does not dismiss the fact that while social media has amplified the voices of those who would "cancel" others over real or imagined missteps, it has also amplified—particularly on loosely moderated platforms—the voices of hate. The more time we spend online, the more racism, homophobia, transphobia, antisemitism, Islamophobia, misogyny, and other forms of bigotry are unfortunately present in our lives. Actions can, and often should, have consequences. In today's environment, however, it becomes difficult to match the punishment to the crime, and this book can help.

Evan and Mark's trailblazing six-part framework for identifying true examples of cancel culture will help readers parse the previously fine line between unfair cancellation and the rightful, even the righteous, opprobrium sometimes owed to the worst actors in society—which, sometimes, can itself help to save a reputation or a business.

While this book is aimed at anyone who faces potential reputational risk, which is to say, nearly everyone, it will be an indispensable tool for communications professionals. This is precisely the kind of accessible, practical text that I like to assign to my undergraduate and graduate students at the University of Southern California's Annenberg School for Communication and Journalism, because it provides concrete advice and specific recommendations from practitioners who are deeply immersed in their fields of expertise.

I have advised corporations, nonprofits, and individuals on high-stakes strategic communications matters for nearly three decades, and I have had a front-row seat to some of the most consequential corporate and political crises during that time period—from the Whitewater Investigation to the BP oil spill to countless small businesses and entrepreneurs who had to weather potentially disastrous, but ultimately manageable, situations.

Bringing almost any of these assignments to a successful conclusion would have been exponentially more difficult in today's environment. *The Cancel Culture Curse* is the handbook we all need for the crises of today and the future. The pages that follow will arm you with the tools to protect yourself, both on- and offline.

Dave Quast
Adjunct Faculty University of Southern California
Annenberg School for Communication and Journalism

How to Read This Book

The Cancel Culture Curse was written to expose the harmful practice of cancel culture, and to help put an end to it as soon as possible.

While the chapters are assembled here in a logical order, you do not have to read this book sequentially. So please feel free to jump around, spending more time on the sections of particular interest to you.

To make navigating easier, and to highlight the most fundamental points, we have included a summary of key points at the end of each chapter.

For those who prefer to read this book in the traditional manner, from cover to cover, we certainly will not object. As in every aspect of life, we each need to find our own path. At the end of the day, all we really ask for is your open-minded consideration of our perspectives and the ideas we share.

In addition to defining cancel culture for the first time, we also have endeavored to provide a playbook for survival, while also sharing ways to help you avoid getting canceled in the first place.

Moving forward, we will continue to make the case against cancel culture until the practice has been eliminated and the term relegated to an outdated reminder of a regrettable bygone era that arose quickly but faded fast.

We look forward to continuing the conversation in the American spirit of intellectual debate. We want to recognize how grateful we feel to live in a country that guarantees its citizens the greatest measures of freedom, and to be alive at such an exciting time of rapid technological advancement that can be wielded in wonderful ways. Our nation is like each of us: imperfect works in progress, but with limitless potential.

This book is neither intended to settle all arguments nor to be the final word on this topic. We remain hopeful that it will spark more discussions and, ideally, contribute in some small measure to making the world a more positive and forgiving place.

Sincerely,

Evan Nierman and Mark Sachs

Why This Book Matters

The only thing we have to cancel is cancel culture itself.
—Evan Nierman (with appreciation to
Franklin Delano Roosevelt)

Put simply, this is a book that matters. Because if you think that cancel culture affects only large corporations or A-list celebrities, then think again. In fact, it is the average person who is most at risk. Every single human being who walks the planet makes mistakes and is therefore in danger of being struck down by cancel culture. This is true for individuals from every background imaginable, and for organizations across all industries.

We in the United States used to love nothing more than a good comeback story, but in twenty-first-century America, it is increasingly difficult to rebound once you take a fall. To date, cancel culture has been heavily concentrated in the United States, but should cancel culture leave our shores, the reputations and livelihoods of people all over the world could be in jeopardy.

To be clear, this is not a political book, nor is it a thinly disguised attempt to advance a partisan agenda. Our principal aim is to expose the ugly face of cancel culture, and to make the case that this hateful and harmful practice needs to stop.

For those looking for a comprehensive accounting of canceled people—living and dead—you will need to look elsewhere. Unfortunately, that list is long and growing by the day, and it would have been grossly out of date by the time this book hits the shelves. We thought it more useful to define for the first time the elements of cancel culture, based upon research, and share a playbook born from own experiences counseling cancel culture victims through traumatic times.

We intend to illustrate how cancel culture is fundamentally un-American, running counter to the values upon which the United States was created and that were forever enshrined by the Founders in the documents that form the basis of our government and culture.

While all persons found guilty of offenses and crimes should face consequences, we also believe that every accused American should continue to enjoy the right to due process and a presumption of innocence. Mob justice must never become a preferred, let alone acceptable, method for silencing or punishing fellow citizens with whom we disagree.

In these pages we will examine the trends that have led to making cancel culture possible, looking at how cancel culture campaigns have been employed, and by whom. We will also share best practices and offer guidance for what to do if you or those you know find yourselves the target of a cancel culture mob. We call these people "cancel vultures" because they thrive upon picking apart others, shutting down debate, making all mistakes permanent, and removing the opportunity for people to atone for their sins and seek salvation.

The cancel culture curse is presently afflicting our society. But for the good of our nation, our culture, our world, and our future, we must band together to break the spell.

Introduction to Cancel Culture

"We are watching you. Racist bitch. We will make sure your business will always suffer. Accuse us and will [sic] accuse you. Burn in hell and will [sic] piss on your grave."

The email arrived from a sender using the name Black Lives Matter. Similar emails followed, as well as posts submitted via the general feedback form on the website.

"Lisa, you are one UGLY fucking whore !!!!!! Eeewww. Have you looked in the mirror? You are a seriously ugly cunt. How on EARTH did you ever become the CEO of a skincare company????? You filthy, ugly old cunt. Do you have any kids, bitch? I bet you don't. I bet your husband has to hold his nose while fucking you, cause you are one disgusting piece of dogshit. Fuck you, you fucking old ugly CUNT."

"Hello RACIST. I hope you never earn another dollar. You are the scum of the earth. You think you're better than the HOMEOWNER you were harassing. You're NOTHING ma'am. Absolutely NOTHING!! There's a special place in hell for bigots like you!!!"

"Fuck you, Karen. You're a bad person."

"I hope you trash get what you deserve. Cancel culture got your bitch asses quick. Can't wait to see what's next!!"

Years after a video lasting less than two minutes went viral, attracting global attention and media coverage, skincare CEO and entrepreneur Lisa Alexander is continuing to receive similar hate mail messages.

Out for a walk in her San Francisco neighborhood on a pleasant summer day, she came upon a man drawing on the wall adjacent to a historic home owned by a neighbor she knew. At the time, she was unaware that her neighbor rented rooms to boarders. She did not recognize the person, whose back was to her and who was wearing a mask, since this was during the coronavirus pandemic in June of 2020. As she addressed the stranger, asking him, "Sir, do you live here? Pardon me sir, do you live here?" he spun around with his mobile phone at the ready, recording the encounter.

A testy exchange ensued in which the man asserted that Alexander was "accusing me of a crime," suggesting to her that she call the police. She said she did not want to do that and in fact never actually did. The man then demanded to know her name, while refusing to tell her his, saying, "I'm asking you the questions." Narrating his video once the conversation ended, the man said, "And that, people, is why Black Lives Matter." He then aimed the camera at the stencil on the wall before turning the camera back to the woman, following her down the street. "That's Karen, and she's calling the cops. And this is gonna be really funny. Because she knows the people who live here . . . personally." The details of the encounter are addressed later in the book alongside an interview with Lisa Alexander, who is stepping forward for the first time to tell her side of the story.

Several days after that chance encounter on the street, the man who filmed the incident posted the video online with the assistance of a public relations firm. Within days, Alexander's cosmetics company LAFACE was utterly destroyed, and the stress from the ongoing ordeal nearly ended her life. The Better Business Bureau and various reviews sites were bombarded with negative posts and complaints that completely erased years of positive reviews and a stellar reputation.

A furor erupted on Twitter, where Alexander was "doxed," meaning her name, address, and phone number were posted online. Death threats began barraging her via text, phone calls, and voicemails. A group of people arrived at the building where she lived—she saw them as she peeked out from the windows in her home. According to Alexander, some members of the assembled mob were armed with baseball bats, and even firearms.

One person was able to secure entry to her building and began banging on her door, threatening her and demanding that she come out. Strangers began calling her family members, promising they would make the harassment go away in return for money.

An avalanche of stories aired in the media, making headlines across the globe. Her business associates broke off all ties, essentially ruining the company. Under duress, Alexander issued an apology, but the threats kept coming. Ultimately, the stress forced her body's nervous system to shut down, and she was rushed to the hospital for emergency surgery from which she has never fully recovered.

Years after this experience, she and countless others like her who have endured similar assaults are left to wonder: Is there life after cancellation? Is there a way to survive the cancel culture curse?

CHAPTER 1

Cancel Vultures

The Trolls Who Justify Their Cancel Culture Antics

There are too many people in the world today who think nothing of canceling someone else. Many of them, in fact, wear it as a badge of honor, proud to have taken part in a cancel cultural campaign that claimed a victim. A term that we use to describe those who participate in cancel culture assaults is *cancel vulture*.

Other than the word "vulture" rhyming with "culture," making it particularly convenient as a phrase for bullies who target and attack a weaker victim, it is a term that accurately depicts what takes place when a mob descends on its target. After all, vultures are large, ugly birds who thrive by picking apart others who have perished. Drive along any highway and you will eventually come across a piece of roadkill. And where you find roadkill, you will find vultures congregating nearby.

Vultures like to travel in groups. A group of flying vultures is called a "kettle," which is an odd term but fittingly suggests that they may be cooking up trouble. A group of vultures feeding on carrion is termed a "wake," reminiscent of the identically named gathering that comes in the wake [pun intended] of a person passing away. Meanwhile, vultures at rest are called a "committee," which parallels nicely with groups of people sitting behind computer screens who then come together to target, tar, and tear apart other people. In essence, a cancel culture attack is trial and summary execution by committee—an unelected group bringing their collective efforts to bear to achieve their destructive desired outcome. Cancel vultures are like nature's vultures in many ways, and not just because of the just-discussed nomenclature. Both types of vultures do not care too much about what prey they find, so long as they can feast on the remains.

Cancel Vultures and the Roadkill That Sustains Them

If you think about the people who engage in cancel culture as vultures, then their victims are a lot like the mangled animals left for dead somewhere alongside the highway. Roadkill victims—like cancel culture victims—usually suffer severe blows and must fend for themselves in a state of incapacitation or severe injury. People who have become embroiled in reputational crises often refer to the experience as being "run over by a truck" or "hit by a bus." The sentiment is meant to convey that, with shocking speed and perhaps unexpectedly, they have been stunned and harmed, with their entire world turned upside down.

Comparing life in the digital age to being on a highway is a simile that was previously explored in the book *Crisis Averted: PR Strategies to Protect Your Reputation and the Bottom Line* by Evan Nierman. In that instance, a person receiving unwanted media attention was described as a slow-moving turtle seeking to avoid being destroyed by fast-moving cars whizzing past, which represented the press and public opinion. The book cautioned that inaction and seizing up in "analysis paralysis," where you do nothing out of fear and fail to defend your own reputation, place you at high risk of being crushed to death like a turtle on a highway.

To carry that same construction forward, once you have been hit by cancel culture, your reputation and future career prospects are in mortal jeopardy. Stunned and wounded, lying on your back, you nevertheless need to pull yourself together and seek to save yourself. The cancel vultures, like nature's vultures, will in short order begin circling overhead, perceiving your death to be imminent and preparing to devour you.

Another Source of Sustenance

Cancel vultures come in all shapes and sizes. At present, no hard data exist to reveal the typical profile of a person who chooses to target others in activist assaults. After all, this is part of cancel culture's potency. You never know who is behind that Twitter handle, posted comment, or Reddit thread. The Internet demands neither accountability nor transparency.

People are not obligated to reveal themselves online. Much of the time, people online are playing a role, donning masks, disguising themselves, and hiding behind obscured identities. People who participate in cancel culture attacks can include anyone who has access to the web. This could include children, teenagers, young adults, and adults. Essentially anyone from eight to eighty or beyond.

Participating in a cancel culture attack often results in no negative consequences for the cancel vultures who make them possible. After all, if you play a role in taking someone down, then most people are unlikely to be aware that you have done so unless you choose to brag about it online. Proxy servers, hidden ISP addresses, and made-up usernames enable people to go online and savage someone's reputation or target them with heinous messages or threats and never get caught.

As Internet access continues to expand by leaps and bounds and the world grows increasingly digital, there is no limit to the number of people who can participate in cancel culture unless a shift occurs and the practice is dropped. Most people never peer behind the curtains to see the magnitude and lasting impact of cancel culture. They read about scandals in the media, watch videos of "Karens" or "Brads," and consume information about the incidents that generated headlines without ever speaking to the actual human beings involved. But in our case, we have met and conversed with many of these people. We have listened to their stories and learned about the stress and trauma they experienced during, for many, the darkest hours of their lives.

We have also seen firsthand the horrifying messages that cancel vultures, spurred into action by their own motivations—self-righteous or not—have delivered to others. In many instances, the communications are shocking, intimidating, and designed to instill horror and fear. The words of the vultures are wielded as menacing weapons. During an attack, cancel culture victims typically receive an onslaught of these messages through a variety of media, including text messages, phone calls, voicemails at home or their places of business, and email messages to their individual and work email accounts, as well as the general inboxes of their employers. They take the form of horrifying statements posted in the comments sections of mainstream press and more fringe outlets. They occur in discussion boards, online social media threads, and virtual rooms and meetups where strangers congregate to share their perspectives in the public square.

Many cancel vultures never pause for a moment to consider the harm they are causing. If they took the time to learn the facts or had the opportunity to speak with the objects of their derision or to learn more about the context surrounding controversial events, then perhaps they would pause before participating.

Reality Check

For many of the vultures, there is a significant difference between what they are willing to do or say online anonymously, as opposed to what they are willing to do or say face-to-face, in real life. One example involves the husband of a woman who was the target of online abuse. Her crime was putting herself "out there" as a candidate for public office. By doing so, she instantly became a public figure, and a critical mass of people in her community suddenly had someone to target with strident but untrue accusations. She was labeled a criminal and cheater. She was accused of defrauding other companies, acts that she had certainly never committed; the charges were patently false.

In this case, the man attacking her on a Facebook page heavily followed within the local community was posting under his own name, so the identity of the cancel vulture was never in doubt. As luck would have it, the candidate's husband ran into the online detractor at a community event and confronted the individual. He approached him in a calm manner but told him firmly: "Stop insulting my wife and spreading lies about her. You know they are not true, so cut it out."

The cancel vulture was shocked. For him, being forced to confront real-life consequences for his online behavior was a scary thing. He immediately began to stammer, raising his voice and bringing his hands up defensively, palms outstretched toward the candidate's husband as if to calm him and de-escalate the situation. In mere seconds, a group of others, including friends of the online gadfly, gathered to separate the two men and ensure that the encounter did not turn physical.

The event went on without incident; the vulture retreated and hours later emerged where he felt most at ease: seated safely behind his computer keyboard at home. He proceeded to recount the incident for the public from his perspective. He wrote that he simply could not believe that this person had been so rude as to confront him verbally in a public forum. After all, his statements were merely Internet banter. In other words, he freely admitted to the world that the things he would do and say online to attack someone else were things he would never even consider doing in real life.

The online detractor being forced to confront the humanity of the people he was attacking should be an eye-opening episode. It illustrates the mind-set of a critical mass of cancel vultures in our society today. The vast distance in the digital space between cancel vultures and their targets frees them to insult, abuse, and wound people in ways they never would in person.

Like nature's vultures for whom they are named, cancel vultures sustain themselves by picking apart the remains of others. Is there any hope that they might channel their energies elsewhere and stop feasting upon women and men who have been hurt and could be facing their demise? Perhaps. And that is one of the core goals of this book.

SUMMARY OF KEY POINTS

- Cancel vulture is a term for describing someone who participates in cancel culture assaults.
- Groups of cancel vultures are called a "committee," which is fitting because cancel culture is trial, conviction, and execution by an unelected committee.
- The anonymity of the Internet makes it possible for cancel vultures to strike with impunity.
- Those who cancel others do not consider the serious harm they are causing.
- There is a gap between the behaviors of people online and those in the real world.
- Like nature's vultures for whom they are named, cancel vultures sustain themselves by picking apart the remains of others.

CHAPTER 2

Defining Cancel Culture

The topic of this book is cancel culture, but how exactly should we define this phenomenon? The Merriam-Webster online dictionary defines one form of the verb *cancel* as: "to withdraw one's support for (someone, such as a celebrity, or something, such as a company) publicly and especially on social media."[1] It defines cancel culture as "the practice or tendency of engaging in mass canceling as a way of expressing disapproval and exerting social pressure."

We live in a time of near continual controversy, but not every situation in which someone faced negative online attention is a cancel culture event. People and organizations are often criticized or suffer consequences from bad behaviors. They receive unflattering publicity or scrutiny. Do such actions always qualify as cancel culture events?

Cancel culture is talked about with increasing frequency in the media—the subject of discussions on the Left, the Right, the Center, and everywhere in between along the political spectrum. It is a topic that touches business, politics, music, entertainment, and each area of life. At the end of the day, cancel culture is coercive, illiberal, and destructive. It creates an environment of fear, of knowing that your behaviors, perspectives, actions, or ideas can be seized upon by a group of people whose only mission is to destroy you.

On the Left, there is a tendency to downplay the impact of cancel culture or deny that it is really a problem. In some quarters, cancel culture is praised. It is seen as a necessary tool for holding powerful people accountable and mobilizing the masses to ensure that those in positions of influence cannot get away with whatever they wish. The Right, on the other hand, uses cancel culture as a political weapon. It decries it as a creation of the "woke" movement on the Left, brushing off scandals involving a conservative as the result of a so-called cancel culture campaign. To the Right, cancel culture is a buzzword, a natural successor to political correctness run amok, put on steroids, and activated by the liberal media and leftist elites.

This book gives an overview of the underpinnings of American society: a commitment to free speech, a free marketplace of ideas, and individual liberty and expression. At its core, cancel culture is completely at odds with each of these values. We examine the crushing consequences that cancel culture is visiting upon everyday citizens. We provide recommendations for how people who find themselves under fire should conduct themselves if their hope is to emerge with the possibility of reclaiming their livelihoods and dignity.

Valuable Observations from Previous Explorations

To date, several instructive and valuable books have been written on this topic, adding to the understanding of its harmful effects. In *Cancel This Book* (also published by Skyhorse Publishing), Dan Kovalik provides a litany of shocking examples of cancel culture in action. He reveals that his own family was hesitant that he would become a target simply by taking on a topic that he correctly noted "involves public humiliation and job/career loss." Kovalik expresses his concern "that the goal of canceling . . . is not to educate or to advance the cause of social justice, but to punish and ostracize; it is not a means to an end; it is the end."[2]

Polarizing British media personality Piers Morgan has for years shone a bright light on "illiberal liberals" in his book *Wake Up* and various other opinion pieces and interviews in which he fearlessly criticizes the "woke" movement. "The origin of woke was well-intentioned," Morgan told *60 Minutes* in an interview with Karl Stefanovic. "It was to have an awareness, to be awake to racial and social justice. We can all sign up to that. But it's been hijacked by a bunch of extremely illiberal people professing to be liberals, who have now become the modern-day fascists."[3,4]

Morgan himself was temporarily, though not permanently, canceled when he lost his job on leading English television program *Good Morning Britain*. Reportedly, 41,000 complaints were filed with his employer, including by Meghan Markle herself, after Morgan reacted to Prince Harry and his wife's blockbuster interview with Oprah Winfrey by saying, "I'm sorry,

I don't believe a word she said, Meghan Markle. I wouldn't believe it if she read me a weather report."[5]

After storming off the set of the show and with his job hanging in the balance, Morgan then stated publicly, "I said I didn't believe Meghan Markle in her Oprah interview. I've had time to reflect on this opinion, and I still don't. If you did, OK. Freedom of speech is a hill I'm happy to die on."[6] Given an ultimatum by his bosses to apologize on-air to Markle or give up his right to voice his opinion without fear of retribution, Morgan left the program he hosted.

Bill Maher is another media personality who regularly uses his show to express opposition to the practice of cancel culture. "We have to get past this endless, unforgiving, zero tolerance mind-set bent on punishing and disappearing anyone caught saying the wrong thing. The right response to speech you don't like is more speech, not the lazy, cowardly response of canceling people," Maher said on his show *Real Time* on Feb. 11, 2022.

Meanwhile, one of America's most prolific writers and well-known First Amendment champions, Harvard Professor Alan Dershowitz, has written extensively on the topic of cancel culture. He has done so in a compelling book titled (aptly enough) *Cancel Culture,* as well as in *Guilt by Accusation: The Challenge of Proving Innocence in the Age of #MeToo* and a vast number of opinion pieces appearing throughout top-tier media.

In *Cancel Culture,* Dershowitz describes the phenomenon as "a cancer on American democracy," deriding its fundamental denial of due process and lamenting that it not only harms the accused, but also deprives others of the opportunity to benefit from the teachings or perspectives of the people who have been canceled. He calls for the practice to be replaced by debates "contested in the marketplace of ideas" and warns of the "great dangers to liberty that lurk in the insidious encroachment by men and women of zeal, well-meaning, but without understanding."

Dershowitz's conclusion is as powerful as it is chilling:

> Cancel culture causes more problems than it solves. It falsely accuses; it applies a double standard of selectivity. It fails to balance or calibrate vices and virtues. It has no statute of limitations; it provides no process to challenge cancellations. It is standardless, unaccountable, not transparent, and often anonymous. It hides personal, ideological, and political agendas. It can be abused for revenge, extortion, and other malign motives. It is un-American to the core. It must be stopped lest it destroy the heart, soul, and values of our nation.[7]

In a later chapter, we will dive into some of Dershowitz's observations related to cancel culture and due process, exploring how legal trials are being impacted by PR warfare and reputation assassination. We will also share excerpts from an interview with us in which he spoke about the personal impact of being canceled.

This book seeks to build upon the work done before by these and other authors, academics, and journalists who have written about the topic and related areas of inquiry. While we interviewed numerous people who have been canceled, it would have been an impossible task to speak with, or even to enumerate, every example. There are simply too many cases and new incidents arising every day.

Through our readings of history and contemporary thinking, we have arrived at the conclusion that cancel culture sits in direct opposition to American values, and that cancel culture must itself be canceled. But to do so effectively, we believe it valuable to define—for the first time—the elements that comprise cancel culture.

It is important to recognize at this juncture that there are innumerable instances where people have lost their jobs, become the targets of lawsuits, or been subjected to public scrutiny, mockery, or worse. Many claimed to have been cancel culture victims, when in fact, they were not.

This country has always possessed effective mechanisms by which people could be held to account for their actions. Due process is a fundamental concept in the United States, and a critical aspect of our democracy. We have a judicial system that, while imperfect, has operated effectively for centuries. The American justice system is predicated upon the idea that all people are entitled to due process and should have fair opportunity under the law to be heard, present evidence, and make a case for themselves. In this country you are innocent until proven guilty.

Since the beginning of time, people have been making bad decisions and doing harmful things for which they have been punished. Societies have always enacted certain standards, mores, laws, and legal structures to hold people accountable. Those institutions have become more robust through the years owing to centuries of legal precedent and evolving scholarship. We do not need cancel culture to hold people accountable. And we certainly cannot allow justice to be farmed out to vindictive lynch mobs that subject people to threats, force them into financial ruin, and permanently destroy their ability to gain employment or function in society.

The Elements of Cancel Culture

Our review of preexisting literature on the topic and review of hundreds of specific instances in which people were targeted has led us to conclude that there are six fundamental elements to cancel culture.

Just as we have derived value from contemporary writers on the topic, we have arrived at this first-of-its-kind definition of cancel culture owing to the scholarship of others who came before. Albert J. Bergeson is a professor of sociology and member of the graduate faculty at the University of Arizona. He wrote a 1978 paper for the *Journal for the Scientific Study of Religion* called "A Durkheimian Theory of 'Witch-Hunts' with the Chinese Cultural Revolution of 1966–1969 as an Example."[8]

"Durkheimian" refers to Emile Durkheim, a French academic regarded as the father of sociology, who wrote extensively on the forces undergirding society and religious groups. In *The Division of Labor in Society*, written in 1893, Durkheim describes with uncanny prescience the same societal forces that Bergeson related to witch hunts, and which we see playing out today in the form of cancel culture. Durkheim cautioned that "we should not say that an act offends the common consciousness because it is criminal, but that it is criminal because it offends that consciousness."[9]

In the following passage, Durkheim describes the nineteenth-century process of collective outrage, which in the twenty-first century proves to be even more potent owing to widely available technologies and the Internet, which accelerate and amplify scandals and facilitate cancel culture attacks:

> We have only to observe what happens, particularly in a small town, when some scandal involving morality has just taken place. People stop each other in the street, call upon one another, meet in their customary places to talk about what has happened. A common indignation is expressed. From all the similar impressions exchanged and all the different expressions of wrath there rises up a single fount of anger, more or less clear-cut according to the particular case, anger which is that of everybody without being that of anybody in particular. It is public anger.[10]

In his work, Bergeson used the groundbreaking writings of Durkheim to draw conclusions about what constitutes a political witch hunt, identifying three aspects of political witch hunts that also apply to cancel culture.

The first is **accusations of crimes against the collective**. Writes Bergeson: "The various charges that appear during one of these witch hunts involve accusations of crimes committed against the nation as a corporate whole. It is the whole of collective existence that is at stake; it is The Nation, The People, The Revolution, or The State which is being undermined or subverted."

The second is that **political witch hunts arise quickly:** "Witch hunts seem to appear in dramatic outbursts: they are not a regular feature of social life. A community seems to suddenly find itself infested with all sorts of subversive elements which pose a threat to the collective as a whole. Whether one thinks of the Reign of Terror during the French Revolution, the Stalinist Show Trials, or the McCarthy period in the United States, the phenomenon is the same: a community becomes intensely mobilized to rid itself of internal enemies."

The third is that **the charges are often trivial or fabricated:** "These crimes and deviations seem to involve the most petty and insignificant behavioral acts which are somehow understood as crimes against the nation as a whole. In fact, one of the principal reasons we term these events 'witch-hunts' is that innocent people are so often involved and falsely accused."

In their book, *The Coddling of the American Mind*, First Amendment expert Greg Lukianoff and social psychologist Jonathan Haidt write about the current state of American universities. The authors assert that three untruths have been taught to the generation studying at institutions of higher learning and preparing to enter the workforce. These three untruths are: their feelings are always right, they should avoid pain and discomfort, and they should look for faults in others and not themselves. Lukianoff and Haidt contend that these three untruths have led to rising rates of depression and anxiety and have produced intense divides that manifest themselves on American college campuses.

Writing in Chapter five, titled "Witch Hunts," the authors reference Bergesen in the context of dramatic and strident controversies happening on American college campuses. Lukianoff and Haidt cite the three elements outlined above, while adding an additional witch hunt feature that consti-tutes the fourth defining element of cancel culture: **fear of defending the accused:** "When a public accusation is made, many friends and bystand-ers know that the victim is innocent, but they are afraid to say anything. Anyone who comes to the defense of the accused is obstructing the enact-ment of a collective ritual. Siding with the accused is truly an offense against the group, and it will be treated as such. If passions and fears are intense enough, people will testify against their friends and family members."[11] In the case of cancel culture, this could also be extended to totally abandoning them.

While we believe these elements of witch hunts identified by scholars should be applied to cancel culture, we wish to add two additional elements.

The first is **disproportionate response.** Without full consideration of facts or context, a coalition forms around the aggrieved. The reaction is often furious and far-reaching, involving efforts to shame, embarrass, punish, and cause lasting, sometimes permanent, harm.

The second element we suggest adding to the definition of cancel culture is **moral absolutism.** Those engaged in cancel culture do so with the conviction that their beliefs and actions are morally just, and therefore justified. To the cancel culture mob, people expressing or demonstrating heretical ideas are believed to have transgressed; therefore, they warrant whatever punishment the mob ultimately deems necessary.

CANDEM—The Cancel Culture Elements

For the first time, we are now able to put very clear markers around what is—and what is not—an instance of cancel culture. These six elements can be remembered easily through the acronym CANDEM (pronounced *condemn*). It is a fitting mnemonic device, considering cancel culture entails a mob engaging in the practice of condemning a target, condemning their behavior, condemning their perspectives, and ultimately condemning them to consequences with life-altering repercussions.

To reiterate and clarify, the core elements that define cancel culture as represented by CANDEM:

C   Collective considered victim of the crime
A   Arising and accelerating quickly
N   Nature of the offense is trivial or fabricated
D   Disproportionate response
E   Everyone is afraid to defend the accused
M   Moral absolutism by those doing the canceling

We think about these elements as constituting a checklist. If five or six of the elements are present, then it certainly qualifies. However, if only three or four of the elements are present, then questions exist as to whether the incident actually deserves to receive the cancel culture label. If only one or two of the elements are present, then the situation should not be described as cancel culture.

The **C** in CANDEM refers to the fact that a perceived objectionable statement or action is often viewed as an affront to some collective—a much larger group—rather than to a single individual. This plays out time and again, whether the collective relates to race, gender identity, religious affiliation, sexual orientation, or otherwise. When one person insults another, or has a disagreement, then it is a one-to-one incident. But cancel culture demands that a larger group of people is brought into the discussion, expanding the controversy to represent a person's contempt or disrespect for a larger group of people. That collective group of "victims" then becomes the aggressors, mobilizing to exact justice against the alleged offender.

The **A** refers to the rapid rate at which the outrage around a person or incident arises and accelerates. This is largely due to the power of the Internet, which can transform an issue from a small, insignificant exchange into a global conversation in mere moments. The speed of the Internet, fed in part by the 24-hour news cycle and often with a critical role being played by the media, amplifies incidents and catalyzes action related to the controversy.

The **N** in the acronym is a reminder that the natures of the offenses at the root of cancel culture events are almost always insignificant, and sometimes even fabricated. A poorly worded tweet alone does not constitute racism. Too often, a video or social post that goes viral is taken out of context. The actual transgression, when viewed in context, is often far less damaging than the mob purports it to be.

The **D** in our cancel culture checklist is for disproportionate response. Few among us would say we are infallible, and those who would can more accurately be described as delusional. Errors in judgment happen. Mistakes happen, and quite regularly consequences result from those mistakes. As the saying goes, actions have consequences. What is critical, however, is that fair consequences be applied by the rule of law and through reasonable considerations. In the context of cancel culture events, the consequences far outweigh the alleged transgression, and in many if not most cases, the disproportionate consequence is in response to words or ideas, and not actions.

The **E** in CANDEM is included because everyone is afraid to get involved once a cancel culture campaign gets underway. In the days of the Salem Witch Trials, neighbors turned on one another. Once a person was falsely accused, their family members and friends were under pressure to disavow them lest they be charged with also being witches. The modern-day version means that anyone who sympathizes or expresses allyship with a cancel culture victim runs the risk of having the mob turn on them. This explains why many organizations are quick to dissociate from employees who come under fire. Even corporations are terrified of attracting the mob's ire. "The main problem with 'cancel culture' as I see it is that it suppresses speech and coerces people into staying silent about things they believe and that others also believe too, but about which they are afraid to speak," writes attorney, author, and peace activist Dan Kovalik in *Cancel This Book*.[12] The result of all of this is that the accused is left isolated.

CANDEM's **M** refers to the moral absolutism declared by the cancel vultures who dedicate themselves to attacking and picking apart the remains of those taken down. Cancel culture would not be possible if those engaged in the process were not certain of their own moral superiority. Those engaging in mob rule allow no doubt that they are right, and the accused is wrong. Facts are never in question. Cancel vultures believe themselves to be morally and absolutely right and are willing to go to great lengths to prove it.

A group's perceived moral supremacy over others, combined with the conviction to enforce that view, presents a danger to society. The willingness to physically, emotionally, and financially destroy others for the good of a collective has been at the root of all significant, large-scale tragedies throughout human history. Kovalik correctly notes in his book that "now many seem to see it as a badge of honor to effectively get someone fired, so long as they are fired in the ostensible interest of social justice or anti-racism."[13] To a cancel vulture looking to shut down someone else, the ends justify any means.

Based on the CANDEM elements, a more precise and accurate definition of cancel culture is warranted: "The use of intimidation by a morally absolute coalition to isolate and disproportionately punish an alleged transgressor."

Illiberal Punishment

When directed at people for their ideas, cancel culture presents itself as the latest incarnation of an age-old practice: silencing those perceived as pushing dangerous views. In the sixteenth century, Galileo proved Copernicus's heliocentric theory. The Catholic Church declared him a heretic for contradicting Biblical teachings, and he was sentenced to house arrest for the remainder of his life. In the seventeenth century, more than 200 people were accused of practicing witchcraft during the Salem Witch Trials.

Is today's cancel culture any worse than or different from historical efforts to cancel people? In some ways, there are similarities. Historically and now, publicly shaming, silencing, and discrediting is wielded against those espousing beliefs deemed harmful to the collective. While the means for punishing the accused may be less violent today, the underlying anger and overall approach are the same.

Contemporary writers, academics, artists, and countless others have faced campaigns waged to discredit them. The brutal stabbing of writer Salman Rushdie at Chautauqua Institution, described on its website as a "community of artists, educators, thinkers, faith leaders and friends dedicated to exploring the best in humanity," is an example of how far some people will go to literally silence those with whom they disagree.[14]

The illiberalism that led to a religious decree authorizing Rushdie's murder is not a consequence of cancel culture, but it does reflect the exact same illiberalism and hostility inherent in cancel culture. Two hundred years ago, a man accused of violating public norms could be faced with mob justice that included lynching, tarring and feathering, or death by firing squad. Today, however, that same man would face public shaming, the loss of his job, abandonment by friends, and social isolation.

Having arrived at the CANDEM framework for defining cancel culture, we can now use these elements to evaluate and help determine a more appropriate response. It also provides a useful lens through which to reflect on what took place, both in real time and after the fact. Our hope is that we, as a country, will eschew mob mentality and bring about the end of cancel culture, not just in our lifetimes, but ideally, as soon as possible. Hopefully, years from now we will look back on this era of cancel culture as a blemish—an age of rage in a world gone mad.

Who knows? Perhaps the 2020s will prove to be as shameful a chapter in the history of American society as the Salem Witch Trials of the 1600s. Witch trials are natural precursors to cancel culture attacks, since the same elements exist across both. Moving forward, when you hear stories of people or organizations being deplatformed, avoid a rush to judgment, apply the CANDEM criteria to their circumstances, and properly and reasonably consider what should be done.

SUMMARY OF KEY POINTS

- Not every situation involving public shame or scorn is cancel culture.
- The political Left downplays or ignores cancel culture, while the Right uses it to its advantage.
- Some media personalities from across the political spectrum have led the charge against cancel culture.
- Cancel culture is antithetical to American values and must itself be canceled.
- Cancel culture is the modern-day incarnation of witch hunts, pogroms, or lynchings.
- Much has been written about the topic, but until now nobody has truly defined cancel culture.
- Our definition of cancel culture is "The use of intimidation by a morally absolute coalition to isolate and disproportionately punish an alleged transgressor."
- *The Cancel Culture Curse* identifies six elements that are hallmarks of cancel culture, which can be remembered using the acronym CANDEM:
    o Collective considered victim of the crime
    o Arises and accelerates quickly
    o Nature of the offense is trivial, minor, or fabricated
    o Disproportionate response is enacted
    o Everyone afraid to get involved
    o Moral absolutism by those doing the canceling
- The Six Elements of Cancel Culture provides a means by which to evaluate incidents and correctly classify them as cancel culture or otherwise.

CHAPTER 3

A Brief History of American Liberty

It is liberty that fundamentally comes under assault when cancel culture attacks are pursued.

This book is not primarily about philosophy or political science. However, because cancel culture is at odds, and in constant tension, with the foundational American value of liberty, it is important to examine why the Founders placed such primacy on this concept and what it means in the American context, both at the time of the founding nearly 300 years ago and today.

Doing so reveals how our understanding of this most important philosophical underpinning of our democracy has evolved into something the Framers of the Constitution probably would not recognize.

Foundational Freedom

The Founders, and particularly those who framed the Constitution, believed in government by the people, but they knew that a pure democracy, unchecked by countervailing institutions, could lead to mob rule. Understanding human nature, the Founders knew that mob rule could stifle civil liberties and allow the majority to trample on minority rights.

That is why they established a constitutional republic—a form of democracy, not an alternative to it—to codify key democratic provisions to protect civil liberties, while also establishing nondemocratic institutions to protect against tyranny. The Constitution creates a system of checks and balances, which include undemocratic institutions like the Supreme Court, and a complex electoral system for selecting a president, with the hopes of foreclosing on the possibility of pure majority—meaning, potentially, mob—rule.

It is frequently noted that the Constitution describes a government of enumerated powers, while the people enjoy unenumerated rights. To resist the temptation of governmental overreach, the Constitution restricts the federal government's powers to only those it enumerates. The Bill of Rights, on the other hand, sought to restrict government power to impinge on individual liberties. Though the Bill of Rights does enumerate certain rights—free exercise of religion, free speech, protections against self-incrimination, to name a few—the Ninth Amendment says that "the enumeration in the Constitution, of certain rights, shall not be construed to deny or disparage others retained by the people."

When viewed in its entirety, the US system of government outlined in the Constitution can be seen as protection against the rise of a demagogue.

The Federalist Papers, as they are now known, was a series of eighty-five essays and articles written to rally support for the ratification of the Constitution. Future Treasury Secretary Alexander Hamilton wrote most of the essays, with future President James Madison, and future Chief Justice John Jay, penning the rest.

In Federalist #17, Hamilton wrote of the challenges that would arise from a federal government that sought to administer the private justice between individuals:

> It is therefore improbable that there should exist a disposition in the federal councils to usurp the powers with which they are connected; because the attempt to exercise those powers would be as troublesome as it would be nugatory; and the possession of them, for that reason, would contribute nothing to the dignity, to the importance, or to the splendor of the national government.[15]

George Washington, John Adams, Thomas Jefferson, James Madison, and Alexander Hamilton, regardless of which side of the Democratic-Republican and Federalist divide they found themselves, all agreed that a federal government should have no ambition to manage the individual affairs of its citizens. To do so would create a government so large and complex as to:

form so many rivulets of influence, running through every part of the society, cannot be particularized, without involving a detail too tedious and uninteresting to compensate for the instruction it might afford.[16]

The Founders understood that a limited government would leave open the opportunity for individuals to take advantage of their liberties, often at the expense of others. That is why John Adams warned Americans that the "Constitution was made only for a moral and religious people. It is wholly inadequate to the government of any other." Not least, the Constitution requires people of good faith and of all political persuasions, especially those who take an oath to defend it, to respect and abide by its tenets. There is some evidence that there has been some erosion of that good faith in recent years and that some have sought to take advantage of this by acting in more demagogic ways than politicians have acted in the past.

The Idea of Liberty

The Founding Fathers and Framers of the Constitution were greatly influenced by the philosophies of Thomas Hobbes and John Locke, two great minds of the seventeenth century, as well as eighteenth-century thinkers David Hume and Adam Smith. In their various writings, these philosophers explored heady topics including the meaning of liberty, the proper role of government, and the nuanced aspects of democracy that would form the philosophical foundation of the United States of America and inform our founding documents.

Thomas Hobbes argued that man's state of nature, which he defined as man's life in the absence of government to provide structure and safeguards, would be a constant state of fear and war. Never knowing who would attack and when, man would be predisposed to wage war preemptively, attacking others before he could be attacked: "I put for a general inclination of all mankind, a perpetual and restless desire of power after power, that ceaseth only in death."[17]

Hobbes believed that man's passions alone would guide him, casting reason aside in favor of survival. Without a government possessing absolute power, which he called a leviathan, man's state of nature would consign man to a life that would be "solitary, poor, nasty, brutish, and short."[18] Moreover, unless citizens lived under a strong government that could wield power and deliver consequences, covenants would only have the strength of words "and [be] of no strength to secure a man at all."[19]

Hobbes recognized that man's passions could lead to a constant state of war, positing that a government formed by a consenting people, and imbued with absolute power, could mitigate such violence. However, in doing so, he also raised the question of whether man had rights beyond those required merely for survival.

John Locke examined that very question. The philosopher and physician, considered one of the founders of classical liberalism, believed that man could, in fact, govern his passions by reason and moral principles. Thus, "every man, by consenting with others to make one body politic under one government, puts himself under an obligation . . . to submit to the determination of the majority."[20]

According to Locke, the primary purpose of government was to pass laws enshrining the rights of people to "life, liberty, and property." This idea was later slightly adapted and permanently enshrined in the American Declaration of Independence:

> We hold these truths to be self-evident, that all men are created equal, that they are endowed by their Creator with certain unalienable Rights, that among these are Life, Liberty and the pursuit of Happiness. That to secure these rights, Governments are instituted among Men, deriving their just powers from the consent of the governed.

With those liberties granted to them, Locke believed people would be free to willfully engage, without fear, in all aspect of commercial and social life.

In essence, Hobbes believed man's worst instincts could only be harnessed by the imposition of absolute rule. Conversely, Locke believed that mankind would enjoy a nobler, happier, and more fruitful life by "agreeing with other men to join and unite into a community for their comfortable, safe, and peaceable living one amongst the other, in a secure enjoyment of their properties, and a greater security against any, that are not of it."[21]

What's more, Locke argued, "the end of law is not to abolish or restrain, but to preserve and enlarge freedom: for in all the states of created beings capable of laws, where there is no law, there is no freedom."[22]

Self-Rule and Self-Restraint

Well-versed in Greek, Roman, and Enlightenment philosophy, the Founders sought to create a polity that could adequately balance an individual's right to liberty and the government's need to exercise some reasonable constraints.

If the people possessed adequate moral principles and the disposition to self-regulate their behavior, defined by a general set of established mores—grace, gratitude, and generosity, which promote life, liberty, and happiness—the government could be expected to resist the ambition to grow too large or too powerful.

Over time, these mores inevitably evolve, and our scope of the Framers' emphasis on individual liberty evolves, as well. This is to be expected in a free and open society, where many behaviors previously deemed unacceptable eventually normalize. Consider, for instance, how public acceptance has evolved in the past century on a wide range of issues including everything from the acceptable length of a man's hair to couples cohabitating before marriage to interracial relationships and the use of marijuana.

During times of transition, people naturally respond to changing realities by demanding or seeking to regulate the behavior of people displaying what society happens to consider unacceptable behaviors at that moment in time. This, of course, flies in the face of the idea of a government with enumerated powers protecting, rather than impinging on, individuals with unenumerated rights.

In these examples and so many others, demands by some to regulate the behaviors of others result in illiberal societal restrictions that reduce individual liberty. Economist and philosopher F.A. Hayek, author of *The Road to Serfdom*, argued passionately against imbuing states with too much economic and financial power, lest they lead to regimes that crush individual rights and invite destructive conflicts.

Put another way, a Hobbesian march toward illiberalism, where some individuals seek power over other individuals, is a march away from the values that have made democratic societies vibrant, successful, and free.

John Stuart Mill, a nineteenth-century political philosopher committed to Lockian principles, wrote that:

> [Liberty] comprises, first, the inward domain of consciousness; demanding liberty of conscience, in the most comprehensive sense: liberty of thought and feeling; absolute freedom of opinion and sentiment on all subjects, practical or speculative, scientific, moral, or theological. The liberty of expressing and publishing opinions may seem to fall under a different principle, since it belongs to that part of the conduct of an individual which concerns other people but, being almost as much importance as the liberty of thought itself, and resting in great part on the same reasons, is practically inseparable *from it*.[23]

Mill goes onto profess that:

> No society in which these liberties are not, on the whole, respected, is free,
> whatever may be its form of government; and none is completely free in
> which they do not exist absolute and unqualified. . . . Mankind are greater
> gainers by suffering each other to live as seems good to themselves, than
> by compelling each to live as seems good to the *rest*.[24]

Limits on individual liberties can be imposed by people or governments.
They can emanate from the political Right or the Left and be undertaken by
communists or nationalists, by blackshirts or skinheads, by theocratic governments or secular ones. In fact, the only common value shared by these
ideologies, which possess such contradictory views, is that they are authoritarian—or populist (authoritarianism's less-scary sounding little brother)—
in their belief that individualism and the liberties that define it should be
subordinate to the will of the majority, as long as the majority agrees with
the ideologues. Authoritarian populism on the political left and the political
right are, in fact, very similar, but antithetical to individual liberty as the
founders of the United States, and the classical liberal thinkers who inspired
them, understood it.

So, present-day culture shows us that Hobbes, Locke, and the Founding
Fathers were largely correct. In a society that loses its philosophical and
moral moorings and where citizens are fearful and perhaps even hateful,
what results is a global citizenry all too willing to engage in increasingly
populist, if not authoritarian, behaviors based solely on the ideas expressed
by those with whom they disagree. Whether attempts to "cancel" arise from
the Left or Right, cherished democratic principles are eroded.

For generations, America has prided itself and has been held up as a
global model for maintaining the rule of law, upholding due process, and
sustaining a free and open marketplace of ideas. But that world is slowly
being distorted into an Orwellian and dystopian one that seems to share as
much with the seventeenth century as the twenty-first.

Life in America during the seventeenth century included the Salem
Witch Trials, where more than 200 people in one town in colonial
Massachusetts were accused of practicing the devil's magic and nineteen
were summarily executed. In many cases, these people were convicted based
upon hearsay and false accusations from neighbors. Harsh societal punishments were exacted on citizens in the form of town square lynchings,
public shamings, and the enforcement of strict moral codes that greatly

limited individual liberty. Nathaniel Hawthorne's work of historical fiction *The Scarlet Letter* refers to the letter "A" emblazoned upon the clothes of a woman convicted of adultery as a means of calling attention to her sexual transgressions. Indeed, devices such as stocks and pillories were employed to imprison people and subject them to public scorn in the form of hurled stones and verbal abuse.

In the twenty-first century, cancel culture has produced modern-day witch hunts in which people are accused by others and consequently subjected to threats and sometimes even physical violence. Many current forms of intolerance share strong similarities with the religious fundamentalism practiced by the Puritans in colonial America. Today's scarlet letters come in the form of destroying a person's online reputation, and permanently hindering their personal and professional aspirations.

Our latest technologies, like the Internet and the myriad devices that we use to connect to it throughout the day, are employed to enforce rapidly changing moral codes through public shaming and humiliation, while simultaneously curtailing people's rights, including, as the Declaration of Independence states, their rights to "life, liberty, and the pursuit of happiness."

Liberty as an Intrinsic versus Instrumental Value

In moral philosophy, something is defined as possessing instrumental value if it helps to achieve a goal. Intrinsic value, on the other hand, is a goal in and of itself. For example, financial resources or an impactful job are means to an end, and therefore of instrumental value. Happiness and unfettered freedom are intrinsically valuable.

In the context of liberty, the instrumental value of liberty implies that freedom is good only to the extent it confers some benefits to society at large. If liberty does not advance us toward a better end collectively, then it is not necessarily good. Conversely, the intrinsic value of liberty implies that personal liberty is an end to itself. You can see where the tensions lie in those two definitions.

Viewing liberty as merely an instrumental value to its fullest and most dangerous degree produces authoritarianism, where the state controls every aspect of individuals' lives. On the other hand, the most extreme expression of the liberty-only-has-intrinsic-value argument could lead to anarchy, with each person choosing entirely the limits, if any, of their actions based on what provides the most benefits to them alone. In a balanced context, people would be willing to subordinate some intrinsic liberties in pursuit of goals that have instrumental value to the society in which they live. In other words, there is a balance between responsibilities to society and rights as individuals.

At the root of our society's most difficult ethical questions is this push and pull between instrumental and intrinsic values. And people's unique vantage points and life experiences lead them to see things through different lenses. For instance, is assisted suicide an instrumental or intrinsic liberty? Is it of greater instrumental value or intrinsic value to provide drug addicts with syringes? To what extent is same-sex marriage and a person's right to marry the person they love an instrumental or intrinsic liberty?

Whether we recognize it or not, nearly every policy decision we make is analyzed through these lenses. In healthy societies, answers to these deeply complex questions are arrived at through an exchange of competing ideas, resulting in either persuasion or compromise.

To flourish, our system of debate and problem solving for the common good requires certain elements: tolerance, forgiveness, trust, mutual respect, the principle of charity which presumes universal fallibility, and relative happiness or at least the absence of fear. Also, there must be general faith in governance as a social compact requiring concessions by all citizens out of acceptance that we are all part of something bigger than ourselves.

Left, Right, and Off-Kilter

In the United States, and in other Western-style democracies, there has been a consistent shift toward liberal values, laws, and cultural mores. If one needs any proof of this, just take a moment to think of all the laws that did not exist just sixty years ago protecting the rights of individuals and groups: civil rights, prisoner rights, women's rights, LGBTQ+ rights, animal rights, employee rights, passenger rights, patients' rights, children's rights, and so on.

It is fair to say that most of this has been extremely good for our society. More liberties are protected now than ever before in history; and more people can express themselves freely and with the requisite legal protections to do so. This should be welcome and unsurprising in a nation that strives for the ideal of unenumerated rights.

In fact, there has never been a time in American history, much less human history, where people have as much freedom as they do today. You would think that people would be happier and more fulfilled in twenty-first-century America than ever before, but sadly that is not the case.

According to many on the authoritarian Left, there is little redeemable in either America's history or its future, and the entire system warrants total (second) reconstruction. In this narrative, the United States was founded by men who were racist, and they wrote a constitution that explicitly contradicted its supposed focus on liberty by not, for example, banning slavery. While some of this is objectively true, according to the extreme version of this view, the Founders' white heirs remain the sole beneficiaries of the country's success and continue to embody and espouse racism consciously or unconsciously because of their privilege. While this is not a majority view on the left side of the political aisle (authoritarians are a vast minority in the Democratic Party, for instance), it is a more common view in the academy and among younger activists.

In the authoritarian Left's telling, "all of the bad aspects of American history were highlighted, amplified, sometimes exaggerated or even fabricated, and then repeated endlessly to create a picture of a nation in whose DNA racism and conquest was inescapably imprinted. The solution to the crisis of America's past and present was nothing less than revolution—a dismantling of America's classical liberal founding and its replacement with illiberal structures that used the force of law and government to uproot entrenched power structures and re-order society from the top down," writes David French in a piece titled "Against the Demolition of the American Spirit."[25]

Those on the left of the political spectrum—liberals and populists alike—have achieved more than any political or ideological movement in the world, but some have been willing to recraft history and to move in an illiberal direction to achieve its goals. In accordance with Newtonian physics, it did not take long for an ideology and movement headed in the opposite direction to meet the Left head-on with a force that was equal to or greater than its own.

In 2016, the populist and even authoritarian Right, along with enough less ideological voters who gave credence, without irony, to claims that the Left was becoming too authoritarian, voted former President Donald Trump into office. Many saw him as the only bully capable of pushing back against the turning tide in America, a tide that included some far-left overreach even though, as we note in Chapter 6, those efforts expanded liberty and protections for individuals like never before in history. During Trump's campaign and throughout his four years in office, his consistent use of belittling, demeaning, and crass language obliterated what remained of civil discourse. Of course, casting political opponents in unsavory and unflattering ways has always existed in politics. However, Trump was the first major candidate and president to embrace mockery, insults, and bigotry in a full-throated way. He upended notions of what was acceptable, in terms of rhetoric and decorum, and we have for years been living with the repercussions.

Since the rise of Trump, violent, demonizing rhetoric has become commonplace, employed by presidents, congressional leaders, and pundits across the political divide. We have also seen rising violence fueled by white supremacist and white nationalist groups.

Indeed, while this impulse of course exists for authoritarians of all stripes, thankfully, no credible attempts to dismantle the Constitution have yet emanated from the far Left. However, there was a literal attempt from the authoritarian Right to not only physically attack the United States Capitol, but in so doing, attempt to disrupt the certification of the 2020 presidential election and, in effect, overthrow the duly elected government of the United States.

During the Trump and Joe Biden administrations, and the Barack Obama and George W. Bush administrations immediately before them, the country continued to grow increasingly polarized. The two-party system in the United States has been producing increasingly extreme authoritarian/populist candidates, and these candidates pander to their most vociferous and engaged primary voters, who demand more audacity and less civility. Populism has become the favored ideology of the present-day base of the Republican Party, and the congressional GOP caucuses contain supporters of former President Trump and his ideology, although a number of Trump-endorsed candidates suffered high-profile losses in the 2022 midterm elections. This is currently less true on the Democratic side, where populist and more authoritarian candidates (often called "true progressives" in current-day parlance) in the mold of Bernie Sanders have not yet been able to secure a presidential nomination. When Democratic populists do occasionally prevail in primaries for down the ballot races, even in otherwise winnable districts for their party, they then tend to lose in the general elections, rejected by the broader population.

The surge of far Right and far Left political candidates, and the echo chambers of media outlets that cater to these constituencies, are producing a body politic that has become more extreme in both its rhetoric and actions. David French has observed that "The radical left seethes with fury at the

America that was and believes that the America that is cannot escape its horrific past, at least not without revolutionary change. The radical right longs for the America that was, loathes the America that is, and believes the America that will be is doomed, at least not without revolutionary change."[26] While French probably overstates the influence of the "radical left" in electoral politics, this is an astute observation.

The political Left and the Right view each other as enemies, to be at least defeated and at best destroyed. Too many on both sides of the aisle consider liberty a fair casualty so long as their side triumphs, with the two groups arguing that restriction of the other's liberty has instrumental value because they perceive it as better for the country and its future. Along with many other ills in society, it is out of such disregard for liberty that cancel culture can arise and flourish.

What We Gain through Pain

Why, in a twenty-first-century society where an infinitely larger number of people have more freedom, flexibility, and tools than at any time in history, are people so mad? And why, in the safest and most comfortable time in human existence, are people experiencing so much fear?

One answer might be that as more and more people enjoy rights that others have taken for granted for centuries (marriage, bodily autonomy, education, etc.), some in the previously in-group—in most cases this means white males—start to feel singled out and resentful. It is a common observation that, when a group has enjoyed elevated status for a long time, newly acquired equality feels like oppression. But it cannot be only this. Those whose rights are increasingly protected and celebrated seem to have the same tendency, in today's world, toward anger and fear.

In the context of cancel culture, it is helpful to understand Plato's answer to the question of what constitutes intrinsic value, because it lies at the root of happiness and is as relevant today as it was over 2,300 years ago. It also lends a perspective that helps set up discussions of cancel culture, witch hunts, and the tendency to view others as enemies rather than colleagues, all predicated on fear and pain, and an absence of happiness.

Plato argued that "pleasure is, in fact, good as such and pain bad, regardless of what their consequences may on occasion be." The consequences, whether good or bad, are irrelevant to those searching for intrinsic value so long as the individual's need for pleasure is satisfied. But are all pleasures intrinsically good and all painful things intrinsically bad?

The Stoic philosopher Seneca is known for his thoughts on enduring pain and suffering. "We suffer more often in the imagination than in reality," he wrote. Adding: "It does not matter what you bear, but how you bear it."[27]

Then there is Hamlet's wise advice that "there is nothing either good or bad, only thinking makes it so." And, of course, we have all heard Friedrich Nietzsche's aphorism that that which does not kill us makes us stronger, or its modern version: no pain, no gain.

The point is that pain can be intrinsically good.

In nature, the strong survive, having endured triumphs over adversity. Our bodies rebuild broken bones stronger in the places where they break. The pressing of the mind, as difficult as learning may be at times, yields a more formidable intellect. Bodies placed under significant and repeated stress respond by developing stronger, denser bones, and larger, stronger muscles that produce greater power. A person placed under extreme duress can respond with exemplary growth that takes him or her well beyond the points of discomfort. In fact, science has found that there is such a thing as post-traumatic growth, providing evidence that pain can be intrinsically good.

Advancing through Adversity

The ability of humans to not just persevere through pain, but to advance because of adversity bears keeping in mind, especially as we explore the concept of *safetyism*, coined by Jonathan Haidt and Greg Lukianoff in their book *The Coddling of the American Mind*.

While cancel culture is expressed in several different ways, expressions of outrage often, but by no means exclusively by those on the illiberal Left, center around *safetyism* and perceived traumas: who experiences them, who causes them, and to what extent people are required to go in order to avoid them taking place.

For centuries, Americans have worked, debated, and fought their way to create a society that continuously removed limitations to individual liberty, recognizing there was intrinsic and instrumental value in doing so. From freeing slaves to repealing Jim Crow laws to ratifying the Nineteenth Amendment recognizing women's right to vote, and then passing the Civil Rights Act of 1964, the Voting Rights Act of 1965, and the Fair Housing Act of 1968, all benefit and make the United States "a more perfect union."

The succeeding liberties afforded to women, the LGBTQ+ community, Americans with disabilities, and various other groups of citizens that have sought equality under the law were in recognition that these individuals possessed intrinsic liberties that should be guaranteed and that any mob, even a majority, cannot take away. What must be celebrated, however, was that these liberties, which conferred substantial intrinsic value to each of these communities, also conferred enormous instrumental value to society.

What stood as a constant for much of human history was recognition that adversity was a great catalyst for growth. While government's role is to remove structural impediments to liberty, it has never been expected to fully eliminate adversity. The Reverend Dr. Martin Luther King Jr. professed deep belief in the power of struggle when he said, "The greatness of man cannot be seen in the hours of comfort and convenience, but rather in the moments of conflict and adversity." Modern-day self-help books are full of idioms that inspire people to face adversity head-on, knowing the only way forward is through those challenges.

Though adversity is, by definition, never easy, social scientists like Albert Brooks, applied psychologists like Martin Seligman and Angela Duckworth, and self-help inspirational authors and speakers such as Tony Robbins and Ryan Holliday have researched and written profusely to uncover mechanisms for overcoming adversity.

Not all trauma is "perceived," and true harm and hardship are obviously not things that we wish upon anyone regardless of their power to teach beneficial lessons. However, as a society and individually, we also should not expect to move through the years with the total absence of adversity, pain, or the feelings stirred by great discomfort.

In the normal course of our lives, discomfort will arise in many forms. As Seneca noted, it is hardest to protect a person from the pain that forms in the mind. Despite the benefits of positive thinking, learned optimism,[28] Cognitive Behavioral Therapy, Stoic philosophy, and other means for taming our inner thoughts, the present-day default to outrage and naked embrace of cancel culture is starting to overpower these measures.

A World of Hurt

Global trends are converging to produce a tidal wave of fear, hatred, and violence. Unfortunately, schools of higher learning that are supposed to be bastions of dialogue, intellectual exploration, and complex critical thinking have in some cases become ground zero for illiberal attacks on free speech and discourse.

Ilya Shapiro was the incoming executive director for the Georgetown Center for the Constitution until he sent a poorly worded tweet regarding President Biden's promise to select a Black woman for the Supreme Court. Shapiro rescinded that tweet within hours, recognizing that he had not artfully conveyed his critique of Biden's position. He also apologized the next day, but by then demands for his firing had already erupted.

Within hours, a petition signed by more than 1,000 Georgetown law students had circulated demanding his immediate termination. Though pundits, lawyers, and judges across the political spectrum defended Shapiro, others sought to deliver a digital age tarring and feathering by tweeting, blogging, and editorializing about his supposed racism.

In an apology he publicly issued, Shapiro offered to speak with anyone who felt hurt by his words. When interviewed for this book he was asked if anyone took him up on the offer. "No" was the answer.

His situation is highlighted later in one of the cancel culture case studies. In short, he was placed on suspension, a period that he referred to as "purgatory," before publicly resigning when he felt he could not do his job without the constant threats of harassment or firing hanging over his head.

During Shapiro's suspension, he was scheduled to speak at UC College of the Law, San Francisco. Hecklers won out by shouting him down long enough to prevent him from offering his thoughts on constitutional law. Sadly, and perhaps ironically, there is arguably no better place than a law school for people with opposing views to make evidence-based cases.

Instead, those who reflexively rejected Shapiro limited not only their own intellectual enrichment by foregoing the chance to hear from him, but also denied that same opportunity to other less hostile students who arrived at the event eager to engage in dialogue and learning. Sadly, the trend of activists seeking to silence people with views that have fallen out of favor is going strong, as of this writing.

Perhaps the skills that American students apparently need the most are the ones they cannot presently get at hypersensitive and hyperpolitical campuses: learning to listen, avoiding leaping to conclusions, thinking critically, engaging in intellectual debate, and recognizing the intrinsic value in philosophical or intellectual differences.

SUMMARY OF KEY POINTS

- Liberty is a foundational value of the United States, and cancel culture is a direct assault on it.
- Demands by some to regulate the behaviors of others may result in illiberal societal restrictions that reduce liberty.
- Illiberalism moves us away from the values that have made democratic societies vibrant, successful, and free.
- American citizens are increasingly willing to engage in destructive behaviors based solely on the ideas of those with whom they disagree.
- Cancel culture events are the twenty-first-century version of witch hunts.
- Our system of debate and problem solving for the good of society requires tolerance, forgiveness, trust, mutual respect, the principle of charity, happiness, and the absence of fear.
- The body politic is becoming more extreme in its rhetoric and actions.
- Expressions of outrage, mostly but not exclusively on the illiberal Left, center on safetyism and perceived traumas.
- Adversity creates opportunities for growth.
- Colleges and universities have become ground zero for illiberal attacks on free speech.

CHAPTER 4

Examining the "Culture" Supporting Cancel Culture

Trigger Warning: Original Ideas Ahead. Proceed with Caution

Disclaimer: More than in any other part of this book, this chapter addresses and offers opinions on multiple hot-button issues. Some readers may find our perspectives objectionable, or even disagree with our views. Please know that we would never seek to threaten the emotional or physical safety of anyone, nor do we intend to create trauma. We accept that our words may induce feelings of anxiety or anger. We hope, however, that careful consideration of these circumstances and the fair warning issued in the form of this clear disclaimer will override any impulses to immediately muster a cancel vulture mob, send us death threats, or visit physical violence upon us.

Cancel culture is not just defined by those events where collective action is applied against an individual for a real or perceived transgression. The term actually describes a "culture" of illiberalism and censoriousness, which can lead to a culture of fear, intimidation, and anger. In this chapter we examine the key forces shaping our culture and setting the stage for the illiberal practice of canceling others.

We live in a world of multivariate causality. This is a fancy way of saying that there are lots of forces at play in our society. No single factor, alone, can explain how we got to where we are: unprecedentedly free and mostly prosperous, but angry and afraid.

The corruption of language is a good place to start. Language serves to transmit ideas, not only across finite space and time, but across generations. However, the most well-articulated ideas will fail if they are not communicated properly. Why? Because every time we use language to express a thought, there is a person receiving that communication who possesses different perspectives, biases, beliefs, and sometimes even definitions for the very words just spoken.

Conversation and debate require some degree of mutual agreement by each party about the meaning of the words being exchanged. It is another way of understanding the words attributed to long-serving US Senator Daniel Patrick Moynihan: "Everyone is entitled to his own opinion, but not to his own facts." Cancel culture seems to flourish when there are no agreed-upon definitions of words, or when people purposely obfuscate the meaning of terms to advance an agenda. An example of this is the right-of-center media's overuse of the term "the Left" in an attempt to discredit mainstream Democratic policies and politicians that, in the realm of elected officials, are arguably more centrist than today's mainstream Republican politicians. Outlets like Fox News typically use the term not to refer to some of the illiberal authoritarian populists on the Left whom we have discussed; instead, they attempt to conflate these populists with Center-Left Democrats.

Making matters worse is the fact that our political discourse has largely been reduced to the simplicity of bumper-sticker slogans. Consider the medium and you start to see part of the problem: to fit on a bumper sticker, words must be short and memorable, and there is simply no room for complex discussion or context. Modern-day adaptations of bumper stickers are quick information bursts like TikTok videos, YouTube reels, and Instagram stories.

In his book *The Better Angels of our Nature,* Steven Pinker explores the phenomenon of integrative complexity, a concept put forth by Philip Tetlock and other political psychologists. To illustrate this concept, Pinker attributes a numerical score to integrative complexity in order to measure the "balance, nuance, and sophistication" of political discourse. Words that imply certitude, such as *absolutely, always, certainly, definitively, entirely, forever, indisputable, irrefutable, undoubtedly,* and *unquestionably,* for example, reduce the integrative complexity score a passage would receive. The more those words are used, the lower the integrative complexity score, and the less balanced and nuanced the argument. However, words such as *usually, almost, sometimes, but,* and *maybe* add to a statement's perceived moderation. Invoking pros and cons, tradeoffs, and compromises into a discussion raises the integrative complexity score even more.

According to Pinker, there is a relation between increases of low integratively complex language and levels of violence. Not surprisingly, people whose language is replete with low integratively complex ideas, meaning they approach issues and circumstances with intellectual or moral certitude, are more prone to react to frustration with anger and violence. You see this reflected in the "M" element of cancel culture, in which the moral certitude of cancel vultures leads them to justify whatever actions they take against the offending party.

As a result of years of decaying political rhetoric, we have seen first-hand the degree to which Americans are willing to support, excuse, and engage in political warfare. Perhaps no more fitting example exists than the January 6 insurrection at the US Capitol, which we have already mentioned. In a shameful display of political violence, organized extremist groups, as well as everyday citizens who had been subjected to weeks of inflammatory, low-integratively complex language about the need to "stop the steal" of an American presidential election, converted words into deeds by attacking Capitol Police and breaching and desecrating the seat of American democracy. Examine the political statements in the run-up to January 6, and the rally speeches directly proceeding the rioting, and you will find plenty of examples of this low-integratively complex language.

Two groups are especially prone to political violence, according to research cited in The *Journal of Democracy*.[29] The first group is white, Christian, evangelical conservatives who comprise the bulk of supporters of political violence and Q-Anon, a "decentralized, far-right political movement rooted in a baseless conspiracy theory that the world is controlled by a 'deep-state,' a cabal of Satan-worshipping pedophiles, and that former President Donald Trump is the only person who can defeat it."[30] The second group likely to embrace political violence is made up of men, from across the political spectrum, who feel aggrieved and harbor resentment against women.

Words, their definitions, and syntax are critical elements to effective communication. Articulate language is essential for clear and critical thinking. But if both parties to a conversation fail to agree upon even the basic meaning of their words, then problems arise. George Orwell, in his essay *Politics and the English Language*, captured with keen insight the reverse language alchemy taking place, in which the meaning of words has become fluid and manipulative. Such ambiguity leads to more misunderstanding and frustration, which in turn often manifest political and verbal violence—and cancel culture:

> A man may take to drink because he feels himself to be a failure, and then fail all the more completely because he drinks. It is rather the same thing that is happening to the English language. It becomes ugly and inaccurate because our thoughts are foolish, but the slovenliness of our language makes it easier for us to have foolish thoughts.[31]

The Danger of Safetyism

To better understand the present culture fomenting cancel culture, let us return to the concept of *safetyism*. According to Haidt and Lukianoff, safetyism is defined as a "culture or belief system in which safety has become a sacred value, which means that people become unwilling to make trade-offs demanded by other practical moral concerns. 'Safety' trumps everything else, no matter how unlikely or trivial the potential danger."[32]

Safetyism seems to have taken firm hold, according to psychologists and academics, right around 2013. That date is significant, because 2013 saw unprecedented degrees of unrest and verbal conflict on the campuses of American colleges and universities. The year 2013 is the date when the cohort referred to as Generation Z or iGen—those born between 1995 and 2012 and raised with the Internet—started college. According to research, iGen suffers from "far higher rates of anxiety and depression than did Millennials at the same age—and higher rates of suicide."[33]

For iGen/ Generation Zers, the emphasis on safety includes concern not just for physical safety, but also for "emotional safety" that can be sparked by the expression of opposing ideas. This form of safetyism has been increasingly creeping into parenting, education, corporate life, and the media. Around 2014, safetyism crossed the Rubicon to an entirely new and heightened level of societal impact when rhetoric and safety became equated with violence. This shift meant that any person's subjective belief that his or her safety was being imposed upon could be construed as an act of "violence" being committed by the other party. This is not to suggest that parents, educators, bosses, and the media dismiss the emotional needs of those they love, care for, oversee, and write about. It does mean, though, that in elevating, and especially institutionalizing, the idea that avoiding discomfort, for example, is as fundamental a value as free speech and open inquiry, then we start on a path to illiberalism at a time when (small-"l") liberal values, under assault from the authoritarian Right and Left, have never needed defending more.

To help protect students from having to hear ideas with which they might disagree or deem unacceptable, some colleges and universities in 2013–2014 started imposing trigger warnings. Such trigger warnings were not references to the triggers of actual guns, which have produced a massive cultural problem in American society in the context of mass shootings in schools. The two authors of this book unfortunately understand all too well the devastating impacts of this phenomenon given that our children attend a public high school devastated by a horrific mass shooting.

As opposed to physical threats, the trigger warnings that have proliferated since 2013 refer to potential emotional damage. For more than a decade, schools have also been offering "safe spaces" and cautioning professors to protect the safety of students in their classrooms. Mind you, not their physical safety from a gunman in the context of a lockdown or active shooter scenario. They mean the students' emotional safety. Again, we are not calling for students' emotional needs to be disregarded; we are arguing that many institutions of higher learning have a tension between a commitment to good-faith scholarly exploration and the risk that this exploration will cause discomfort to students.

The culture of safetyism has constructed a new syllogism: Words can create harm. Harm can lead to violence. (So far, so good.) Therefore, words can be violence. The "words are violence" argument can too easily escalate into a case for using actual physical violence to counter words. In other words, if I believe your words and ideas are harmful to my identity and a threat to my "safety," then I am justified by responding violently to what you say. In the context of cancel culture, someone who hurts someone else's feelings or offends a group of people can subsequently and justifiably be punished with cancellation or even violence.

What this means is that any affront to another's self-defined "safety" is increasingly deemed to have produced actual trauma. Long gone are the days of "never let them see you sweat" or "putting on a brave face" or "maintaining a stiff upper lip." American society at present has replaced admiration for steely strength with an overcorrection toward safetyism. The primary goal of many now is to protect the psyches of those who demand trigger warnings prior to being exposed to alternate viewpoints that they believe may make them feel uncomfortable or threatened.

Downgrading trauma to a level that is purely subjective allows anyone to claim a traumatic experience, thus increasing the risk that someone who unwittingly disturbs another's sense of safety will be met with attacks and cancellation. "[N]ow that some students, professors, and activists are labeling their opponents' words as violence, they give themselves permission to engage in ideologically motivated physical violence. The rationale . . . is that physically violent actions, if used to shut down speech that is deemed hateful, are 'not acts of violence' but, rather acts of self-defense."[34]

The message that some institutions in American culture are sending the iGen/Gen Zers—and simultaneously allowing them to promulgate—is that there is no such thing as oversensitivity to perceived traumas, even trauma caused by words, and not actual physical threats or real violence. This trend is leading, in some spheres, to a culture of victimhood, which, in turn, serves to further foment and encourage cancel culture as people, especially students, become scared to discuss controversial or potentially triggering ideas. As we have noted previously, there should be ample room for politeness and grace when debating ideas with those who are sensitive to the subject matter. And there is certainly some speech that is beyond the pale in an academic or other environment, but what we should not do is make it a cultural norm to shut down free speech at the drop of a hat and to abandon our general commitment to free inquiry.

Idea Laundering and Manufactured Consent

Idea laundering is a process whereby illiberal ideas infiltrate society by appropriating legitimate and liberal-sounding concepts. Manufactured consent—a phrase coined by reporter and commentator Walter Lippmann in his 1922 book *Public Opinion*—acts as the vehicle through which these ideas infiltrate organizations and society.

Idea laundering involves advancing an agenda through the creation of scientific-sounding concepts and terminology and corresponding studies that convey credence to those concepts. The idea was artfully explained in a *Wall Street Journal* op-ed by author and philosopher Peter Boghossian, who described a process by which new, more "progressive" jargon was "imbued with an air of false authority."[35]

We do not mean to suggest that modern terms like whiteness, heteronormativity, and intersectionality (Boghossian even includes fat shaming) have no value to add to the discourse. Boghossian argues that terminology like this can be used as a cudgel in cancel culture when a group of academics feels strongly about a topic, creates quasi-academic journals around the topics with only ideological in-group peer review, and gets these publications to become ubiquitous in libraries and classrooms. They then impart their views—which, whether they are right or wrong, are derived from moral impulses and not scientific study of the phenomena—to droves of students who cycle through their classes every year and eventually go out into the world further disseminating these concepts.

The tie-in to cancel culture happens when individuals who have bought into the viewpoints espoused in the "academic" literature and been taught these concepts by professors at institutions of higher learning decide to become activists enforcing adherence to those concepts. The moral absolutism inherent in many of these concepts, and thus in the people espousing or arguing about them, is a key red flag that cancel culture might be around the corner. People holding opposing views, especially ones who express them publicly in some fashion, and even if those views are as, or more, academically grounded, run the risk of facing vitriolic dissent and being shut down.

In an article in Intelligent.com, Professor James M. Patterson, who has taught at both conservative and left-of-center institutions, points out that "many students simply have no idea how to disagree constructively, or even if constructive agreement is possible."[36]

Like our politics, academic discourse has over time been reduced to one side against another, with an ever-shrinking middle ground at which the two sides can meet and agree.

Manufactured consent serves as a litmus test to determine who is on which side of a cultural divide. The symbiotic relationship between idea laundering and manufactured consent is illustrated by Diversity, Equity, and Inclusion (DEI) initiatives. This represents ideas that on the surface might be deemed indisputable and positive by almost everyone. After all, who does not believe diversity is a good thing and that others should be included? Equity sounds a lot like equal, and Merriam-Webster defines equitable as "dealing fairly and equally with all concerned."[37]

We will say this clearly: DEI is predicated upon good intentions, and most people supporting it are aiming to produce positive effects. Creating environments that bring together people with a range of different experiences and perspectives provides huge benefits to communities that embrace them. Efforts to remove barriers and provide opportunities for each person to become the best versions of himself or herself are responsible and noble. We are clearly better as a society when we welcome other people into the fold.

However, when implemented by those with illiberal tendencies, DEI initiatives can help elevate tensions, rhetoric, and actions that do not serve the noble ends of diversity, equity, or inclusion and, in fact, increase cancel culture contagion. Given the fraught state of our present-day politics and the lack of nuance wielded by critics quick to err on the side of outrage, few people are willing to even question the concept, let alone its implementation, for fear of being canceled.

Those who believe without question that diversity should be the primary principle upon which hiring, firing, and college admissions should be based are welcomed as members of one side. If, however, someone raises questions about the challenges or fairness of insisting upon equity, then they are deemed part of the opposition. Buy in totally, and you are part of the team. Ask questions or pause to ask for more discussion, and you are considered an apostate at best, and a racist at worst. This not only immediately shuts down any conversation or opportunities for mutual growth, but it has serious implications for the remainder of someone's life and career: the ultimate cancellation.

Manufactured consent serves to subordinate a group's members to the group's interests. Group membership offers significant emotional and psychological benefits to an individual. If the choice is to maintain your status as part of the group that is fighting for social justice or being cast out as a racist, which are you likely to choose? In other words, manufactured consent works as a coercive force.

DEI is an example of manufactured consent in the context of a certain strain of left-wing ideology, but manufactured consent is also commonly employed on the Right. Make America Great Again is an example of manufactured consent. Don't all its citizens want America to be great? Don't they stand to benefit from the greatness of their country? In reality, MAGA filters in those who buy into the political implementation of its ideology and separates out those who question it or object. If you are part of the Make America Great Again team, then you proudly wear your red MAGA hat, fly your Trump flag, or display your Let's Go Brandon bumper sticker. Conversely, if you are on the opposing side, you likely call out MAGA devotees and their methods as threats to democracy.

Illiberalism versus Liberalism

While most may be Left-leaning in their political orientation, American institutions of higher education have become hotbeds of illiberalism with professors and students being canceled at an alarming rate. This trend is a major focus of the nonpartisan Foundation for Individual Rights and Expression (FIRE), an organization that declares its "mission is to defend and sustain the individual rights of all Americans to free speech and free thought—the most essential qualities of liberty." Led by President and CEO Greg Lukianoff, FIRE focuses on research and education, also helping to fund litigation to protect free speech as a basic human right.

The censuring of professors, implementation of Bias Reporting Systems across hundreds of campuses, creation of safe spaces and trigger warnings on campuses, and utilization of protests and the heckler's veto to shout down invited speakers are just some of the illiberal tactics increasingly used to stifle free speech on college campuses.

One probable reason for this trend is that colleges and universities are becoming much more ideologically homogenous, creating environments where students engage with others who have very similar ideological predispositions. The chart below illustrates this:

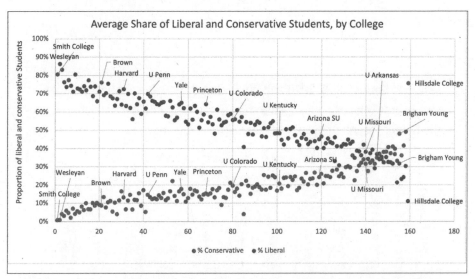

Figure 1. Source: FIRE 2020 and 2021. Survey weights applied. (Reprinted with permission from the Center for the Study of Partisanship and Ideology.)

At Smith College, students who identify as liberal make up 80 percent of the student body, while those who identify as conservative are statistically 0 percent. At Brown, Harvard, the University of Pennsylvania, Yale, and Princeton, liberal students outnumber conservative ones by a ratio of at least 4:1.

Interestingly, the ratios of liberal students to conservative students at schools with the most Left-leaning student bodies are dramatically higher than the ratios at schools with the most Right-leaning student bodies. At the ten most conservative schools, all but two had student bodies between 30 percent and 37 percent liberal. Conversely, of the ten most liberal schools, all but two had student bodies that consisted of less than 8 percent conservative, and six of the schools had less than 5 percent:

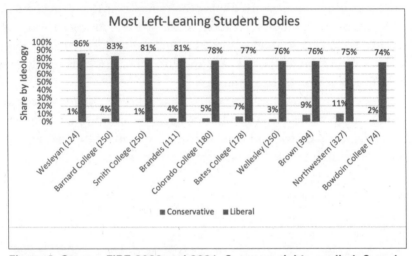

Figure 2. Source: FIRE 2020 and 2021. Survey weights applied. Sample size in brackets, excludes moderates. (Reprinted with permission from the Center for the Study of Partisanship and Ideology.)

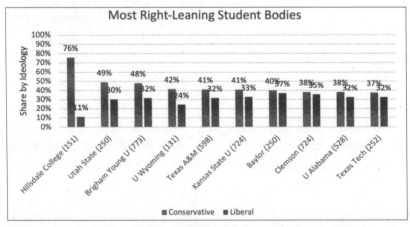

Figure 3. Source: FIRE 2020 and 2021. Survey weights applied. Sample size in brackets, excludes moderates. (Reprinted with permission from the Center for the Study of Partisanship and Ideology.)

It should thus come as no surprise that, by the numbers, cancel culture is driven by Left-leaning students and faculty more than Right-leaning students by a ratio of almost 2:1. Sixty-eight percent of cancel culture incidents emanate from the Left, while thirty emanate from the Right, according to FIRE. This does not necessarily make left-wing students more censorious than their right-wing peers; there are simply many more of them, so this makes sense, as their greater number provides more opportunities to censor.

But while college campuses lean heavily left-of-center and produce the majority of cancel culture sanctions, students on the Right have been active enough to comprise almost forty percent of the sanctions aimed at college professors. Based on information provided by FIRE, between 2015 and 2022, sanction attempts by students on the Right range from a low of 4 in 2016 versus 14 from the Left, to as high as 53 in 2021 compared to 49 from the Left. As of October 2021, the sanction attempts remained even.

The story of Jack Cocchiarella illustrates how the right-wing students employ the same takedown tactics that we often see coming from the Left. In 2022, Democratic student Cocchiarella asked a loaded, albeit reasonable, question to former Republican Member of Congress Madison Cawthorn at a public event, and a modestly heated back-and-forth ensued.

That is not where it ended, however. Two days after that interaction, anonymous social media accounts reportedly operated by a conservative student published and promoted false and defamatory information about Cocchiarella on social media platforms. These posts accused Cocchiarella of raping and sexually harassing multiple women.

Despite the evidence being highly suspect, news outlets such as *Inside Sources*[38] and *The Washington Free Beacon*[39] reported the story as fact. According to the *Dartmouth Review*, Dartmouth's independent conservative newspaper, "more than a year after the initial episode, not one anonymous source has come forward through an official channel beyond Librex," a now-defunct social media app, "to corroborate the severe accusations of sexual violence and serial rape against Cocchiarella."[40] None of this really mattered in the court of public opinion. His reputation damaged at Dartmouth, Cocchiarella was forced to transfer schools. According to his attorney, he "is always looking over his shoulder at Columbia. This is a case of cancel culture."

According to FIRE's 2021 Scholars Under Fire report, "537 incidents targeting a scholar for some form of professional sanction" have occurred since 2013, with almost two-thirds of these incidents resulting in sanction and almost a third resulting in termination.[41]

Peter Boghossian, who helped to inform our discussion of idea laundering, taught philosophy at Portland State University and is one of these sanctioned professors. Throughout his career, he has attempted to counter illiberal ideas with what is called street epistemology. Street epistemology is a fancy description for testing John Stuart Mill's proposition that if all you know is your own position, then you do not even know that very well. In other words, you test how committed you are to a position by being willing to hear and consider the arguments of those on the other side of an issue.

In an interview we conducted with Boghossian to better understand the ideological struggles playing out on campus, he pointed out that the "schism is not liberal-conservative; it is liberal-illiberal." He observed that our two-party political system forces us to think bilaterally: you are either considered a "liberal/ progressive" or "conservative." But in the real world, most people do not fit neatly into either box, but hold varied views that fall on different points along a spectrum. Someone who considers herself conservative may also hold very liberal social views. A person who votes Democrat may be antiabortion, although the position is more closely aligned with the Republican party. As Boghossian points out, we are in a "more difficult political and social milieu now."

Boghossian draws distinctions among the *political* liberal, the *ideological* liberal, and the *classical* liberal. *Politically* liberal defines where a person falls on the political spectrum, such as classifying a person as a Democrat. *Ideologically* liberal he defines as a person whose certitude in his beliefs is so entrenched that he espouses and enforces illiberalism. *Classically* liberal applies to a person who recognizes that issues are complex, accepts the nuances required to pursue the truth, and is willing to engage in the complex process of street epistemology in an effort to determine whether or not their position is correct. Someone who is classically liberal can be either a Democrat or a Republican because the measure of their liberalism is the extent to which they employ reason, debate, and deliberation to arrive at their positions. These are practical definitions useful for this discussion, in contrast to our earlier philosophical definition of the classical liberal ideas in the Enlightenment tradition that animated the Founders, embodied in the Bill of Rights.

Several trends are coalescing to make college campuses some of the most illiberal places in the country. Let's start first with the ideological perspectives of college professors, and how they have changed in recent decades. Generally speaking, there is recognition that college professors as a group—particularly in the humanities and social sciences—tend to lean more Left than Right. But, so long as the left-to-right ratio is less than 3:1, a leveling process called institutionalized disconfirmation can take place.

Institutionalized disconfirmation is the process of ensuring that various opinions are represented in any group, so the group arrives at a well-informed position on a topic. Research has shown that in a homogenous group of like-minded people, such as those comprising a college faculty, it takes a certain number of opposing views to tip the scales, not to a mathematically ideal place of "balance," but to ensure that an entire swath of viewpoints is not missing from important discussions.

Between the 1930s and 1990s, academic psychology had a Left-to-Right ratio of between 2:1 and 4:1. As of 2016 that ratio had increased to 17:1, with other fields across the humanities and social sciences in excess of 10:1.[42] These trends of dramatically increasing the Left-to-Right ratio in favor of one side has effects on how teachers instruct, which studies get published, and what students learn. We should note that the American Right took a rather dramatic ideological detour beginning in 2015, and what were traditionally thought of as "conservative" views shifted in a dramatically rightward, populist, and authoritarian direction. Thus, faculty that might once have considered themselves small-c conservative or libertarian may have found a new, more comfortable, ideological home in the middle or even Center-Left of the political spectrum.

Still, it cannot be denied that in an environment like Smith College, where the student body is comprised of 80 percent liberal students, 20 percent moderate students, and 0 percent conservative students, and where there is virtually no viewpoint diversity, it is unlikely that an outside opinion could disrupt the cycle of confirmation bias. Who would be willing to stand up and take on the majority opinion? Even the most liberal or progressive person should be able to concede this. A similar dynamic would no doubt hold at Hillsdale College, where students on the Left would feel the chilling effect of right-leaning homogeneity. Research has clearly shown that "in the most vivid experiments involving group influences . . . individuals were willing to abandon the direct evidence of their own senses,"[43] which means a student is far more likely to suppress his/her opinion than stand against the majority campus opinion.

Moreover, "research shows that reviewers go easy on articles and grant proposals that support their political team, and they are more critical of articles and proposals that contradict their team's values or beliefs."[44] In a

college environment, where there are often overwhelming consensus opinions, there is almost no mechanism by which institutionalized disconfirmation can occur or critical thinking can be developed.

This is exactly what Boghossian sought to prove. He attempted to take
on the culture within higher education by publishing academic papers
employing faux-academic buzz words, phrases, and ideas to prove absurd
theses. One such paper explored canine "rape culture and queer performa-
tivity." His sole intention was to test the integrity of a system that purported
itself to be based on science. His thesis was proved when some of these
articles were, in fact, published. But his efforts proved disastrous for him.

He analogized it this way: if someone successfully brings an inert bomb
through a TSA checkpoint to prove how fallible security was, then he should
at least get a pat on the back for exposing how vulnerable everyone is, not
a knife in it.

Boghossian and many other professors have had the deck stacked
against them. Over the past five years, colleges and universities have been
hypersensitizing students to bias and perceived harm by implementing Bias
Reporting Systems on their campuses. According to Speech First, which
describes itself as "a nationwide community of free speech supporters," 456
bias reporting systems had been implemented through 2022, a 230 percent
and 175 percent increase, respectively, at private and public institutions over
the preceding five years.[45]

According to Speech First's report "2022 Free Speech in the Crosshairs:
Bias Reporting Systems on College Campuses," bias reporting systems
(BRS) are "designed to silence dissenters, stifle open dialogue, and encourage students to report speech they deem unacceptable." University teams
or systems are established to identify, report, investigate, and respond to
reports of bias incidents. While, of course, objective standards for the most
incendiary and vile speech exist, students or faculty are encouraged to report
speech *they* deemed to be biased. In fact, they do not even have to have been
part of the conversation; they can report things they heard about from others and do so anonymously.

While there may be some merit in knowing, as early as possible, that a
faculty member or even a student is a vocal and inveterate racist or misog-
ynist, campuses clearly are not teeming with people whose speech exceeds
the bounds of even the most permissive definition of free and open debate.
However, the result of bias reporting systems is that every student and faculty member must effectively censor what he/she thinks and says aloud.
According to polling, 24 percent of liberal students and 68 percent of

conservative students self-censor for fear of retribution or punishment. After all, they are operating in an environment where they must fear being anonymously reported at the risk of being forced to undergo anti-bias training or public shaming. All of this is enough to chill, if not cancel altogether, free speech on college campuses.

Against this backdrop, it is not surprising that Boghossian was met with a hostile response. Portland State, like hundreds of other universities, has little viewpoint diversity and no institutionalized disconfirmation to counter strong institutional bias. The result is that Boghossian angered people, and his questions made people feel unsafe, unheard, and uncomfortable.

The response to his ideas was an illiberal effort to make his life miserable. Ultimately, he offered a lengthy public resignation wherein he reminded everyone that "every idea that has advanced human freedom has always, and without fail, been initially condemned. As individuals we often seem incapable of remembering this lesson, but that is exactly what our institutions are for: to remind us that the freedom to question is our fundamental right. Educational institutions should remind us that that right is also our duty."[46] Given what he exposed, Boghossian's was a very public, and incredibly hypocritical, cancellation.

Living Lives of Fear

Albert Brooks is a prolific academic and respected social scientist who teaches a course at Harvard Business School called Leadership and Happiness, which is so popular that it fills up and closes within minutes. Brooks researches, studies, writes, and teaches about the elements of happiness, particularly in the context of high-performing individuals.

In one of his talks,[47] Brooks explores the concept of the Mortality Paradox and its impact on love, fear, and hate, which carries important lessons related to cancel culture. The Mortality Paradox is the cognitive phenomenon to describe the fact that, although our brains are capable of understanding that we are all going to die, our brains cannot conceive of not existing. The tension that exists between these ideas creates fear.

Brooks argues that love and hate are not opposites; rather, love and fear are opposites. This philosophical principle derived from ancient philosophers has been shown by modern neuroscience to be true, based on how emotions are processed in the brain. Love can turn off fear and, conversely, fear can turn off love. When fear takes the lead, hatred is not too far behind. So why are people today so filled with fear and hate and less inclined to love?

Studies show that today's ninety-year-olds—members of the Greatest Generation born between 1901 and 1927—are significantly happier than today's 20- and 30-somethings. The lessons that these two groups—at opposite ends of the life and longevity spectrums—have learned are markedly different. Those in their nineties were born around the Great Depression, when resources were scarce and nobody had computers, let alone televisions or even air conditioning. The world was a tough place, and they had to learn how to maneuver through challenges without the support systems that we all have today.

Haidt and Lukianoff contend that the lessons of perseverance not giving in to fear are contradicted by three untruths that young people are being taught today, whether explicitly or implicitly:

1. The Untruth of Fragility, which implies that adversity is harmful rather than formative;
2. The Untruth of Emotional Reasoning, which teaches us to always trust our feelings;
3. The Untruth of Us versus Them, which teaches that people are in a state of constant war against others and can be classified as either oppressors or victims.[48]

However literally these "lessons" are being taught, and we do not doubt that these are messages kids are taking more from their entertainment sources than their parents and teachers, they combine into a wicked mix of emotional reasoning, anxiety, fear of the known and unknown, and demands for safety above all else. The Mortality Paradox at work creates fear so intense that record numbers of young people are choosing to commit suicide, kill others, or take their aggression out on others in the form of public shaming and silencing.

Yet, at the same time kids are being pumped full of fear, they are also being told they are special. Given the amount of information available to young people today, most parents would acknowledge that kids are far more knowledgeable than they were at the same age. But knowledge is one thing, and wisdom is another.

What happens when young people possessing fragile egos, filled with fear and anxiety as a consequence of environmental and parenting factors, attend colleges or step into careers where ideas that they thought they fully understood from watching online videos are challenged or otherwise called into question? Since many have no experience debating their "truths," they instead shout others down, flee, or ban them from speaking.

Consider the case of Nicholas and Erika Christakis, a married couple who both taught at Yale University. Erika is an early childhood education expert who has "long been critical of ways that adults deprive children of learning experiences by over-policing their behavior," according to a story in the *Atlantic* about how the Christakises were canceled.[49]

The scandal erupted when Erika Christakis offended Yale students by questioning an email previously sent by Yale's Intercultural Affairs Committee regarding Halloween. That email expressed "genuine concerns about cultural and personal representation" and praised the "spirit of avoiding hurt and offense." But she also questioned whether it was the role of administrators to police behavior of the students.

"Have we lost faith in young people's capacity—in your capacity—to exercise self-censure, through social norming, and also in your capacity to ignore or reject things that trouble you? . . . What does this debate about Halloween costumes say about our view of young adults, of their strength and judgment? Whose business is it to control the forms of costumes of young people? It's not mine, I know that."

But the section of the email that most prompted outrage was a thought she attributed to her husband: "Nicholas says, if you don't like a costume someone is wearing, look away, or tell them you are offended. Talk to each other. Free speech and the ability to tolerate offense are the hallmarks of a free and open society."

Amazingly, the email underscoring fundamental American values of free speech and encouraging open debate to address and resolve differences sparked virulent protests. Petitions circulated, amassing signatures from hundreds of Yale students and alumni. A face-to-face encounter ensued with Nicholas Christakis filmed listening to his detractors as they expressed their outrage. Posted online, the clip shows Christakis attempting to engage in a rational discussion as a student points a finger at him and yells for him to "be quiet!" She then screams, "Who the fuck hired you, you should step down, it is not about treating this as an intellectual thing, it is not. It's about creating a home!" Her public rant carries on for a little more than a minute before she storms off. But not before she closes with a final barrage, "You should not sleep at night. You are disgusting!"

It was an outright verbal assault illustrative of the concepts explored by Brooks, Haidt, and Lukianoff. Light on love, heavy on fear, and brimming with anger. Shortly thereafter, Nicholas stepped down as Head of Silliman

College at Yale, canceled by an illiberal culture that those doing the canceling no doubt thought of as tolerant.

SUMMARY OF KEY POINTS

- Productive conversation requires that each party agree about the meaning of the words being exchanged.
- Cancel culture flourishes when there is no agreed-upon definitions of words or terms.
- Safetyism, which took hold around 2013, is a concept that makes a person's self-perception of safety a sacred value, trumping all else.
- Integrative Complexity (IC) measures the amount of certitude in any given statement or thought.
- Low IC, meaning moral absolutism or certitude, correlates to higher levels of violence.
- The year 2013 is significant because it is when iGen/GenZers started college.
- Safetyism became more impactful when rhetoric was equated with violence, prompting "trigger warnings" on campus.
- A culture of victimhood foments and encourages cancel culture.
- Idea laundering is a process of infiltrating society with illiberal ideas using liberal concepts.
- Manufactured consent is the means by which idea laundering works:
  - Functionalizes ideal laundering
  - Produces group litmus tests
  - Enforces group member subordination
- Street epistemology uses questions to test a person's commitment to their ideas.
- In the context of the work of Peter Boghossian:
  - Politically liberal relates to party identification
  - Ideologically liberal is a dogmatic position that can lead to acting in an illiberal manner
  - Classically liberal is defined by using reason, debate, and deliberation to reach a conclusion
- Institutionalized disconfirmation is a process of representing various opinions within a group to arrive at a balanced, well-informed position.

- Many American college campuses have very low viewpoint diversity.
- Bias reporting systems, though well-intentioned, are chilling free speech on college campuses.
- American kids are dealing with record levels of anxiety, fear, and anger.

CHAPTER 5

Dangers to Democracy: Mob Rule and Accusatory Justice

America's Founding Fathers cautioned about a particularly poisonous threat to democracy, which we are presently seeing play out before our eyes: the danger of mob rule. They feared that man's tendency toward passion could give rise to unsavory leaders who could successfully manipulate those passions to improper ends. In fact, only 52 percent of Americans believe our democracy is working.[50]

Humans have an innate system for navigating the world, an idea John Tooby, the founder of Evolutionary Psychology, called *Coalitional Instinct*. Tooby contends that our neural networks have evolved over millennia to endow us with the instinct for maneuvering through life in solidarity with, or opposition to, others. We join, organize, trust, support, defend, and subordinate ourselves to others who share the same needs and beliefs as us. Likewise, we are quick to oppose, attack, condemn, destroy, distrust, and seek to defeat others and groups of others whose needs and beliefs differ from our own.

In our current age of identity politics, turbocharged through the pervasive power of social media, groups and subgroups form coalitions or compete for power. Those who are not part of that power coalition are essentially powerless. Tooby writes:

> The primary function that drove the evolution of coalitions is the amplification of the power of its members in conflicts with non-members. . . . Since

coalitional programs evolved to promote the self-interest of the coalition's membership, even coalitions whose organizing ideology originates to promote human welfare often slide into the most extreme forms of oppression, in complete contradiction to the putative values of the group.[51]

It is a short leap from what Tooby describes to those who claim to seek social justice while using unjust means. Coalitional instincts driving those on the political Right and Left have moved our society away from the classically liberal ideas of moderation, reason, and tolerance and toward an illiberal, dog-eat-dog, zero-sum, destroy-at-all-costs mentality. Rather than promoting advancement, coalitional movements have devolved into coalitional ideologies promoting destruction.

The Changing Face of the Mob

A global network—the Internet—enables otherwise disparate communities to unite as online mobs fixated upon bringing down an accused. In the age before social media or the Internet, news traveled slowly, so the odds of coalescing a large group of people around a perceived grievance took a lot more time. In part because people were given the chance to gather more information, weigh the facts, and make more reasoned decisions about right and wrong. Now, you can instantly absorb a limitless trove of news and information that aligns with and confirms your preconceived perspective.

The introduction of Apple's iPhone in 2007 and the explosion of similar Android devices around the same time turned on a spigot of endless content. Today, every smartphone is designed as a global gateway to billions of pages of material, bombarding viewers with often highly emotional and biased information in real time. Making matters worse are algorithms purposely constructed to take advantage of confirmation bias. Social media platforms utilize this to their advantage and our detriment in the form of encouraging more clicks and spending more time in their platforms.

Humans are genetically predisposed to believing information that aligns with their beliefs.[52] Rather than seeking to disprove their already-held beliefs by examining information to challenge them, most people seek out additional information that further confirms and cements their views. That is why people tend to watch Fox *or* MSNBC, or Fox *or* CNN, but usually not both. That also explains why most people's Twitter followers and feeds, and favorite talk show pundits, are people who share their beliefs and not those with whom they disagree.

The result is that people on the Left are exposed to ever-greater amounts of left-leaning viewpoints and vice versa for those on the Right. Any hope for disconfirmation that prompts people to evolve their thinking or change their minds is obliterated by the sheer volume and intensity of incoming, ideologically homogenous information. Notably, this binary appears to be changing as more people like Bari Weiss, Kmele Foster, Sam Harris, and John McWhorter and groups like The Foundation Against Intolerance & Racism (FAIR) bring diverse ideas from the Left and Right to those who align themselves on the opposite side of the spectrum. This growing trend could prove to be an important way to reduce the rush of an ideological and irate public to employ cancel culture.

From Due Process to Accusatory "Justice"

So fundamental was the right to due process in America that it was codified in the Fifth and Fourteenth Amendments to the Constitution, with laws to ensure the enforcement of due process inserted into the Sixth Amendment. Due process remains a universal and vital concept for democracies willing to balance the rights of accusers against the accused. Due process is a moral principle with significant instrumental value to society.

If you were accused of committing an act or expressing an idea that another person or group found damaging, dangerous, or hurtful, then wouldn't you want your side of the story heard before being punished? It is hard to imagine that any person would prefer receiving a death sentence (reputational or otherwise) before being given a fair hearing to present evidence and make a case for himself/herself.

Global history—ancient and modern—is replete with examples where mobs ruled the day, with violence, suffering, and destruction the expected outcomes. Examples include family-led honor killings, pogroms, lynch mobs and public executions, riots and looting, and public shaming of others denied true legal representation and due process under the law.

A major problem with "mob mentality," or coalitions such as cancel culture mobs, is that they feed off one another's energy, dismissing information that could otherwise be instrumental to the group making more balanced, thoughtful, and sound decisions. As different coalitions with competing ideologies proliferate, group polarization sets in, pulling each coalition ever farther from a central point around which reasonable debate and deliberation can take place.

In his books *Cancel Culture, Guilt by Association,* and *The Price of Principle,* Harvard Professor Alan Dershowitz correctly points out that cancel culture has no statute of limitations, and that it is "a direct attack on due process" because it cancels innocent, guilty, and those who fall somewhere in between without a systematic method for arriving at the truth. To address this, Dershowitz proposes in his book *Cancel Culture* the formation of a "cancel culture court" that "could be established by the bar association, media organizations or other credible groups interested in the truth."

Dershowitz has a vested, personal interest in such remedies being introduced, given that for years he described himself as a victim of cancel culture based upon allegations of sexual assault that he vehemently and consistently denied and repeatedly declared "categorically false." In a series of books and articles, Dershowitz, with the same tenacity, persistence, and persuasive reasoning that made him a globally recognizable jurist who delivered results for his clients, sought to clear his name.

The attempted cancellation of Professor Dershowitz took place after he was accused of sexual abuse by a victim of his client, convicted pedophile Jeffrey Epstein. Virginia Giuffre, and her attorney David Boies, separately sued Dershowitz for defamation in 2019 when he denied her assertions publicly in media interviews, suggesting that she and her attorneys were making false accusations to extort financial settlements. Counterdefamation charges were brought by Dershowitz against Giuffre and Boies.

The matter was eventually settled in November 2022. Attorneys for Giuffre, Boies, and Dershowitz filed joint stipulations requesting that the claims be dismissed with prejudice, meaning that the matter is permanently resolved and cannot be refiled. The following joint statement accompanied the filings:

*

AGREED STATEMENT

FROM ALL PARTIES:

Virginia Giuffre, David Boies and Alan Dershowitz have today dismissed with prejudice all pending litigation. The resolution of the litigation is accompanied by the following statements. The resolution does not involve the payment of any money by anyone or anything else.

FROM VIRGINIA GIUFFRE: I have long believed that I was trafficked by Jeffrey Epstein to Alan Dershowitz. However, I was very young at the time, it was a very stressful and traumatic environment, and Mr. Dershowitz has from the beginning consistently denied these allegations. I now recognize I may have made a mistake in identifying Mr. Dershowitz. This litigation has been very stressful and burdensome for me and my family, and we believe it is time to bring it to an end and move on with our lives.

FROM DAVID BOIES: I agree with Mr. Dershowitz and Ms. Giuffre that the time has come to end this litigation and move on. I know that Alan Dershowitz has suffered greatly from the allegation of sexual abuse made against him—an allegation that he has consistently, and vehemently, denied. I also know that this litigation has imposed, and continues to impose, a significant burden on Ms. Giuffre. I appreciate Mr. Dershowitz's recognition that I was not engaged in an extortion plot or in suborning perjury. I accept each of their statements in the spirit in which they are made, and I wish each of them well.

FROM ALAN DERSHOWITZ: As I have said from the beginning, I never had sex with Ms. Giuffre. I have nevertheless come to believe that at the time she accused me she believed what she said. Ms. Giuffre is to be commended for her courage in now stating publicly that she may have been mistaken about me. She has suffered much at the hands of Jeffrey Epstein, and I commend her work combatting the evil of sex trafficking. I also now believe that my allegations that David Boies engaged in an extortion plot and in suborning perjury were mistaken.

*

During the research-gathering phase of this book, we interviewed Professor Dershowitz about his thoughts. At the time we spoke, his case had not yet been resolved. When asked who was most responsible for the spread of cancel culture, he did not hesitate to call out "the hard-left Progressives—the wokes," while also noting how the Left learned from the example set by the Right during the era when being falsely labeled a Communist was tantamount to total cancellation. Said Dershowitz: "The Left, of course, learned from the Right. The Left today are the new McCarthyites. I grew up during the old McCarthyism, and the Right employed many of the same tactics of cancel culture. If you represented somebody who was accused of being a Communist, you no longer could practice law, no longer could be accepted in polite society."

In answer to the question of where to draw the distinction between cancel culture and legitimate or fair criticism of people, Dershowitz said, "It is an old term that goes back into the beginnings of philosophy: ad hominem. When you take on arguments, that's fair. When you take on people, that's unfair. And what's happening now, and the reason I wrote *The Price of Principle*, is because the arguments have shifted from reason and rationality to attacks on people. It's the shift from reasoned argumentation to McCarthyite ad hominems, which is the major manifestation of the new cancel culture."

The case of Alan Dershowitz is a particularly interesting one, because it sits at the nexus of a fight in the legal arena and a spirited battle for the hearts and minds of a mostly uninformed public. Dershowitz proceeded on both fronts simultaneously, employing a legal strategy at the same time that he executed a strategic communications/public relations strategy. And in the end, he prevailed.

Those who are falsely accused would do well to gather both instruction and inspiration from Dershowitz. He proved that refusing to be canceled, and that countering fictional allegations with factual evidence, can defeat cancel culture.

Media's Impact on the Legal Realm and Due Process

Given their ostensible role exposing the truth, why do so many media outlets turn out to be complicit in the takedown of innocents or people on the receiving end of disproportionate punishments that do not fit the crime? In some cases, there may be low-integrity members of the press who willfully advance false narratives to drive agendas. They could more accurately be called advocates than journalists. When exposed as such, they should either be required to immediately raise their standards or find a line of work better suited to such endeavors.

While some bad apples certainly spoil the bunch, many other reporters fall into this trap unwittingly, the consequence of which is driving stakes into the hearts of innocent victims and depriving them of future careers. In many cases, this happens in part because steep financial declines in many quarters of the press have left journalists stretched too thin, pressed for time, harried by the frenzied competition, and without adequate training, guidance, or thoughtful oversight from seasoned editors. This problem is massively compounded by salary constraints that result in outlets foregoing more highly paid veterans in favor of a platoon of young, inexperienced, and far less compensated cub reporters who nevertheless possess extreme levels of power because the reach of their work is so enormous thanks to the Internet.

Add to the mix clever PR people and lawyers seeking to advance their clients' agendas, and this can be detrimental to fair outcomes. In fact, many media-savvy attorneys seek to take advantage of the fact that assertions—true or false—made within legally filed documents can be disseminated far and wide by media outlets without fear of being hit with defamation charges. After all, the outlets can always justify their stories by saying that they are simply reporting allegations contained within publicly available documents. Given that there is no way for a reporter to determine whether what is asserted in the court documents is true or not, why should they be permitted to repeat them and thereby amplify them?

A clear explanation of this catch-22 appears in Alan Dershowitz's book *Guilt by Accusation*. This complex notion is so artfully distilled by the author in a chapter titled "The Weaponization of the Media" that it bears repeating, verbatim, and in its entirety here:

> This is how this dangerous partnership works: the lawyers pressure a client into making a false accusation, but they are careful to make it only in court documents that are protected by the so-called litigation privilege. Even if it's irrelevant to the court proceeding, as the judge ruled it was in my case. This privilege protects anything said in a court document or proceeding from a defamation suit. The false accuser or her lawyers then leak the judicially protected false accusation to the media, which is also protected against a defamation suit, for reporting on what was said in court papers or proceedings. The media then publish the false accusation without requiring the false accuser to repeat the accusation to the journalist outside the protection of the privilege. The false accuser and her lawyers can, in this way, launder the defamatory accusations through the media and achieve the same result they would have achieved had they made the accusation directly to the news media. But, and here is the critical element—without incurring the risk of a defamation suit by making a false accusation. Moreover, because the accusation is made in

court papers, some readers believe it has the imprimatur of the courts and therefore is more credible than if it had been made directly to the media. The victim of this false accusation then has only three options:

The first and most obvious is that he can immediately respond to the media report of the false accusation in the media. But his response may not be protected by the litigation privilege because it is not made in court papers or proceedings. He can, therefore, be sued for defamation merely for denying the accusation and saying it's a lie.

The second option is to respond in court documents, or proceedings, and thus be protected by the privilege. But filing court papers or appearing in court takes time and it is imperative to respond to false accusations immediately within the news cycle if the denial is to be reported and credited. A court filing made days or weeks after the initial accusation was reported in the media will either not be reported, or if reported, will be buried.

The third option is to ignore or no comment the accusation and hope it will go away. An entirely innocent, falsely accused victim should not be satisfied with the story going away. He should categorically deny and disprove the false accusation.[53]

The part of option three that demands denying and disproving false allegations is squarely in line with our position that the best way for an individual to communicate, on issues involving controversy or otherwise is to press the truth. See Chapter 10, "The Cancel Culture Playbook," for a full explanation of this concept.

View from the Top: A Lawyer's Perspective

Attorneys advocating aggressively for their clients must consider this brave new world in which people have unprecedented levels of access to information. Increasingly, lawyers must contend not only with prevailing inside the courthouse, but in the court of public opinion, as well.

Jonathan Missner is the managing partner of Stein Mitchell Beato and Missner, regarded as one of the most connected and effective law firms in Washington, DC. For nearly twenty-five years, he has also taught at the Georgetown University Law Center. Seated at the conference table in his regal offices just blocks from the White House, Missner and his law partner Philip O'Beirne shared their insights into how top-tier counselors operating at the highest levels, and at the center of power, think about the challenges presented by the media and cancel culture.

"The reason we have a legal system, as imperfect as it may be, is it provides every citizen the opportunity to prove their facts, engage in discovery, take depositions, give testimony, and have their day in court," said Missner. "But that is in jeopardy in a cancel culture world, where people lose any meaningful right to due process. The mob skips to sentencing, and the sentence can be permanent. Proving a negative is almost always impossible, so cancel culture acts as a form of weaponized bullying that can have a life-long impact on your business, relationships, and ability to make money and defend yourself."

Missner and O'Beirne noted that a principle our society has always held dear—the right to representation, having someone advocate for you and help you make your case when faced with charges—means lawyers have a uniquely constructive role to play in eliminating the practice of cancel culture. Asked to contrast every citizen's right to trial by a jury of their peers with what plays out in public cancellations, O'Beirne said, "Trial by mob entails all the downsides of people making collective decisions without any of the controls and protections to ensure fairness. The number one basic requirement of being a juror is that you have not prejudged a matter. But Twitter mobs are comprised almost entirely of people who have already made up their minds about an issue and have no interest in understanding any new facts, only validating their own conclusions." He added: "Cancel culture is the polar opposite of a fair jury, since it involves impassioned people with incomplete views of the facts and prejudiced views of the individual being charged."

Missner spoke about how much more complex it has become for attorneys to try cases in today's media-fueled environment: "The legal landscape has changed in the sense that many lawsuits are now public. You must take for granted that anything that emerges publicly may immediately be unfairly characterized and used against you with hardly an iota of goodwill or common sense, but the maximum amount of unfairness. This raises the stakes on your ability to convey the truth and advocate for your position." Concluded Missner: "Attorneys must be able to advise and guide our clients as they navigate challenges inside and outside of the courtroom."

Because of the manner in which information spreads globally, much discussion takes place in the public square long before any matters are litigated in court. It is incumbent upon people seeking to prevail long-term both legally and reputationally to drive their narrative and win people over to their perspective. Otherwise, they could already be canceled—losing sponsorships, customers, brand equity, or respect—well before an actual trial gets underway and they have their day in court.

In Too Depp

The legal battles between Johnny Depp and his ex-wife Amber Heard provide another compelling anecdote highlighting how a public figure who became a victim of cancel culture ultimately was able to be "uncanceled."

Johnny Depp and Amber Heard's marriage was relatively short-lived, even by Hollywood standards. Married in 2015, Heard filed for divorce just 15-months later, alleging that Depp had physically abused her. The accusations were denied by Depp, who reached a $7 million out of court settlement with Heard when the two split. Then, in December 2018 with the #MeToo social movement in full swing, Heard authored an op-ed in the *Washington Post* that did not name Depp but claimed that she was "a public figure representing domestic abuse." Shortly thereafter, in 2019, Depp sued Heard for defamation, and she responded with a defamation lawsuit of her own. At the time, Depp claimed that the false allegations against him had effectively led him to being canceled, and that movie studios were denying him the opportunity to secure lucrative work due to the allegations casting a dark shadow upon his reputation.

In 2020, Depp brought a lawsuit in the United Kingdom, suing the publisher of *The Sun* newspaper for repeating allegations that Depp was an abusive husband who beat his wife. The trial attracted enormous press attention and featured explosive testimony from Depp and Heard. The court ruled against Depp, denying him an appeal.

Undeterred, Depp continued with his $50 million defamation lawsuit against his former partner, which culminated in a trial in Virginia in April of 2022. The court proceedings could aptly be defined as a major public spectacle, attracting fawning fans to the courthouse and generating stunning quantities of national and international media coverage.

Most of those standing outside throughout the trial, craning their necks for sight of the Hollywood A-listers and cheering and jeering their arrival, were fans of Depp who professed their support in the form of hand-crafted signs that they held aloft for the television and still cameras to capture. As events unfolded in the Fairfax County courthouse, the salacious testimony gave birth to a seemingly endless torrent of content in the mainstream press, as well as on social media, especially on the increasingly popular platform

TikTok. Self-declared members of Team Johnny and Team Amber squared off, with Depp attracting the lion's share of support.

Videos of the proceedings were picked over, analyzed, and posted alongside commentary and analysis by amateur content creators whose content was viewed by legions of followers. They also turned out daily videos and memes after slicing and dicing a feast of images captured by Court TV television feeds.

Tawdry details from a deeply toxic relationship were conveyed from the stand, and social media lit up with conspiracy theories, snarky observations, and coverage slanted from the perspective of whoever was producing it.

In the run-up to the trial, it seemed like an exceedingly steep challenge confronting Depp. The bar for winning a libel case is extremely high, requiring you to show an article was published with malice using information known to be untrue, and with the intention of causing harm. Setting the record straight in a packed courtroom is rarely the best crisis communications strategy because litigating your case in court comes with the very real threat that you might end up permanently harming your reputation and making a bad situation even worse. But in the case of Depp, he and his team evidently felt that the potential upside outweighed the risks.

Over the course of the trial, Depp's representatives discredited Heard's narrative. The jury unanimously ruled that Depp had been defamed by his ex-wife Heard, and she was ordered to pay him $15 million in damages. Countersued by Heard, Depp was found guilty of just one of the three charges, and Heard received $2 million in compensatory damages.

Despite the fact that the trial brought into public view embarrassing personal details that painted Depp and Heard in a very negative light, there were some lessons that each should have drawn from the saga. By any measure, Amber Heard lost big. Because she was ordered to pay a staggering sum to her ex-husband, the verdict reflected the jury's determination that she was a vindictive liar. Dishonesty and cynicism are now the hallmarks of her brand, aided mightily by recorded videos and conversations unearthed during the trial that showed her to be haughty and mean. Unfortunately for her, Heard's attempt to drape herself in the flag of the #MeToo movement was judged a failed ploy to win fame or sympathy from the public.

Legitimate victims of abuse also suffered a setback as a result of the Hollywood starlet's attempt to declare herself a representative of victimized women. Following the jury's verdict, Heard released a statement in which she claimed that once again a powerful man was silencing her. Her representatives put out a statement trading the #MeToo flag for an American flag, saying she had been denied her right to free speech. Whatever positive benefits she may have enjoyed from the publication of her op-ed were completely overshadowed and overwhelmed by negative attention during and after the trial. It is likely that her brand has been indelibly marred. It also should serve as a cautionary tale to people who dishonestly step forward as self-proclaimed victims. The trial showed clearly that it is not enough for them to go public with "their truth," but they must actually speak "the truth."

For Johnny Depp, on the other hand, things began looking up immediately after the jury found in his favor. Despite his complaints about being "canceled" and losing out on leading film roles, and even before he secured a positive result in court, Depp was always likely to find work in the entertainment industry. After all, he has for decades been one of Tinseltown's most bankable leading men. The talented actor has starred in a range of iconic roles: *Edward Scissorhands, Donnie Brasco*, Willly Wonka from *Charlie and the Chocolate Factory*. He has received three Academy Award best actor nominations for his roles in the *Pirates of the Caribbean* franchise, as well as *Finding Neverland* and *Sweeney Todd*.

Almost immediately after prevailing over his ex-wife at trial, Depp began increasing his public visibility. He appeared before concert crowds at gigs with his band, jamming onstage with the guitar legend Jeff Beck, who passed away in January 2023. At the MTV Video Music Awards, Depp made light of his past struggle to secure a leading man role. His face superimposed onto the graphical figure of MTV's iconic astronaut, he quipped: "And you know what? I needed the work." In the weeks that followed he made a cameo at a fashion show featuring the lingerie line of musical artist Rihanna. Meanwhile, Depp got involved with at least two movies, including one with him slated to direct. Despite revelations of a deeply dysfunctional marriage to Heard, the airing of profane comments directed toward her showcased in trial, and the circulation of photos and videos displaying a rapacious appetite for drugs and alcohol, Depp appears poised to reclaim the stratospheric level of stardom that predated his marital and legal woes.

Both Dershowitz and Depp brought separate strengths to their legal fights. Dershowitz faced down attempted cancellation with conviction, boundless energy, and legal acumen, while Depp brought his willingness to pursue justice, impressive financial resources to fund the fight, and legions of fans and supporters willing to aggressively advocate for him online. Average people on the receiving end of cancel culture assaults, however, rarely have a legal remedy or their own "mob" to turn to for support.

A bedrock principle of American justice—the presumption of innocence until proven guilty—is turned on its head by cancel culture. Salacious accusations, especially those of a sexual nature, quicken pulses, get people excited, and tend to grab headlines. Whatever denials are proffered pale in comparison to the tidal wave of attention attracted by the charges against them. When it comes to cancel culture, the person on the receiving end of an allegation starts with the deck stacked against them, and at a tremendous disadvantage. Unfortunately, false accusations tend to be much more exciting than truthful denials.

SUMMARY OF KEY POINTS

- The Founding Fathers presciently warned against the dangers of mob rule.
- Humans employ coalitional instinct to navigate the world: joining, organizing, trusting, supporting, defending, and subordinating ourselves to others who share our same needs and beliefs.
- Turbocharged through the pervasive power of social media, groups and subgroups form coalitions or compete for power.
- Those who claim to seek social justice through cancel culture do so in unjust, illiberal ways.
- Widespread adoption of the smartphone has set the stage for cancel culture.
- Humans are genetically predisposed to believing information that aligns with their beliefs, leading people on the Left and Right to harden their views because of repeated exposure to self-selected content that confirms their biases.
- Due process, a long-held American value codified in multiple amendments to the Constitution, is being replaced by accusatory justice.
- Global history is filled with examples of mob justice resulting in death and destruction.
- Cancel culture mobs feed off one another's energy, dismissing information that could otherwise be instrumental to the group making more balanced, thoughtful, and sound decisions.
- Coalitions with competing ideologies are polarized, moving further from reasonable debate.
- Countering fictional allegations with factual evidence can defeat cancel culture.

- Overworked and inexperienced journalists can unwittingly damage the reputations of people through their reporting.
- A catch-22 exists that makes it possible for media to report and amplify unproven or false allegations without the threat of being sued for defamation, provided they quote from publicly available legal documents.
- Attorneys have a unique role to play in demanding an end to cancel culture and the extending of due process.
- Trial by mob is the antithesis of trial by jury, eliminating safeguards for fairness and due process and embodying prejudice.
- The legal sagas involving Johnny Depp and his ex-wife Amber Heard illustrate that it is possible to survive cancellation by simultaneously prevailing in court and the court of public opinion.
- A bedrock principle of American justice—the presumption of innocent until proven guilty—is turned on its head by cancel culture.
- A major danger of cancel culture is that salacious accusations are often more memorable and powerful than factual denials.

CHAPTER 6

A Perfect Storm: Why Cancel Culture Is Happening Now

It is no exaggeration to say that cancel culture is one of the biggest threats to free speech, due process, artistic expression, and democracy. It is ironic that the United States, arguably one of the freest, safest, healthiest, and most advanced nations on the planet, albeit far from perfect, has become ground zero for a belief system that directly undermines the democratic and classically liberal ideas that have made these successes possible in the first place.

We have already examined, in some detail, the various social forces and trends that have contributed to the rise of cancel culture. But what is it about this unique moment in human history that makes the practice so pervasive? The answer is that there is a confluence of elements creating a "perfect storm" in which cancel culture can thrive.

Age of the Internet

It is no accident that cancel culture has caught on during an era that could be appropriately termed the Age of the Internet. With the proliferation of affordable smartphones that are web-enabled, previously disconnected people all over the world can now pull from their pockets devices with more computing power than supercomputers possessed as recently as the 1990s.

Statistics around connectivity and activity clearly illustrate the incredible global reach of the Internet. With the average growth rate of Internet users increasing by 8.2 percent annually, you can expect these numbers to require updating on a continuous basis. But a few key numbers provide a useful snapshot in time.

Today, a staggering 5.47 billion people are active online. This represents about 66 percent of the total global population, which at the time of publication was hovering near 8 billion people. Of those users, 4.32 billion individuals around the world use their mobile devices, including phones and tablets, to access the Internet. Roughly the same number (over 4.3 billion) are currently active on social media. In the United States alone, there are nearly 310 million Internet users[54] who visit 198.4 million active websites, more than 25 percent of which are in English. As large as these numbers are, we should expect to see the number of people online continuing to expand as more people gain Internet access across the developing world, aided by low-cost handheld devices that quite literally put the power of the Internet into the hands of women, men, and children across the globe.[55]

The Internet has produced a global community no longer divided by physical, geographic, or time barriers. Instead, immediacy and interconnectivity keep people intimately linked 24 hours a day, seven days a week and 365 days a year. News and information—especially dramatic content that produces widespread interest and can coalesce into a cancel culture attack—moves instantaneously to potential audiences of billions of people.

From #MeToo to #CancelYou

No substantive discussion of cancel culture can ignore the movement known as #MeToo. For decades, if not centuries, some men in positions of power wielded it as a weapon against women in the form of harassment, sexual misconduct, and even abuse. While this dynamic had slowly changed over the course of the last century, a social movement called #MeToo emerged in 2017, becoming large and powerful enough to rapidly alter the status quo.

Using the hashtag #MeToo, a symbol used within social media to call attention to key words and phrases and aid searches for them, the movement enabled women all over the world to join a global coalition. Sharing or liking posts using #MeToo was a way to express solidarity with women who suffered this humiliation and injustice.

The #MeToo movement sought to hold accountable (mostly) men who used positions of power to subjugate women in the most humiliating and abusive ways and had, until that point, gotten away with it. Let us be crystal clear: supporting women against predators is a good thing. #MeToo served as a clarion call, bringing about a collective takedown of bad actors whose deeds had gone unpunished for far too long, and a recalibration of culturally acceptable principles pertaining to power dynamics between men and women.

In October 2017, the #MeToo movement turned its attention and energies toward Hollywood mogul Harvey Weinstein. This was a watershed moment that signaled the power of the #MeToo collective. Before allegations of despicable behavior came to light, Weinstein was regarded as a God-like figure in the film industry. In fact, during Meryl Streep's acceptance speech of a Golden Globe award for best actress in a motion picture drama, she said, "I just want to thank my agent Kevin Huvane and God— Harvey Weinstein," as the latter laughed from a prime seat near the front of the stage. Streep was kidding, but it was a telling joke because it reflected Weinstein's perceived omnipotence.

In the end, women bravely stepped forward to tell their stories, and the media amplified their messages. Their allegations were investigated, corroborated, and ultimately resulted in bringing Harvey Weinstein to justice. Within three days of the story breaking in the *New York Times*, he was fired from the company he cofounded and that bore his name. Other exposés, including by Ronan Farrow in the *New Yorker*, brought to light allegations by eighty-seven women. Weinstein was convicted of rape and sexual abuse at trial in New York and sentenced to twenty-three years in prison. Once regarded as the most singularly powerful person in Hollywood, the name Weinstein is now synonymous with the Devil rather than God.

The Danger of False Accusations

#MeToo represented real victims of sexual harassment and abuse, both male and female. Unfortunately, the success of this movement also opened opportunities to abuse its power. It served as a way for victimhood seekers to instantly garner attention and admiration. Those seeking to damage another's reputation could appropriate it, since the mere lodging of #MeToo allegations can be enough to cause lasting damage. Finally, it inadvertently lowered the bar so low on power dynamics and sex that flirting, dating, and even conversing now come with new risks and often unclear paths forward.

A number of women and men have used the power and influence of the #MeToo collective to level accusations that lacked any evidence, and in many cases proved false. That is not to say that anyone who reports abuse— even if they do not have supporting evidence—is lying or an opportunist seeking to force a payoff or legal settlement. Sadly, though, there are plenty of people who are abusing #MeToo in that way, and the result undermines the integrity of the #MeToo movement.

We have had discussions with individuals whose businesses and lives were shattered when people accused them of sexual misconduct. In one case, a woman posted a video on social media using the hashtags #MeToo and several others, complaining that a misogynistic male boss took advantage of the power dynamic to sexualize her and harm her career. According to her story, when she declined to engage in a romantic affair with this person, he blackballed her in their industry. The woman who made these accusations did so voluntarily, posting a tearful video online that instantly made her the object of public discussion. However, a quick investigation revealed that the facts did not support her allegations.

It turned out that *she* was the aggressor. When her boss rebuffed several requests for dates, she pressed harder and upped the ante by sending him unsolicited nude photographs of herself. He still had them in the message thread on his cell phone, and they proved to be vital evidence that helped resolve the situation. After his lawyers confronted her with the evidence, she recanted her allegations, took down the video, and disappeared from public view. Her #MeToo moment was a lie, intended to target, embarrass, and smear a person against whom she wanted to exact revenge for not being interested in her. Had this individual not fought back with the assistance of legal and crisis communications experts, it is likely that his business and reputation would have been irreparably harmed.

During preceding decades, women were subjected to abuse because it was the men who held positions of sway over them. However, in the age of the Internet, this dynamic has shifted somewhat. Women (and sometimes men) making #MeToo allegations are the ones with more power, because "he said, she said" has become "he said, mob said," with droves of highly motivated and enraged online activists directing rage at a single individual as soon as allegations are levied. Often, the accusation is dreadful, and people react quickly, assuming that it is factual. When this happens, men (and in some cases women) accused of #MeToo offenses become radioactive almost instantly, even before having the opportunity to refute, rebut, or reveal the truth. When it comes to #MeToo, mere accusations can be enough to destroy careers, rip apart lives, damage familial relationships, and wreck reputations.

In one fascinating case, a man's life was turned upside down because he was accused of sexual abuse by nine women. But he had only met one of the women in person, and nothing even remotely sexual occurred between them. The other eight women all met him online within a virtual world where their avatars engaged in fully consensual, virtual sex acts. These women, all legal adults, had never met this man in person and lived hundreds or even thousands of miles away from him. Angered by his avatar's philandering, they banded together and nearly ruined him.

When It Comes to Cancel Culture, #BlackLivesMatter

The Black Lives Matter movement is aimed at guaranteeing that Black people receive equal justice under the law in the United States, and particularly ensuring that Black Americans are not victims of violence at the hands of law enforcement. The hashtag #BlackLivesMatter first emerged in social media after the acquittal of a Florida man who shot and killed Black teenager Trayvon Martin.

According to the mission statement on its website, "#BlackLivesMatter was founded in 2013 in response to the acquittal of Trayvon Martin's murderer. Black Lives Matter Global Network Foundation, Inc. is a global organization in the US, UK, and Canada whose mission is to eradicate white supremacy and build local power to intervene in violence inflicted on Black communities by the state and vigilantes."[56]

A series of additional tragic deaths at the hands of police catapulted #BlackLivesMatter to major national and international recognition. These tragedies included the fatal shooting of unarmed eighteen-year-old Michael Brown in Ferguson, Missouri, in July 2014. Thereafter, BLM activists, but also others glomming onto the movement to cause havoc, took to the streets confronting police. Other violent protests occurred after Eric Garner was choked unconscious by police and died in August of that same year and Freddie Gray died in the custody of Baltimore police in 2015. All the while, the Black Lives Matter organization, which became indistinguishable from the sentiment that Black lives matter, was gaining momentum, influence, and power, all of which coalesced into a powerful eruption of violence in 2020 following the killing of George Floyd.

With bystanders recording the horrifying incident on video, a white police officer in Minneapolis, Minnesota, knelt on the neck of the restrained Floyd for nearly ten minutes, ending his life. This appalling event set off historic nationwide protests, prompting the *New York Times* to report that #BlackLivesMatter may have become the largest protest movement in the history of the United States.[57]

Like the #MeToo movement, #BlackLivesMatter started with positive intentions and noble goals, achieving much. Writing for the Brookings Institution, where he is a senior fellow in governance studies, Rashawn Ray clearly articulated the key accomplishments:

- Black Lives Matter shifted public opinion. For example, a 2017 Pew study[58] found that 54 percent of white people viewed officer-involved shootings involving Black people to be signs of a broader problem. . . . This attitudinal shift created a policy window for local, state, and federal changes to policing and the criminal justice system.
- Black Lives Matter helped usher in a series of policy and organizational changes to policing that include implicit bias trainings, body-worn cameras, and bans on no-knock warrants.
- Black Lives Matter helped illuminate the inordinate amount of money spent on policing and civilian payouts for police brutality that come out of taxpayer pockets.
- Black Lives Matter helped stimulate federal oversight for problematic cities such as Ferguson, Louisville, Baltimore, and Minneapolis.[59]
- Black Lives Matter altered data collection efforts[60] in the academy, police departments, and the federal government to better assess which law enforcement policies do and do not work to reduce racial disparities.[61]

But through the years, accusations of racial discrimination have been invoked in a range of situations, some of which undoubtedly have warranted that label, as well as other incidents where it could not honestly be applied. Complicating things even more, the phrase Black Lives Matter has become a catch-all rallying cry for anyone believing in social justice for people of color.

As with #MeToo allegations, finding yourself on the receiving end of charges of racism with the hashtag #BlackLivesMatter attached to it can sound the death knell for the reputation of an organization or individual.

Adding to the confusion is the fact that the name of the organization Black Lives Matter has been comingled and made indistinguishable from the belief—held by all except racists—that Black lives matter. By using an unassailable fact as its organization's name, it became almost impossible for someone to question the organization, its principles, or tactics without the risk of being labeled a racist.

Life in the Age of Rage

Another key factor that has brought cancel culture to the center of national discussion is a level of rage and political frustration that has not existed in decades. It was on display, perhaps most prominently, during the presidential campaign of Donald Trump, who regularly used unprecedented degrees of inflammatory rhetoric. In his speech announcing his candidacy for president, he said of Mexicans: "They're bringing drugs. They're bringing crime. They're rapists. And some, I assume, are good people." During campaign rallies he mocked political opponents with derisive nicknames and as president spoke in coarse terms about "a total and complete shutdown of Muslims entering the United States." Make no mistake: Donald Trump was not the cause of the schisms in American society. Rather, his election was a manifestation of them.

To his "credit," Trump was able to harness the rage and frustration of a critical mass of American citizens and ride it into the White House. However, one of the long-term consequences of Trump's presidency has been the tolerance and acceptance of more bombastic (and worse) rhetoric. The biggest problem is not necessarily Trump's use of colorful language; after all, he spent many decades making a media spectacle of himself. The issue is that half the country saw his rhetoric as completely inappropriate and fundamentally unpresidential, while the other half reveled in his take-no-prisoners approach that provoked his detractors into frothy fits of rage.

Since Trump left office, other politicians have attempted to use some of his tactics and rhetorical devices. To put it another way, they calculated that if it worked for Trump, then it would work for them. But the results of the midterm election after Trump lost his bid for reelection showed that not to be the case: the candidates most resembling Trump in their bombast, election denialism, and extreme rhetoric were defeated.

The silent majority in the United States, located in the Center-Left and Center-Right, is being drowned out and overshadowed by the most polarizing and passionate voices at the fringes of the two major parties. And the federal electoral system in the United States has exacerbated the problem. The process by which candidates are selected in primaries is a recipe for the types of extreme rhetoric, strident politics, and dramatic accusations that characterize cancel culture. In the primary process, the ardent party faithful are the ones from whom candidates must receive the approval and votes. As a result, Democrats must constantly guard against primary challenges from radical candidates far to the left of where mainstream Americans are politically and socially. And the Republicans must contend with primary voters tacking well to the right of most of their fellow countrymen.

In generations past in Washington, members of opposing parties could engage in spirited debates on the floors of Congress and then go have drinks together in a spirit of mutual respect. In other words, they could disagree on the best path forward but express mutual admiration for their respective love of country. Over the past few decades, however, Washington's law-makers on both sides of the aisle have moved in opposite directions, largely losing their willingness to prioritize country over party. Most members of Congress no longer maintain friendships with people on the other side of the aisle. As one former member told us, it is not unusual for members of Congress to have no personal relationships, let alone deep friendships, with members of the opposing tribe. This era of extreme partisanship has grid-locked Washington and altered the tone of nearly every policy debate. This is another key aspect of why cancel culture has gained prominence at this moment in time.

Media Matters

The mass media consistently chides Washington's lack of decorum and chastens its political leaders for failing to reach across party lines to put the country and its people first. However, the press itself has been a vital tool in the creation of unprecedented striation and political strife, because people can now self-select their news outlets based on ideological leaning. In essence, citizens can completely enclose themselves within the confines of their media comfort zones. Instead of challenging their perceptions, the press ends up reinforcing Americans' preexisting views. If you are a Republican looking for proof that your perspective is right, then tune in to Fox News and feel your perspectives harden into concrete. A steady stream of guests, many of whom are even more extreme in their approach than you are, rein-forces not only why you believe you are correct, but also why the other side is not just misguided and wrong, but evil and unpatriotic.

On the other hand, there are diehard progressives who decry conser-vative ideology and the present-day Republican Party. They can choose MSNBC or other outlets and expect to be fed a steady diet of coverage that demonizes people with viewpoints that do not necessarily align with their more liberal (conservatives might say "coastal elite") perspective. By section-ing off America based on political affiliation and political views, the media has played a central role in fostering an environment in which a culture of illiberalism can thrive. In our view, cancel culture would have far less power were it not for the immense and immediate amplification that takes place when mass media latches on to a story or manufactured controversy, holding it up as an example for whoever happens to be the preferred consumer of its content.

Furthermore, people can access news and analysis around the clock in their self-selected echo chambers via the Internet.

The tribal nature of our politics and the partitioning of information sources and social media by political slant is another reason why the six elements of cancel culture introduced in this book have been able to thrive. People who form opinions and seek to reinforce them with tribes of like-minded individuals connect online and in real life through the power of the Internet. It was much more difficult in the past, when enormous time and effort had to be spent finding—let alone meeting in person with—your clan. However, the Internet's accessibility has enabled people to rapidly identify and congregate with droves of other people who share their views. Mobs can form faster and on a larger scale than ever before, wielding further-reaching and more lasting impacts. When your tribe is always there for you and you know where to find it, this by default creates a dynamic in which there is the "other," which is someone outside your clique who does not share your worldview. Today's political and media environment pits sides against each other, making it easy for one tribe to target, attack, and demonize the "other" groups.

Another reason cancel culture is pervasive is that editorial processes still exist but have faded from view in many quarters. There are alternative methods of obtaining information, especially content that masquerades as news but that does not necessarily follow ethical editorial processes. Reporters used to be held to certain standards, which they learned in journalism schools, and which were reinforced by their editors and by the structure of the media itself. In the old days, before a journalist could publish, and thus amplify, a story, there were checks and balances built into the system to ensure factual accuracy as well as a commitment to seek and present multiple points of view and perspectives. The Internet has weakened if not outright demolished true editorial standards across a wide range of information sources. The distinctions between legitimate and respectable news outlets and those who push an agenda are often hard to discern.

Cancel culture can also flourish because the veracity of claims is increasingly difficult to establish. Every day, a staggering amount of information is circulated online that is either completely false or materially inaccurate.

Sites and individuals, whether on purpose or unintentionally, propagate and proliferate these falsities. At the same time, while attention spans may not truly be shorter than those of goldfish, we are undeniably overwhelmed by the digital onslaught of information coming at us from every direction. In the context of observing a cancel culture attack that is underway, this means that even if all the information exists to prove that someone does not warrant punishment, people cannot find the needle of truth within a haystack of lies. In other instances, they simply do not care because they have not given it more than a moment's thought before making their judgment. Others hear an accusation repeated over and over again but have already moved on to the next scandal, next news cycle, and next outrage.

Break On Through

Further complicating efforts to separate myth from fact is that it is increasingly hard to break through in the oversaturated online and media environments. Oftentimes, the person who is the loudest and most extreme attracts the most attention. Websites are incentivized to drive traffic, since that, in turn, generates revenue. The more clicks and visitors you get, the more you can charge advertisers or receive as ad revenue, and the more sponsorship deals you can do. The monetization models of the Internet age serve to reward extreme statements, accusations, and hyperbolic headlines.

Add to that the rising status of the "influencer," and it explains how misinformation can spread so effectively. We, as a society, have granted enormous access to, and have placed significant control and power in the hands of, influencers who can impact global conversations. Mind you, these are people who do not necessarily possess the qualifications or relevant experiences that would qualify them to shape public opinion; yet they do. Their power is undeniable, and largely unchecked. Prominent influencers on social media typically have millions, if not tens of millions, of followers who are inclined to believe everything they say, never question it, and almost never take the time to fully investigate the accuracy of the information they may be receiving. Influencers are beloved by their fans and followers, who in many cases support them regardless of what they do or say.

The Internet Is the Great Equalizer

Yet another cause for the current propensity of cancel culture is the Internet's role as a great equalizer. The most insignificant person sitting at home, who has accomplished absolutely nothing in their life, can weigh in on heady and consequential topics on social media and in some cases generate more attention than a head of state, head of government, or head of a large company. Everyone who has access to the web and social media can produce and publish their own content. People who heretofore were largely powerless have become powerful, moving from bystanders and observers to potential influencers of events, their only credential being access to a keyboard.

Disparate groups of varying sizes, including women, people of color, religious denominations, the LGBTQ+ community, and others whose influence was previously held in check have stepped to the fore to wield immense influence online. Used for positive ends, this is undoubtedly a great thing, and long overdue. By the same token, the flip side of ardent activism is that it can produce highly focused constituencies with the power to cancel others. Part of what makes the practice of cancel culture appealing to some is that it affords an opportunity for the powerless to become powerful.

A final element fueling cancel culture is the mentality and mind-set of Millennials (born 1981–1996), and the members of Generation Z (also known as the iGen) who have followed. Studies have repeatedly shown that these cohorts, who have never known life without the Internet, are highly motivated to seek jobs that provide meaningful work in which they believe, which is an inspiring and positive thing. Problems and cancel culture-related incidents often arise dealing with key social and political issues around which their members are closely aligned, especially ones involving race, gender, and the role of government.[62]

Combine that with studies showing Millennials' and Gen Zs' confidence and assurance, and it creates a scenario in which droves of young people are convinced in the rightness of their views.

While it is a positive thing that young people's views are becoming increasingly (classically) liberal and tolerant, there is a potential authoritarian undercurrent when people do not think their views are open to question. This obviously relates directly to one of the six elements of cancel culture: the moral absolutism of those who engage in campaigns to deplatform others. The potential for danger exists when a critical mass of web-savvy activists believe that they possess the moral high ground, justifying whatever punishment may be meted out to their opponents.

One such example was examined in a *New York Times* feature piece titled "A Racial Slur, a Viral Video, and a Reckoning." The article told the story of one biracial male high school student saving a three-second Snapchat video that a white, fifteen-year-old female classmate had sent in a private message to a friend, saying: "I can drive, N-word." Years after the video was recorded, following protests that shook America in the wake of the killing of George Floyd, the girl urged in an Instagram post for people to "protest, donate, sign a petition, rally, do something" in support of the #BlackLivesMatter movement. Her male classmate responded with a public post: "You have the audacity to post this, after saying the N-word," as the video of her uttering the slur was shared across TikTok, Twitter, Snapchat, and other social media platforms. Her classmate had waited years—until she had already been accepted to college—before choosing to publicly call her out.

A furor erupted online, a mob mobilized, and hundreds of cancel vultures made calls and sent emails to the University of Tennessee, demanding that the high schooler not be admitted. Various mainstream media reported on the controversy, further inflaming the situation. Within days, the high school cheer captain was removed from the University's cheerleading team and began receiving threats of physical violence should she come to the campus.

"We just needed it to stop, so we withdrew her," the girl's mother told the *Times*, adding that the cancel culture attack took twelve years of her daughter's hard work as a student and "vaporized" it: "They rushed to judgment and unfortunately, it's going to affect her for the rest of her life." Reflecting on some of the lessons she drew from the experience, the girl said, "I've learned how quickly social media can take something they know very little about, twist the truth, and potentially ruin somebody's life."

A Black friend of the girl told the *Times* reporter that the student had issued a personal apology for the video long before it was made public online. Once it went viral, the friend defended her: "We're supposed to educate people," she wrote, "not ruin their lives all because you want to feel a sense of empowerment."

Meanwhile, the student responsible for the cancel culture attack, who lay in wait for years to target his classmate by publicly humiliating her and denying her the opportunity to attend the University of Tennessee, said he felt no remorse about his actions. In fact, his comments seem to convey a sense of smug self-satisfaction. "If I never posted that video, nothing would have ever happened," he told the reporter. "And because the Internet never forgets, the clip will always be available to watch." He added: "I'm going to remind myself, you started something. You taught someone a lesson."

SUMMARY OF KEY POINTS

- Cancel culture is one of the biggest threats to free speech, artistic expression, due process, and democracy.
- A combination of elements has created the perfect storm of opportunity for cancel culture to thrive.
- The Internet has created a constantly connected, global community.
- News and information can instantly reach billions.
- The #MeToo movement has contributed to the surge of cancel culture.
- People accused of #MeToo offenses become instantly radioactive before they have had the chance to refute, rebut, or reveal the truth.
- #BlackLivesMatter has contributed to an uptick in cancel culture activity.
- We are living in an age of rage and political frustration.
- The most fringe elements from both parties are exacerbating divisions, producing political tribalism and gridlock.
- The media serves to reinforce preexisting views.
- Larger mobs can form faster than ever online.
- Editorial processes have weakened at many media outlets and are nonexistent at others.
- Online it is increasingly hard to separate facts from misinformation.
- Cancel culture efforts can convert the powerless into the powerful, whether they deserve to be or not.

CHAPTER 7

Media Matters: How the Press Accelerates the Devastating Impact

"Shock and awe" is a military strategy that has been employed by American, and other, fighting forces. The idea is to use immense power, very quickly, to weaken the enemy and destroy its will to fight. Shock and awe became a household term in 2003 during the second Gulf War, when the United States military employed it in the initial phase of the conflict to rapidly devastate the regime of Saddam Hussein. Authors and defense strategists Harlan K. Ullman and James P. Wade pointed to a number of successful historical precedents when they coined the phrase and explored the concept in the 1996 book *Shock and Awe: Achieving Rapid Dominance.*

The key to shock and awe is rapidly overwhelming the other side with a disproportionate amount of force such that the battle is essentially over on day one. Shock and awe limits an opponent's ability to respond by putting him on his heels. It also serves the psychological function of disorienting him, creating despondency, and threatening his sense of survival. He therefore has no choice but to simply submit. In most cases, cancel culture attacks follow the contours of the shock-and-awe model.

Most Outrage Begins Online

The Internet often serves as both ground zero for the perceived infraction (in the form of a public statement, an unflattering video, controversial social media posts, etc.), as well as the gathering ground for cancel vultures poised to feast. Typically, a crusading individual takes it upon himself or herself to expose the target of their ire. They use the power of the web to publicize their call to arms, and a critical mass of people are mobilized.

Shouting for assistance from a hilltop is pointless if no one can hear you. On the Internet, however, someone is always listening. And others are always willing to help. Droves of highly motivated people are ever at the ready to spring into action in support of a cause they perceive as just.

With the right environmental conditions, a spark in a dry area of the woods can rapidly transform into a forest fire. One little flame, the wide availability of a fuel source, and a breeze to spread it can produce a raging inferno in no time. This is how cancel culture works, too. The spark is anything that produces anger and catalyzes action, the fuel source is a tribe of crusaders prepared for activism, and the wind to fan the flames and spread destruction is the Internet.

Imagine this sample scenario. A young professional named Ashley is active on social media in her personal life at home, having nothing to do with her work for a respected accounting firm. One day she says something offensive in a reel that she shares using her personal Instagram account, within a finite universe of followers. Another person who follows her sees it and is upset. He makes a copy of it and circulates it to another group of people who constitute his tribe—a network of followers or other contacts with whom he is in touch in some fashion. Before you know it, the offensive reel starts to spread exponentially. Literally within minutes, a topic that was never on the forefront of anyone's consciousness erupts as something front and center in the eyes of thousands, then millions, then tens or hundreds of millions of people. In short order, Ashley is being called out and publicly blasted. Her employer starts receiving phone calls, posts to its social media, and emails demanding that she be terminated immediately. The company and Ashley are now at a critical crossroads, forced to contend with a full-blown cancel culture attack.

The Media Is the Megaphone

The fictional scenario above assumes that Ashley is not a celebrity or a particularly famous individual. Because of this, her rapid downfall came about simply as a consequence of online mobilization, without involving the mainstream press. But for people living in the public eye, or for salacious stories that happen to hit mass media, that level of exposure can often dramatically accelerate the cancel culture process. Despite decades of dire predictions that it was headed for extinction, American and global media outlets have managed to survive and still play a pivotal role in reaching massive audiences and shaping public opinion.

A story that circulates solely in social media circles has limited reach, largely because it is locked within the parameters of interlocking follower-groups. However, when a story, topic, company, or individual becomes the primary focus of media during a time of reputational crisis, it is like dumping a bucket of accelerant on a bonfire. Moreover, there is often a pack mentality in the press that further magnifies the impact.

There is relentless pressure on reporters to deliver a "scoop" and to be the first to "break" a news story. But once the competitors have missed the chance to be the first ones to report on a story, they often pile on and produce their own content on the same topic. This typically happens because the breaking story rapidly becomes a major topic of discussion in society and on the Internet writ large.

All media outlets are forced to meet the challenge of producing enough revenue to stay in operation. Those basic economics used to mean selling advertising in print publications, or airtime in the form of television commercials. But in the modern world, this requires maintaining an Internet presence, driving subscriber revenue, and attracting consumers of your content and digital advertising deals that yield profits. Clicks and eyeballs are the currency of the day. It is impossible to monetize your content and fill your coffers unless you drive traffic.

The way to drive traffic is to produce articles and videos that attract visitors and keep them on your site. And the way to accomplish this goal is to showcase salacious headlines and cover widely discussed and particularly controversial topics. The kind of fodder that works best is dramatic, and it is usually negative. A range of studies have shown that negative content is more likely to be shared online than positive content, and that false news stories are shared more widely on Twitter than real ones.[63]

Wittingly, or otherwise, the press often aids and abets cancel culture by widely distributing content and stories that cancel vultures use to mobilize assaults on their chosen targets. Compounding the severity of the problem for those under fire is that the guardrails that society previously expected from mass media have crumbled. Hampered by reduced budgets and the breakneck speed with which information travels over the web, the editorial process that used to separate respected news outlets from user-generated sites has largely gone by the wayside. Moreover, outlets are unwilling to spend the necessary hours to properly vet and fact-check stories due to increased pressure to move quickly and post content aimed at attracting attention.

Outlets that demonstrate a methodical approach to ensuring accuracy, and that maintain disciplined journalistic practices, are finding it increasingly hard to compete with websites that lack the same principles and are not held to the same high standards. After all, anyone with a phone, computer, laptop, or tablet can post a blog, vlog, or other piece of content with a few keystrokes and a click or swipe. To the general public it has become increasingly hard to ascertain the difference between news stories produced by credible journalistic sources and those lacking a real editorial process or demonstrating basic journalistic integrity.

A Ferocious and Widening Impact

Days, hours, minutes, or even seconds. That is how quickly relationships, careers, financial stability, and reputations can be erased. Thanks to our society's present polarization and bias toward outrage and action, cancel vultures can eviscerate reputations built over decades. An online mob baying for blood typically unites around an issue about which it is passionate, propelled faster by media attention. Strident, far-reaching actions to address the issue are often the default, initiated and sustained by crowdsourced or user-generated calls to action.

In short order, the institutions that employ individuals under fire come under the microscope, as well. In many instances, the mob demands that the target of their ire be terminated. Often, someone who has been judged to have done or said something unacceptable is asked neither to apologize nor to become more educated about a topic. Instead, he or she is encouraged to immediately resign and accept self-banishment from society. The most vicious of the cancel vultures are not above calling for the targets of their derision to commit suicide.

Threats are almost always levied against the employer, with calls for boycotts issued publicly and communicated privately, too. Entreaties to sever ties with the organization often expand to the company's other employees, associates, board members, financial backers, business partners, or service providers. Usually, the coerced employer is left scrambling to take quick and decisive action because that is precisely what the mob demands. Most are fearful of the implications that come with attracting the spotlight of a Twitter mob. After all, unwanted negative action from zealous detractors can lead to financial consequences on a grand scale. A danger also exists for mid-term and long-term reputational damage and tarnishing of that organization's brand equity should they fail to throw the "offender" under the bus and cut ties.

Failure to bend to the will of a mob can turn a company with a sterling reputation into a pariah, literally overnight. In rapid succession, the person judged to have sinned ceases to be the focal point, and in the next moment their employers, friends, family, and network of contacts are inundated, and often impugned. In essence, the sins of the transgressor are transferred to their employer and other associates. Because, the argument goes, unless the organization is willing to condemn this person's words or deeds and fully cut ties with them, then the organization is somehow endorsing or giving tacit approval and should therefore also be canceled for abiding unacceptable or immoral behavior.

This kind of thinking should leave every one of us shaken. It is stunning to consider how quickly a story can evolve from a set of circumstances framed in a certain way—either true or false—to dissemination of information about the target, to calls to action, including expanding the scope of the vitriol from the individual in question to networks of people and organizations associated with them. Cancel culture is wielded as a weapon, a full throttle, escalated "shock-and-awe" attack aimed at annihilating the individual judged to have uttered the unspeakable or committed an unforgivable sin.

Damage Control—How to Keep the Press Out of It

As discussed, it is bad enough when an online mob brings its collective strength to bear on an individual. It becomes truly overwhelming when the media is co-opted and spreads negative or inaccurate information to an infinitely larger audience. For this reason, one of the key elements of successfully mitigating a cancel culture attack is making a full-throated effort to restrict a story from spreading beyond the confines of a niche interest group and into the mainstream media.

Even in an era when the media is attacked for being partisan, slanted, judgmental, preaching to its own narrow audiences, or simply noncredible and fake, stories appearing in the press still carry an imprimatur of authenticity. If a mainstream outlet begins to focus on a certain topic or story line, then reading accusations against someone often leads people to the default position that what they are reading is partially or fully true. The public does not realize that the speed with which a cancel culture attack moves from origination to dissemination makes it virtually impossible for full editorial processes to play out. So, if you are trying to contain a cancel culture attack, then one of the first things you should do is attempt to limit how widely the story spreads.

Another key element to weathering the storm successfully, and over the long haul, is to demand a fair editorial review of the facts should the mainstream media start to cover the topic. This can sometimes be accomplished by prevailing upon the writer working on a story. In other cases, however, it will necessitate going above the reporter and appealing to an editor, whose job is ostensibly to ensure accuracy and fairness. Oftentimes, editors are under pressure to quickly approve an enormous critical mass of stories for publication. They are overburdened, understaffed, and overworked just like their teams of reporters. The target of a cancel culture attack, or representatives working on his or her behalf, should appeal to the editor's journalistic sensibilities and make the case that they need to pause for a beat, take a breath, and ensure the veracity of whatever they are about to report.

Sometimes, the media outlets themselves need a reminder that if they jump fully into the deep end by covering a certain topic, it will ultimately be in their best interests, and prove their credibility, to take care to not just be first when reporting a story, but to be right. The media has a critical role to play when it comes to curbing the cancel culture curse. To change the dynamic, media should adhere strictly to journalistic ethics and demonstrate commitment to professionalism and fairness. Doing so will not just avoid making mistakes that can cost people their livelihoods, but also help restore the public's faith in the credibility of the press, something that has been sorely lacking in recent years.

Imagine two poles: truth on one side and lies on the other. Accurate reporting and facts are usually somewhere in the middle of these two extremes. It should be up to the public to make a reasoned judgment, but only if it can base its decision on factual information rather than hyperbolic rhetoric or wild allegations found both in the mainstream press and online in the form of social media posts or other content.

We, as a society, have a constructive role to play. We owe it to our neighbors and ultimately ourselves—since any one of us could one day be on the receiving end of a cancel culture mob—to withhold judgment until the facts are known. At a minimum, we should ensure that the individual at the center of the controversy is afforded a fair opportunity to set the record straight and share their side of the story. We all would do well to remember that our nation's founders were the first champions of due process, enshrining it in various forms in the Constitution and making it a hallmark of American society that has endured for centuries. It is still needed today, both in the context of our legal system and the public trials that people face to preserve and protect their reputations.

SUMMARY OF KEY POINTS

- With their suddenness and overwhelming impact, cancel culture attacks are reminiscent of the military strategy called "shock and awe."
- In pursuit of scoops and traffic, the media aids and abets the perpetuation of conflicts and scandals.
- Within moments, reputations built over years can be destroyed.
- Reputation firestorms are accelerated by the media.
- The sins of an alleged transgressor are often transferred to their employer.
- Key to mitigating cancel culture is keeping a story from spreading beyond niche audiences.
- Targets of coverage should demand a fair editorial process from outlets that have such safeguards.
- Given that everyone makes mistakes, we should all withhold judgment until the facts of a situation are known.
- People at the center of controversy should be afforded a fair opportunity to share their side of the story.

CHAPTER 8

Cancel Proof: Why It Is Hard to Cancel Politicians

When it comes to the political arena, neither the Republicans nor the Democrats have a monopoly on cancel culture. If you were to scroll through discussion boards or Reddit threads or read political websites, then you might mistakenly think deplatforming people is a tactic employed solely by the "woke" hard Left. Currently in American politics, the extremists on the Left are highly engaged in cancel culture. This group has to date been more vociferous about defending the supposed benefits of taking this approach than the hard Right.

Numerous cancel culture campaigns have emanated from the "woke crowd," whose very name is meant to declare that its devotees are awake and everyone else in the country is asleep. But a predilection for deplatforming has become a bipartisan effort. In fact, when it comes to politics, there have always been concerted efforts by the two parties to cancel each other's candidates. Until recently it was not termed cancel culture; it was simply called politics.

The Old Forms of Political Cancel Culture

Since the earliest days of the United States, our political culture has involved scorching attacks on political enemies. If you rewind the clock to the twentieth, nineteenth, or even the eighteenth centuries, members of opposing political parties were training their fire on candidates from the opposing side of the aisle. In old world America, dirty politics involved seizing the most extreme language or hyperbolic examples of bad behavior and bringing it to the masses in the form of dramatic accusations meant to sully an opponent's reputation. At that time, the options for doing so were much more limited. If you were going to cancel your opponent in the nineteenth century, you had to either take out an advertisement in a written publication and attack your opponent, take to the floor of a legislative body, or debate that individual face-to-face.

In the past, because of the smaller, less dense populations and owing to the fact that there was not an efficient way to reach a critical mass of the citizenry, the audiences were obviously much more restricted and the results of reputational assaults less potent. If you were a prospective voter who happened to be at a debate between two candidates, then you could hear the allegations or slanders and determine whether they seemed credible to you or not. If you lived in the same metropolitan area where a publication was distributed, then it was possible that you might have read something in the newspaper about the debate after the fact.

Alternatively, you could have read campaign literature, which is basically a euphemism for candidate- or party-produced propaganda. Before the era of online ads and negative TV spots, American political attack advertising came in the form of handbills that were posted or distributed. Today's communications tools are more pervasive, instantaneous, and efficient than at any time in history, giving politicians the opportunity to attack their opponents on local, state, regional, national, and even international stages. In fact, the Internet has made it possible to disseminate information—true or categorically false—all over the planet in just seconds.

Political cancel culture of the original variety was largely directed from one individual against another, or one political party against another political party. Earlier in this book, we defined six common elements of the modern-day cancel culture attack. In prior centuries, a number of these elements were missing.

A core element that was absent from attacks in the past was the mobilization of a huge swath of the population into a mob to target and take out an individual. The element of anonymity that the Internet affords was also absent, so if you were going to trash-talk a candidate for office, you had to engage with people and have a conversation. Your comments were essentially for attribution, and the individual with whom you were engaged in dialogue could then spread the word and inform others that you were the source of whatever information you had disseminated. Now, thanks to the

Internet, a nameless, faceless person cloaked in anonymity can be both the source of information and the amplifier of that information.

Political Support Structures

Several factors make it difficult for American political candidates or politicians to be canceled. One is that cancel culture is often based on a large group of people banding together to enact mob justice targeting an individual. Political attacks, on the other hand, are largely tribal in nature. In elections and day-to-day political warfare, one tribe faces off against another tribe, though, of course, in American politics they refer to themselves as "parties" and go by the names Democrat and Republican. In essence, they are two warring factions with a vested interest in attacking the other side and defending their own. The element of banding together in defense of a teammate is one element that reduces cancel culture's effect in politics.

In most cases, a candidate from one political party will have the unassailable support of his or her fellow party members. Entities such as the Republican National Committee and the Democratic National Committee serve are the governing bodies of their tribes. In addition, there are limitless other entities that rally around their candidates and provide support structures, including political action committees (PACs). Under the PAC umbrella are separate segregated funds (SSFs), which the Federal Election Committee defines as "political committees established and administered by corporations, labor unions, membership organizations or trade associations. These committees can solicit contributions only from individuals associated with a connected or sponsoring organization."[64]

Nonconnected committees can solicit money from the public and are not connected with any of the entities comprising SSFs. But the real political muscle comes in the form of—aptly named—super PACs. These are "committees that may receive unlimited contributions from individuals, corporations, labor unions and other PACs for the purpose of financing independent expenditures and other independent political activity." A 5–4 ruling by the Supreme Court in January of 2020 in the case of *Citizens United v. Federal Election Commission* cleared the path for corporations and other outside groups to spend unlimited sums on elections.

In addition to super PACs, hybrid PACs serve to "solicit and accept unlimited contributions from individuals, corporations, labor organizations and other political committees to a segregated bank account for the purpose of financing independent expenditures, other ads that refer to a federal candidate, and generic voter drives in federal elections."[65] Meanwhile, lead-ership PACs are political committees established for the purposes of sup-porting individual candidates for office, with restrictions placed upon how much they can contribute each election cycle.

As part of their work in support of their chosen candidate and tribe, these various structures serve to protect individuals from attacks, promote the positive attributes of their favorite candidates, and direct financial sup-port toward them. A natural by-product of supporting those candidates is that individuals, as well as corporations or other entities who contribute support, become boosters of their candidate of choice, inclined and incen-tivized to help them prevail in elections and motivated to defend them should they become the targets of cancel culture-style attacks.

Defending Their Teammates

The average woman or man who winds up on the receiving end of a cancel culture attack cannot rely upon the same networks or infrastructures of support available to politicians. It can be debilitating for a political party's candidate or officeholder to be attacked by the opposing party. But he or she can take comfort in the fact that help is almost always on the way. In fact, built into the system of candidate and policymaker support is a critical mass of people who will vigorously defend the person to the hilt—and to a fault. Even in cases of deeply troubling allegations of wrongdoing, political entities are increasingly willing to back up the members of their team to avoid losing elections or ceding power.

This shift has been even more pronounced during the past decade. There used to be certain criteria by which politicians and political parties held their own candidates to account. Think of it like the sports of hockey or baseball, in which there is an unspoken code among those in the game. If one team targets the other team's star player for rough treatment, then players take it upon themselves to police the game and strictly enforce certain mores. On the ice this comes in the form of a physically imposing enforcer, with pugi-listic skills on par with or exceeding his hockey skills, always ready for battle and poised to seek revenge or a measure of justice on the other side.

Often, violent on-ice hits or dropping the gloves for a fight is done to "send a message." And that message is this: if you threaten our players or jeopardize their health, then we will do the same to you and come after your players. In a sense, the hockey "code" is a form of mutually assured destruc-tion that prevents players from being targeted.

A similar code exists in baseball, as well. America's national pastime features a lengthy list of "unwritten rules," and the pitchers are usually the ones who enforce the code. If a team is judged to have crossed the line and committed an infraction, then the pitcher exacts justice by hurling a rock-hard baseball at the batter, which can often lead to injury or provoke brawls.

When it comes to politics, the two political parties are increasingly adopting similar approaches when it comes to unifying the self-selecting members of their tribe. Certain behaviors by policymakers or candidates that were once deemed unforgivable and unacceptable are now largely tolerated due to political parties' desire to win at all costs. In other words, power trumps all, and winning elections to maintain power has subsumed the body politic.

In general, the self-interests of the two political parties have been held up as more important and deserving of support than the overall national good. In other words, we live in a time of partisanship over patriotism. This has come to the fore in recent years, in the form of political salvos launched by one side against the other. The two sides have made it clear that they are willing to weaponize federal government institutions in order to achieve objectives through political coercion. And they threaten to employ these tactics to exact their vengeance. This is the first time something like this has happened on such a grand scale in this country, and it is extremely dangerous.

The difference between cancel culture and standard political attacks is that there is a network of individuals ready to defend the person under fire. We are seeing allegations of outrageously bad behavior on the part of elected officials, which in previous years would have prompted the parties to instantly self-police and demand the resignations of their members. Today, however, the voices of the members of the House and Senate are largely silent in the face of not just allegations, but instances with ample evidence suggesting demonstrably illegal or immoral behavior occurred.

Why It's So Hard to Cancel a Politician

As we have underscored, it is much harder to cancel someone when there exists a virtual guarantee that the individual who is the target of ire has an entire cadre of sympathetic compatriots behind him or her prepared to support them, regardless of the charges or fact patterns. This makes truly canceling a politician nearly impossible. But there are additional reasons.

Politicians are uniquely immune to cancel culture in part because they have resources that are not readily available to everyday men and women. If a small business owner finds herself or himself under attack online or otherwise, they are left to contend with it largely on their own. They can enlist the help of advisors they bring in such as lawyers, public relations professionals, crisis managers, friends and family, or their professional networks. But it takes time to identify such specialists and financial resources to hire them; and time is of the essence when a cancel culture attack is mounted. By the time the proper vendors have been located and retained, the person's reputation or revenue may already be irrevocably damaged. According to respected trial attorney Phil O'Beirne of Stein Mitchell, "Political people in DC are incentivized to play gotcha and engage in endless cancel culture-style finger-pointing because they have the roadmaps and the political foot soldiers to defend against those tactics themselves. The problem is that the little guy who is a cancel culture victim doesn't have a mob; the little guy has got nobody."

Politicians on the other hand have entire staffs at their disposal to help them defend against cancel culture attacks. A member of the House of Representatives likely has a chief of staff who is singularly dedicated to defending the boss and helping them navigate challenges as well as a press secretary or communications director who can push their message out to the media and beyond.

Politicians also have the party and political infrastructure we spoke of earlier, including political action committees. Political leaders also have hundreds of colleagues from the same party with their own staffs and the sophistication and platforms to share messages supporting and defending the embattled lawmaker before potentially huge audiences. They also can rely upon their party's leadership. In other words, they have an extremely large critical mass of experienced, well-qualified individuals accustomed to giving speeches and effectively communicating who can ensure that they are not canceled. They live to fight another day, in the form of retaining their positions or prevailing in the next elections.

Another reason politicians are inoculated against cancellation is the shock factor—or perhaps more aptly described as the total lack of a shock factor—when they misbehave. Many times, when individuals are taken out by cancel culture mobs, it is because the public persona that they cultivated over time contrasts sharply with the image that emerges in the wake of a cancel culture attack.

Consider the fate of canceled high-profile celebrities, such as media personality Matt Lauer. His stunning downfall illustrates that when someone has always been perceived as one thing and then they are revealed to be something very different, then it is a jarring experience. For years, Lauer enjoyed global fame and recognition. As the anchor of NBC's *Today Show*, he projected the image of a wholesome, affable, and all-around nice guy. So, when allegations emerged that he had sexually assaulted subordinates, there was a huge outcry and an explosive end to his career.

When TV personality Ellen DeGeneres was revealed to have tolerated, if not promoted, a culture of bullying and negativity on the set of her show, it did not take long for a chorus of people to unite and ultimately force the show's cancellation. In effect, there was cognitive dissonance between the sweet, lovable dancing woman seen on-air and what was alleged to be negative and abusive behavior behind the scenes.

Many times, when it comes to cancellations and other public relations crises, the shock factor and explosive element of hypocrisy prove the hardest to overcome. This is the case for normal, nonpublic figures, but especially people who live in the public eye enjoying heretofore positive reputations. Religious leaders revealed to have serious moral failings, or whose private lives run totally counter to what they preach in church, are particularly susceptible to career implosion if their hypocritical actions come to light. Examples of this abound.

Yet, with politicians, the bar is immediately set very low. Americans reflexively view them through a negative lens and simply assume that they are hypocrites. For many years, studies consistently show most Americans disapprove of Congress and have little faith in how senators and House members do their jobs. Gallup polls taken in October 2022 showed 75 percent of respondents saying they disapproved of how Congress is handling its job. Asked how much trust and confidence they had in the legislative branch, 23 percent chose "none at all" and 39 percent "not very much."

Because politicians are viewed negatively by a plurality of American citizens, when negative allegations or accusations of bad behavior emerge, there is neither cognitive dissonance nor a shock factor. In fact, people would probably be shocked if policymakers did not demonstrate bad behavior. No career-killing dose of hypocrisy is brought to bear because a huge swath of the public already assumed that these people—by virtue of being involved in politics—were not trustworthy and did not have a high moral standing. This is a fascinating, and perhaps disheartening, reality.

After all, if you already assumed someone to be a liar and a scoundrel, then it comes as no surprise when evidence emerges to support that point of view along with your negative prejudice toward them. If it has always been expected, then there is no surprise and no fall from grace because they never enjoyed a respectable reputation. The assumption about politicians is that they are self-serving liars who will do and say anything to advance their careers.

Politicians are increasingly able to get away with anything because the parties are more willing than ever to tolerate bad behavior within their ranks to secure political power. In essence, the tribe or mob's self-interest is deemed more important than national interest. For these reasons, cancel culture poses a far greater threat to average citizens than to those called upon to represent and lead them in government. The tribal aspect of politics means those under pressure can turn every accusation around and point the finger back at the other tribe. When accused of bad behavior, politicians are typically quick to dismiss the charges as partisan political attacks emanating from the other side. And because people have such low opinions of politicians, and American society has been conditioned to expect food fights between the parties, there always exists the possibility that the charges are fabricated, exaggerated, or that the person is a target of a reputational attack by the other political party.

For a politician, the safest way to defend yourself against cancel culture attacks is to simply wave off the allegation and dismiss it as a political ploy emanating from the other side. That is a privilege that the average individual does not have. Most people do not have a built-in tribe of supporters who will not only stand by them, but assume—whether or not there is evidence to support the outrage—that the other side is attacking and seeking to bring them down simply because they belong to an opposing political party.

Political Storms Pass Quickly

Another element that is the hallmark of a cancel culture attack for mere mortals, but seemingly does not apply to officeholders or office seekers, is becoming radioactive forever. That element of permanence is largely lacking in the political arena. There are, of course, a few exceptions and third rails that still exist within our body politic. For example, members who engage in illegal sexual contact or communication with minors are thankfully still largely cast out and forever banned. For examples of this, look no further than repeat offender and disgraced former Democratic congressman and

New York mayoral candidate Anthony Weiner, a.k.a. "Carlos Danger," who was sexting underage girls. Or former Republican Speaker of the House Dennis Hastert, who was sent into political oblivion and then served prison time for hush money payments to a boy he sexually assaulted as his high school wrestling coach.

Another element that keeps politicians from being canceled is the staggering number of public statements they make, which are amplified by partisan media. Most average citizens will never say or do anything in their lifetimes that will produce outrage or draw national media attention. Politicians, on the other hand, find themselves on national television programs, podcasts, radio shows, and in print and online media headlines on a regular basis. For some, it is a near daily occurrence. And because they have so much exposure—and in some cases overexposure—they have an enhanced ability to quickly move past a scandal or controversial statement by issuing plenty of other controversial or noncontroversial statements.

In other words, politicians can flood the system with additional content. The average person who makes a mistake and says something objectionable or false will have a very hard time walking that statement back. The initial outrage and media shaming will be difficult to overcome later should they issue a clarification, apology, or retraction. Organizations that become the target of extremely critical news coverage often see this play out. When a negative story goes viral, the company suffers a huge reputational hit, which many times leads to reductions in sales or the short-term or long-term denting of their brand's value. And then, when the accusations are eventually proven to be false, untrue, or exaggerated, or a retraction or correction has been offered, it has little impact helping them to redeem themselves.

People remember dramatic and hyperbolic headlines, and the accusation becomes ingrained in their minds. In fact, the existence of an allegation alone, whether it has basis in reality or, to borrow a phrase, is completely "fake news," becomes far more powerful than any clarifications predicated upon truth. Politicians understand this; they can make the most outlandish statements knowing full well that they are untrue, because they have party infrastructure behind them. Moreover, they are surrounded by professionals who can help them move forward past the current controversy of the day. Instead of accepting responsibility for missteps or things they have actually screwed up, they can just point to the other side and blame them. And, in some cases, they just move quickly to create more content, more statements, more positions, and more controversies in order to set off a fresh news cycle.

Donald Trump's Cancel Culture

Love or loathe him, former President Donald Trump is undeniably a mas-
ter of the media and a genius when it comes to understanding how to
insert himself into, and even shape, national conversations. What Trump
demonstrated as a candidate and later as the communicator in chief was
an uncanny ability to tap into the emotions of the American public, attract
attention, and create an unyielding litany of media firestorms that all but
guaranteed that he would dominate the news.

His primary opponents ahead of the 2016 election were completely
overwhelmed by Trump's ability to draw attention. They were left impo-
tent, unable to attract even a fraction of the news coverage that he was able
to command, rendering them ineffectual and helping Trump secure the
Republican nomination and ultimately be elected president.

During his time in office, Trump demonstrated an ability to control the
news cycle and be the focal point of the news in ways that no other president
has or likely ever will be. Trump is the ultimate example of an uncancel-
lable politician. Despite two impeachment trials, a mind-boggling amount
of negative media coverage, the storming and desecrating of the United
States Capitol by his supporters, and enough controversies to fill dozens of
breathless tell-all books from his own former staffers, Trump still managed
to become a third-time presidential candidate and continues to keep himself
implanted in the nation's dialogue.

Nobody understands better than the man himself just how uncan-
cellable he is. He said it best during his first campaign. With his fingers
mimicking the firing of a gun, Trump said on-camera at a campaign rally:
"I could stand in the middle of Fifth Avenue and shoot somebody and
wouldn't lose any voters, okay? It's, like, incredible."

Yes, it was incredible. And he was right. The four years of his presidency
proved his prescience. Donald Trump, more than any other human being
on the planet, cannot be canceled. Various members of his party, as well as
members of the opposing party, have attempted to use Trumpian tactics
to dominate the news cycle, manufacturing controversies and saying out-
rageous things that put them in the spotlight, spark outrage, and aim to
generate interest. But many of them have failed to replicate his success or
win elections. In our lifetimes, we are unlikely to ever see a person better
at getting into the heads of the press, generating headlines, staying in the
news, and somehow manipulating both the media outlets and journalists
who love him, and those who despise him, to nonetheless cover him.

There Is Always an Exception

Despite this chapter's focus on politics, it is not intended to be political in nature or to express preferences for either side of the ideological spectrum. The assessments made here about Donald Trump and the others mentioned by name are meant to be seen through the lens of communication around cancel culture. We understand that the mere mention of the name Trump or other political leaders can be enough to trigger outrage, consternation, or controversy—none of which is our intention.

The timeless maxim that there are two sides to every story is not accurate. In our experience, there are usually at least three sides or more. The world is complex, and the truth about every situation is usually located somewhere between black and white in a decidedly gray area.

The general assessment we have made is that politicians are far less likely to be canceled than other people. Which is not to say that it never happens. Few things in life are ever absolute, and there is an exception to every rule. With that in mind, we now recall the case of a famous politician who was canceled: Senator Al Franken.

When Al Franken reported for work in Washington as a senator from Minnesota, he was already a bona fide celebrity. A nationally recognized comedian and former mainstay on the popular weekend comedy show *Saturday Night Live*, he was also the author of a series of bestselling books. After being reelected to a second term, Franken spoke about wanting to be known as a hardworking policy wonk. He was effective as a fundraiser, and one of the highest-profile Democratic senators. Which made his eventual fall from grace even more stunning and spectacular.

A Crushing Tide of Internal Opposition

On November 16, 2017, Franken's office was sent into a tailspin by the arrival of an email from the news director of a local Minnesota radio station. It requested comment from the senator on a publicly posted statement from a woman named Leann Tweeden. She accused Franken of forcibly kissing her against her will while the two of them were on a United Service Organizations (USO) tour entertaining troops in Afghanistan, Iraq, and Kuwait in 2006. A photo already published online showed Franken smiling impishly while pretending to grope the breasts of Tweeden through her flak jacket as she slept.

In the weeks that followed, seven other women came forward claiming improper conduct by Franken. Most of their allegations centered upon unwanted physical contact in some fashion, including that he placed his hands upon their bodies during photo ops. Others cited unwelcome or attempted kisses, with one saying that in 2006 "he had made her uneasy by looking as if he planned to kiss her," according to a detailed story about Franken's undoing in the *New Yorker* by Jane Mayer.[66] Under great pressure from the media, the public, and his constituents, Franken asked Senate Minority Leader Chuck Schumer for an independent investigation into his conduct, a request to which he agreed.

But this investigatory process was overtaken by a series of events that emanated from within the Senate Democratic Caucus itself. Franken's senate colleagues effectively served as a cancel culture mob, publicly demanding his immediate resignation before a full accounting of the facts had been taken or due process allowed to play out. On December 1, according to reporting from Jane Mayer, seven female Democratic senators met with Schumer to alert him that they were close to calling for Franken to resign. Then, on December 6, Politico posted a story in which a Capitol Hill staffer claimed that he attempted to kiss her, which he denied in the story as "categorically not true."

Within minutes, his colleagues began publicly demanding his resignation, and by the end of the day, thirty-six senators from his own party, including their leader Charles Schumer, had joined the chorus. Just weeks after the scandal first broke, and one day after the Politico article published, Franken announced on December 7 his intention to abandon his senate seat. A few weeks later, he was gone.

Of the six elements typical in a cancel culture attack, all were present when it came to the campaign against Al Franken.

Element 1: The Infractions Were Made Against a Collective
Franken's fellow Democratic senators, including a group of female colleagues who led the charge, believed they were doing so in service to victims of sexual harassment and assault and women everywhere.

Element 2: The Controversy Arose and Accelerated Rapidly
Despite a decade in office spanning one-and-a-half terms, in just weeks Franken's Senate career was over.

Element 3: Nature of the Charges Was Trivial or Fabricated

Any unwanted sexual contact, from kisses to touching, are inappropriate and wrong. At the same time, many of the allegations against Franken were on the mild side, with some even accusing him of having intent and preparing to do something without ever having done it. The photograph involving his first accuser appears to be juvenile and stupid, but hardly proof of a serious physical or sexual offense.

Element 4: Disproportionate Response

Senator Franken repeatedly requested due process in the form of an investigation into allegations against him. With no real need for immediate action, he was forced by his own colleagues to immediately resign in shame before that process even got underway.

Element 5: Everyone Afraid to Defend the Accused

His fellow Democratic senators were afraid to stand by Franken during this time. Even long-time friends were quick to abandon him, apparently cowed by criticism from third-party groups and media outlets questioning a double standard for Democrats who at the time were attacking Republican President Donald Trump and Roy Moore, the first for his boasting description of assaulting women overheard by an *Access Hollywood* microphone, and the latter for allegations of sexual assault, some from people who were children at the time, by the Alabama senate candidate.

Element 6: Moral Absolutism

Senator Kirsten Gillibrand from New York provided the best evidence that those demanding Franken resign were supremely confident in the total correctness of their position. She said at a press conference at the time: "Enough is enough. The women who came forward are brave and I believe them. While it's true that his behavior is not the same as the criminal conduct alleged against Roy Moore or Harvey Weinstein or President Trump, it is still unquestionably wrong, and should not be tolerated." Asked by *New Yorker* journalist Jane Mayer years later if she stood by her decision, Gillibrand declared, "The women who came forward felt it was sexual harassment . . . so it was." She also told the reporter, "I'd do it again today."

The sentiments expressed by Senator Gillibrand in the lengthy and robustly reported *New Yorker* piece contrasted sharply with the regrets expressed by many of her colleagues who played critical roles in Franken's undoing. "If there's one decision I've made that I would take back, it's the decision to call for his resignation," said Senator Heidi Heitkamp of North Dakota. "It was made in the heat of the moment, without concern for exactly what it was." Senator Tammy Duckworth of Illinois said the Senate Ethics Committee "should have been allowed to move forward," adding that "we needed more facts. That due process didn't happen is not good for our democracy." Senator Patrick Leahy of Vermont said turning on Franken was "one of the biggest mistakes I've made," while Senator Angus King of Maine said there was no excuse for sexual assault, "but Al deserved more of a process. I don't denigrate the allegations, but this was the political equivalent of capital punishment."

Another regretful Democratic senator, Bill Nelson of Florida, stated: "I realized almost right away I'd made a mistake. I felt terrible. I should have stood up for due process to render what it's supposed to—the truth." New Mexico Senator Tom Udall restated his own belief in due process, especially as a lawyer, and said Franken "had the right to be heard by an independent investigative body. I've heard from people around my state, and around the country, saying that they think he got railroaded. It doesn't seem fair."

At the time when Franken's senate colleagues from his own party were turning on him, Former House Speaker Newt Gingrich made this observation to the *Washington Post*. "This is a party which is losing its mind. They suddenly curled into this weird puritanism that feels like a compulsion to go out and lynch people without a trial." Gingrich's comments were made at a time before the term "cancel culture" had been coined, but you would be hard-pressed to find a better description of a cancel culture attack than the inclination to "lynch people without a trial." It speaks to the very essence of the curse that cancel culture casts upon America today.

Had the same allegations been made today against Senator Al Franken, then he likely would not have resigned, nor would he have been canceled. The various reasons were explored in detail in this chapter, where we discussed how political loyalties, tribal affiliations, and political structures poised to defend their own are a critical factor that normally makes it nearly impossible to cancel politicians. The case of Senator Franken is a remarkable and memorable one since the cancel vultures who picked him apart and left him for dead were Democratic senators from within his own caucus.

SUMMARY OF KEY POINTS

- Both Republicans and Democrats employ cancel culture.
- For hundreds of years, politicians have tried to cancel one another to prevail in elections.
- The Internet makes it possible for politicians to wage large-scale attacks on one another.
- Various elements make it hard for candidates or politicians to be canceled.
- Political parties are "tribes" or "mobs," warring factions with a vested interest in banding together to protect one another and attack the enemy.
- Unassailable support from their own party and its structural organizations serves to keep politicians from being canceled.
- Political entities are willing to form mobs that back members of their tribe to avoid losing elections or ceding power.
- Increasingly, bad behavior by their team members is ignored by parties out of a desire to win at all costs.
- We are living in a time where most leaders place partisanship over patriotism.
- Politicians have resources at their disposal not available to average citizens, which helps them fend off attacks that would destroy average people.
- The powerful shock factor attached to any scandal is muted because people already see politicians through a negative light.
- An available defense to any politician facing a cancel culture attack is to accuse the other side of manufacturing it.
- Politicians are aided by their access to massive media and communications platforms and enjoy many opportunities to get their message across.
- President Donald J. Trump has proven the least cancellable person on the planet, as evidenced by his ability to weather countless controversies.
- Senator Al Franken is an exceptional case; he was canceled because his own tribe/mob turned on him.

CHAPTER 9

Apologies and Atonement

Since childhood, most of us have been raised with the instruction that if you make a mistake or hurt somebody else's feelings, then the proper thing to do is apologize. This, we have been told, holds true whether we hurt the other person on purpose or inadvertently. Once an apology has been offered, then the offended party bears responsibility for considering it, choosing either to accept or refuse it.

Acceptance brings with it the resolution of the immediate conflict, creating a basis upon which both parties can move forward with their lives in some fashion. It may take time to rebuild trust, and the relationship between the two may never be fully mended, but at least there is closure. Rejection, on the other hand, leaves the wound raw and unhealed, and the conflict forever unresolved.

When it comes to cancel culture, the process of destroying someone who has made a mistake more closely mirrors rejection. In fact, not only are their attempts at apologizing in word or deed rebuffed, but they are denied the opportunity for full penitence because a cancel vulture mob decrees them utterly irredeemable.

Neither apologies nor forgiveness are conditional, meaning that a person can still offer an apology with no expectation of receiving absolution. And a person can choose to forgive someone who has sinned against them without ever receiving an apology. An apology offered with the knowledge that it is likely to be rejected or met with apathy is arguably the most meaningful and genuine form of atonement, since it is not being done with any ulterior motive—it is just doing what's right out of a sense of shame, remorse, or regret. Forgiving someone without expectation of an apology can be a way to move past conflict and also unburden you of the stress and anger that often accompany a feeling of being wronged.

Whether a person forgives without expectation of apology or lets go of resentment independent of what anyone else may or may not do or say, it is empowering. It is also a choice to play the role of victor or victim, and to be strong and resilient instead of weak and wounded. Look across the landscape of our present-day outrage culture, and it is not too difficult to see how this equation has been inverted and people are choosing to be victims. Allowing cancel culture to flourish strips the opportunity to apologize from the targets of contempt and conveys undeserved authority and strength upon people who see themselves as wounded victims.

Stroll the aisles of any bookstore or peruse titles online and you will find books aplenty filled with proverbs, adages, and self-help quotes extolling the virtues of inner strength, the nobility of perseverance, fortitude, discipline, love, and overcoming adversity. Unfortunately, cancel vultures conveniently display diametrically opposite traits when they embark on campaigns of character and career assassination. Canceling other people demands that you set aside the idea that other people deserve to be treated as you would want to be treated if the roles were reversed. Our culture seems more filled with rage than ever before, but one answer for moving past the current default to outrage could lie in relearning the lost art of forgiveness.

Scientific Benefits of Forgiveness

Scientific evidence supports the notion that forgiveness is not just good for the soul, but also the mind and body. The degree to which we feel wronged, and how connected we are to the offender, can impact the amount of acute or chronic stress our bodies will have to synthesize. Research has shown, and most of us know from our own experiences, that emotional stress, especially over a prolonged period, can wreak havoc on our endocrine systems. In fact, studies and a field of psychology called Choice Theory® have illustrated that the human body's response to stress is the same, whether the cause was real or imagined. The power an individual has over their stress level hinges upon their choices in how to respond to it.

Stress sets off a reaction in our brain's hypothalamus that influences our autonomous nervous system. Blood pressure, heart rate, breathing, and digestion are involuntarily controlled by this system. In the presence of stress, blood pressure, heart rate, and breathing increase, while other systems such as digestion and reproduction slow. In addition to producing adrenaline, the adrenal glands produce cortisol, which allows the body to use glucose more readily for energy. Elevated periods of stress may lead to digestive problems, weight gain, sleep disruption, infertility, and anxiety.

Perhaps it should come as no surprise that in a society that places more and more emphasis on grievance, with each side claiming grievance and victimhood, forgiveness is in increasingly short supply. We know that anger and resentment have reached catastrophic levels, as evidenced by skyrocketing rates of obesity, low reproduction levels, sleep deprivation, anxiety, and suicide. Might a healthy dose of forgiveness be part of the answer to these ailments?

Research studies have shown that offering forgiveness helps bring down cortisol levels, in turn lowering blood pressure, anxiety, depression, and stress, while reducing the risk of heart attacks. The science is irrefutable: the act of offering forgiveness, whether it is in response to an apology or not, helps lead to a—quite literally—healthier society.

To Forgive Is Divine: Religious Tradition of Forgiveness

The religious arguments for forgiveness predate the scientific arguments by millennia. The world's five major religions, to whose teachings and instruction billions of people subscribe, make the case that forgiveness is essential to one's relationship with oneself, the community, and God. The holy texts of Islam, Hinduism, Buddhism, Christianity, and Judaism all issue spiritual instruction for their followers related to sin, atonement, and forgiveness, albeit in different forms.

In the Muslim holy book, the Qur'an, there are 114 chapters, referred to as *suras*. Every *sura* except one begins with the phrase *Bismillahir Rahmanir Raheem*, which translates to "In the name of God the Merciful, the Compassionate." Of all God's attributes, mercy and compassion are called out and reiterated.

In Chapter 16, verse 3 in one of Hinduism's most revered texts, the Bhagavad Gita, 26 virtues of a saintly nature are articulated in the hopes that adherents to the faith will continually elevate themselves spiritually. One of those highest virtues is forgiveness.

In an interview with Dandapani, a Hindu priest and former monk of ten years who lectures around the world and is the author of the book *The Power of Unwavering Focus*, he challenged the notion that any person should be permanently cancelled: "We are souls living in physical bodies who undergo the process of reincarnation precisely because we have more to learn than can be gained in a single lifetime. Naturally, we all make mistakes, and the goal is to learn from them, take those lessons, and apply them to our lives so that we do not repeat them."

Dandapani reflected upon key aspects of Hindu teaching and philosophy that he sees as inconsistent with cancel culture. "Moral absolutism does not work. We must first understand that we are not perfect, and that people will screw up. Reincarnation allows us to grow and improve," he said. "We each must take ownership of our lives, the good and the bad. Each of us can mitigate mistakes we have made through redeeming acts of atonement. Ultimately, if you can own your own problems and recognize your own flaws, then you can accept others as beings that are evolving."

As for the people who find themselves under attack from cancel vulture mobs, he added: "Divinity is in all of us, energy is in all of us, and rather than criticizing others we should instead empathize with them and show compassion. If the person in question expresses contrition, then instead of taking a cancel culture approach and nailing them to the wall or criticizing them publicly, we should be asking: 'How can I help this person make it right, and how can I support them on their journey to doing so?'"

The concept of forgiveness is not addressed directly in the Buddhist canon of sacred teachings. However, examine the life of the Buddha and you will find a person dedicated to loving kindness, and hardly the type to bear grudges or refuse to give absolution to someone offering an apology.

When it comes to Christianity, the Bible contains a multitude of references to the concepts of sinning, absolution, and forgiveness, and there are numerous practices based upon the belief that Jesus died upon the cross for the sins of all his followers. The Book of Matthew, Chapter 6, verses 14–15 provides a stark warning to those Christians for whom cancel culture seems like an appropriate avenue for attacking others: "For if you forgive men their trespasses, your heavenly Father will also forgive you. But if you do not forgive men their trespasses, neither will your Father forgive your trespasses."

To understand cancel culture through the lens of Jewish law and tradition, we conducted a brief interview with prolific Israeli scholar and author Rabbi Daniel Gordis.

Gordis emphasized the primacy Jewish texts and practice have always placed on justice, as administered by impartial judges and courts: "I believe there is a religious concept of fairness, and the notion of transparency, which I believe Judaism regards as critical to settle conflicts between parties. A huge part of cancel culture is the accuser's ability to secretly or anonymously denounce another, which creates a disparity in terms of vulnerability . . . and makes it fundamentally antithetical to the Jewish take on justice."

Gordis also spoke about the Jewish concept of punishment, noting that "in Jewish life there is no such thing as 'you committed an infraction, you paid your price, but you are guilty forever and ever.' I believe the cancel culture community has completely erased the notion of repentance and forgiveness."

Asked about Yom Kippur, the holiest day of the year for Jews known as the day of atonement, he pointed out that community members are called upon to apologize for sins they have committed, but not for expressing views or taking positions on topics: "Canceling someone for a point of view appears to be a fundamental closure of intellectual discourse. We should not live in a world where people are afraid to express their ideas for fear of being excommunicated, pushed out, or canceled.

"Yom Kippur presumes that one can apologize and there is the possibility of atonement. When you cancel people, you have created a world in which people can't even apologize, devoid of forgiveness.

"You have to be able to say I'm sorry, and the other person has to be able to let go," added Gordis. "A world that does not include repentance and forgiveness is a cruel and mean place."

We concluded the interview by asking why cancel culture, which he said was characterized by "anti-fairness, anti-forgiveness, and anti-intellectual openness" had not been adopted in Israel. His answer: "There is the notion in America of a sacred circle of suffering and victimhood. I'm a victim because of my gender, race, religion, sexual orientation, physical limitations, or whatever the case may be. I believe the whole idea of Israel was to erase victimhood from the Jewish lexicon. I don't think we're going to start sanctifying victimhood, and I don't think the sacred circle of suffering is going to gain traction in this country."

Proceed with Caution: The Risk of Apologizing

In recent years there have been high-profile public apologies by celebrities, academics, athletes, politicians, and others who live in the public eye. Over that same amount of time, endless conjecture has been offered critiquing individual apologies and bemoaning the ineffectiveness of apologies in a world gone mad with cancel culture.

Some apologies seem to work, but many others fall flat. Why is that? What is it about our current cancel culture-friendly society that hardens people enough to resist apologies; and what should we understand about how best to deliver them?

Most people have a difficult time apologizing because it is an admission of failure. A public apology feels even more humiliating because rather than a one-to-one conversation, it becomes public fodder to be picked over by armchair critics and a vicious public accustomed to social media nastiness. Apologizing openly announces to the entire world, "I made an error." Matthew Syed, in *Black Box Thinking: Why Most People Never Learn from Their Mistakes—But Some Do*, offers the following: "When we are confronted with evidence that challenges our deeply held beliefs we are more likely to reframe the evidence than we are to alter our beliefs."[67] In essence, we typically double down, avoiding the admission of failure and succumbing to inner pressure not to apologize.

The public nature of the Internet further compounds and confounds that pressure, given the effect of coalition loyalty pushing us to remain within the comfort of connection to other like-minded people who make up a supportive social circle. But the digital world expands our community so much that it is unlikely—and actually impossible—to ever truly come into contact with all of those on the other end of a publicly issued apology. Given that these are not people with whom we have deep, abiding relationships, we may be even less inclined to care what they think or even see the value in prostrating ourselves before them.

The digital world, amplified by social media, has created a new Hobbesian world, where man's combative state of nature is defined by warring coalitions. These coalitions often see little value in fostering or building relationships with the members of other coalitions. This could, in part, explain the increasingly strident rhetoric directed against the "other" in the form of social media expressions of rage and repudiation. Our current situation reminds us how crucial it is that we somehow find our way back to allowing apologies to facilitate forgiveness.

In an age of cancel culture, there has never been more of a risk to apologizing than now. Doing so can lead immediately to public shaming, online harassment, and even bodily harm. Just as there is immense pressure to issue an apology whenever a conflict arises, there is also pressure in the other direction NOT to apologize. Doing so can risk further inflaming your critics, harming your reputation, and threatening your livelihood, especially in the case where you are concerned that the other party will reject or respond negatively to your sentiments. Apologizing, which is typically an acknowledgment of wrongdoing or error, takes courage. But is it wise to admit an error in the face of potential cancellation?

To Apologize, or Not to Apologize, That Is the Question

Faced with pressure from an online mob to issue an apology, there are some key questions that should be considered when you are assessing the pros and cons of making a public apology.

1. Identify the victim/wounded party

Who is demanding the apology? *Who* was actually harmed by your words or deeds? An apology should be offered to an actual victim; and that victim must have the authority, or be able to assign someone else the authority, to offer forgiveness. Apologizing to an online mob whipped into a frenzy is not likely to absolve you of whatever sin you are accused of having made. Apologizing to someone whom you have truly wronged is another thing altogether.

2. Determine the legitimacy of the claim

What are the reasons to believe the accuser or aggrieved was really harmed, either by your words or actions? Did you express yourself in an inaccurate or inartful manner? Would a reasonable person consider your expression truly hurtful? Apologies for mistakes or causing harm make sense, but not for simply expressing different or unpopular ideas or perspectives on a controversial topic.

3. Issue an apology from a position of strength

If an apology is warranted, and you can clearly identify the person or group from whom you would like forgiveness, then offer a sincere apology that positions you as someone with integrity. Key components to an effective apology often include:

a. Acknowledging the wrong
b. Taking responsibility for your words or deeds without blaming others

c. Forgoing pandering or groveling
d. Asking for forgiveness
e. Following through on any pledges you make
f. Avoiding repetition of the same offense

Cancel Culture and the Hostage Apology

Individuals who have attracted the ire of cancel culture mobs often resort to issuing "hostage apologies." These are rarely a good idea, given that they often fail to rectify controversial situations and can make things worse. The hostage apology derives its name from the videos that kidnappers sometimes force their captives to read on-camera. Often delivered in a flat tone, the captive reads from a prepared script, expressing sentiments or admitting to offenses that advance the narrative of the kidnappers.

While delivered voluntarily, and not as actual hostages, such statements are often seen as reactive, coerced, weak, and disingenuous. If a group of cancel vultures is pursuing a disproportionate response to the offending behavior (a core element of cancel culture), then the mob is not looking to forgive, but to punish. Not surprisingly, the alleged transgressor is viewed completely opposite of his or her intention in the wake of a hostage apology. Instead of being praised for showing integrity, courage, honesty, and humility, they are further denigrated for having failed to demonstrate these qualities.

In early 2021, Chris Harrison, the host of the reality television show *The Bachelor*, was caught up in a scandal that ultimately led to him losing his job. The controversy involved a contestant named Rachael Kirkconnell, who had been photographed attending an antebellum-themed party in college and accused of other racially insensitive actions. When Harrison discussed these issues in a televised interview with former *Bachelorette* star and *Extra* correspondent Rachel Lindsay, he said that the contestant, who ended up winning the season, deserved "a little grace, a little understanding, a little compassion," neither explicitly condemning nor condoning her actions. He did, however, declare that she had been "thrown to the lions" and warned that "the woke police is out there."

With a petition to remove Harrison amassing tens of thousands of signatures, he issued a written apology on Instagram. "To my Bachelor Nation family—I will always own a mistake when I make one, so I am here to extend a sincere apology. I have this incredible platform to speak about love, and yesterday I took a stance on topics about which I should have been better informed.

"While I do not speak for Rachael Kirkconnell, my intentions were simply to ask for grace in offering her an opportunity to speak on her own behalf," he continued. "What I now realize I have done is cause harm by wrongly speaking in a manner that perpetuates racism, and for that I am so deeply sorry. I also apologize to my friend Rachel Lindsay for not listening to her better on a topic she has a firsthand understanding of, and humbly thank the members of Bachelor Nation who have reached out to me to hold me accountable. I promise to do better."

With the scandal continuing to churn and his social media apology falling flat, Harrison was placed on leave from the show and appeared for an interview on ABC's *Good Morning America*. This hostage apology proved to be his undoing. In a haltingly delivered manner, Harrison declared, "I am an imperfect man, I made a mistake and I own that." He claimed to be "saddened and shocked at how insensitive I was in that interview with Rachel Lindsay" and declared: "I am committed to progress, not just for myself, also for the franchise."

The words may have checked the right boxes, but Harrison's body language and voice failed to convey a sense of authenticity, leading his interviewer GMA host Michael Strahan to observe: "His apology is his apology, but it felt like nothing more than a surface response on any of this. I mean, obviously, he's a man who clearly wants to stay on this show, but only time will tell if there is any meaning behind his words." Time did tell. Shortly thereafter, Harrison departed *The Bachelor* for good after nineteen seasons on the job.

This swift fall from grace invites a few key questions: Did Harrison truly believe he had done something wrong, or was he doing what he felt was expected of him? Did he feel like his actions warranted a self-flagellating apology? To whom was Harrison principally apologizing? What's more, did Harrison really expect his apology would help him keep his job, and from whom was he hoping to receive forgiveness?

With the benefit of hindsight, perhaps there were other avenues that could have better resolved this situation. Rather than the theatricality of multiple apologies followed by his eventual removal, the show could have explored a deeper discussion around issues involving race and what constitutes acceptable behavior, effectively educating a massive audience. As discussed earlier in this chapter, the purpose of the apology-forgiveness sequence is to facilitate healthy and positive human interaction from which growth occurs and understanding increases. But in the case of Harrison, there was no ultimate benefit beyond the large group of people demanding his firing being able to celebrate their "victory."

When it comes to hostage apologies, the case of San Francisco entrepreneur Lisa Alexander warrants a closer look. Caught on video confronting a neighbor using chalk to write Black Lives Matter outside of his home, the woman who came to be known derisively as "San Francisco Karen" stepped forward to give an interview telling her story for the first time publicly. The case study contained in this book includes the full text of a hostage apology she was forced to deliver when a cancel vulture mob descended upon her to destroy her company and threaten her life. Issued under "duress," according to Alexander, it is the thing she has said she regrets most about her actions at that time.

Sorry, Not Sorry, and Reluctant Apologies

One of the worst forms of apologies that can be proffered is the type that can be considered "Sorry, Not Sorry." In fact, this precise phrasing is often used as social media slang to share sentiments of someone who wishes to sarcastically share that he or she is guilt-free over expressing a certain action or view. In its truest form, the person who contributes content online will affix the "sorry, not sorry" wording verbatim to their post.

A less explicit version of this, but which reflects the same fundamental idea, is an apology by someone justifying or excusing their behavior while at the same time seeking, on the surface, to make amends for it. This could be referred to as the blaming, reluctant, or nonapology apology. This type of formulation is common when the alleged transgressor refuses to accept full responsibility or does not think they are at fault. Some examples could include:

"I'm sorry if my words offended you."
"I'm sorry, but [followed by a justification].
"I'm sorry that you feel that way."

The Apologies of Winston Marshall

For a fascinating illustration of the nexus between cancel culture at work and the art of the apology, consider the case of Winston Marshall. Marshall, the banjo-playing member of the folk-rock band Mumford & Sons, was forced to resign from the music group he helped found.

Winston is a self-proclaimed autodidact, a claim well supported by his broad literary tastes and diverse thoughts and interests. His intellectual curiosity drew him to learn more about the riots enveloping many US cities following the killing of numerous Black men, especially at the hands of police. Residing in London, Marshall read Andy Ngo's book *Unmasked: Inside Antifa's Radical Plan to Destroy Democracy* to learn more about what was driving these far-off events and to better understand the agents behind it. Marshall said in a lengthy interview with the authors that he felt compelled to weigh in on the discussion because neither people in the music industry nor the "mainstream media" were covering the "danger and damage caused by Antifa."

The trouble for Marshall started when he praised before his approximately 300 Twitter followers the book written by Ngo, a journalist who follows the radical movement Antifa. Tagging Ngo, Marshall wrote: "Finally had the time to read your important book. You're a brave man." In a short time, the rage trended "up, and there was a lot of negative stuff," including labeling Marshall a fascist, which is ironic on two fronts, he told us.

First, that supposed antifascists were using the tactics of repression and intimidation to suppress views espoused by a person who plays folk music for a living. Second, they were affixing that label to a person for whom thirteen members of his "family were murdered in the concentration camps of the Holocaust," said Marshall. "My family knows the evils of fascism painfully well, to say the least. To call me a 'fascist' was ludicrous beyond belief."

The response to Marshall's tweet met every single one of the six CANDEM cancel culture elements. The alleged slight was against a "collective" comprised of a diverse group of violent protestors; the outrage arose and accelerated quickly; the nature of what Marshall said was minor and should not have produced outrage; and disproportionate responses followed, with everyone including bandmates and friends afraid to defend him against the moral absolutism bordering on religious fanaticism by his detractors. Not surprisingly, Winston felt like he was caught in a storm with no warning and without any rudder to guide him through.

The online bullies resorted to repeatedly rewording Marshall's Wikipedia page. According to Marshall, "They just start swarming around you as much as they can. They weren't at my front door, but they were trying to cause as much havoc as they could online." Marshall would later write that he "failed to foresee that my commenting on a book critical of the far-left could be interpreted as approval of the equally abhorrent far-right."

He thought, as so many do who are engulfed in a cancel culture firestorm, that if he just kept quiet, it would all go away. But it didn't. He then started "getting phone calls from friends and family, and then a lot of people close to me who were upset or angry about it."

When the world starts closing in and friends and family start pressuring you to fix the problem, so that their lives are made easier, the pressure builds to do something. Often that "something" is the wrong thing. Winston started questioning himself by thinking, "maybe I don't know the whole story or maybe I don't know everything about the book."

Feeling the weight of his bandmates and family on his shoulders and "under considerable pressure to issue" an apology, he did so. His first apology reads like many other cancel culture/hostage apologies. It is full of self-blame, self-condemnation, and supplication to an amorphous and faceless victim.

In a statement shared via Twitter, Marshall wrote:

> Over the past few days I have come to better understand the pain caused by the book I endorsed. I have offended not only a lot of people I don't know, but also those closest to me, including my bandmates and for that I am truly sorry. As a result of my actions, I am taking time away from the band to examine my blindspots. For now, please know that I realise how my endorsements have the potential to be viewed as approvals of hateful, divisive behaviour. I apologise, as this was not at all my intention.[68]

Following his apology, Marshall delved into research and inquiry and eventually concluded that he "had not done anything wrong" and "the journalist was indeed a brave man." Marshall said he felt like his "apology contributed to the lie that Antifa was a force for good or didn't exist" and that too many in the US were "ignoring the damage and havoc wreaked by Antifa across America." He went on to say that the more he "thought about it, the more I felt like I was lying, or that my initial apology was a lie, or that I was participating in a lie. And then this really tore me up, and my conscience . . . I wasn't sleeping. I wasn't eating properly." He felt that he had paid his dignity as a ransom to cancel culture hostage takers but also concluded how to take it back.

He explains that he drew strength from an Aleksandr Solzhenitsyn essay titled "Live Not By Lies." Solzhenitsyn writes:

And he who is not sufficiently courageous to defend his soul—don't let him be proud of his 'progressive views, and don't let him boast that he is an academician or people's artist, a distinguished figure or a general. Let him say to himself: I am a part of the herd and a coward. It's all the same to me as long as I'm fed and kept warm.[69]

When Marshall learned that the writer Ngo had been physically attacked again by Antifa, it marked a turning point. He realized that for him to live his life free of guilt, he first needed to make one of the most profoundly impactful life decisions he had ever made: deciding to "live not by lies" and leave the band he helped form. He acknowledged this by saying, "I didn't have a choice. I felt like it was more important for me to stand by the truth and keep my soul and conscience—and it did feel like a matter of the soul—than to lie and continue."

More than three months after Marshall issued his initial apology on Twitter, he posted to Medium announcing his departure from Mumford & Sons and marking what would become a defining moment in cancel culture apologies. His letter, dated June 24, 2021, was a well-written account of the witch hunt he endured, explaining why he stepped away from the group he helped start. He knew who had been hurt by his actions and who had not. In that letter, he acknowledged he was "desperate to protect [his] bandmates." The firestorm he unwittingly ignited had blown back on them and their families, and he felt obligated to free them of the torment.

This is the full text, published with permission, of Winston Marshall's departure letter, dated June 24, 2021:

Why I'm Leaving Mumford & Sons

I loved those first tours. Bouncing off a sweaty stage in an Edinburgh catacomb we then had to get to a gig in Camden by lunch the next day. We couldn't fit all four of us and Ted's double-bass into the VW Polo. I think it was Ben who drew the short-straw and had to follow by train with his keyboard. I remember blitzing it down the M6 through the night, the lads asleep beside me. We made it but my voice sadly didn't, completely shot by exhaustion, I had to mime my harmonies. Being in Mumford & Sons was exhilarating.

Every gig was its own adventure. Every gig its own story. Be it odysseys through the Scottish Islands, or soapbox shows in Soho. Where would we sleep that night? Hostels in Fort William, pub floors in Ipswich, even the

Travelodge in Carlisle maintains a sort of charm in my mind. We saw the country and then, as things miraculously grew, the world. All the while doing what we loved. Music. And not just any music. These songs meant something. They felt important to me. Songs with the message of hope and love. I was surrounded by three supremely talented song-writers and Marcus, our singer with a one-in-a-million voice. A voice that can compel both a field of 80,000 and the intimacy of a front room. Fast-forward ten years and we were playing those same songs every night in arenas, flying first-class, staying in luxury hotels and being paid handsomely to do so. I was a lucky boy.

On stage, to my left Ted, a roaring bear, with his double-bass flying high above him. To my right Ben, with his unparalleled passion for music, pounding at the keys. And Marcus leading us with all the might of a hurricane or all the tenderness of a breeze, depending on what the song demanded. What a blessing it was to be so close to such talent as theirs. It will be with immense pride that I look back at my time with Mumford & Sons. A legacy of songs that I believe will stand the test of ages. What we've achieved together has vastly exceeded the wildest fantasies of this shitkicker from Mortlake.

Who in their right mind would willingly walk away from this?

It turns out I would. And as you might imagine it's been no easy decision.

At the beginning of March I tweeted to American journalist Andy Ngo, author of the New York Times Bestseller, *Unmasked*. "Congratulations @ MrAndyNgo. Finally had the time to read your important book. You're a brave man". Posting about books had been a theme of my social-media throughout the pandemic. I believed this tweet to be as innocuous as the others. How wrong I turned out to be.

Over the course of 24 hours it was trending with tens of thousands of angry retweets and comments. I failed to foresee that my commenting on a book critical of the Far-Left could be interpreted as approval of the equally abhorrent Far-Right.

Nothing could be further from the truth. Thirteen members of my family were murdered in the concentration camps of the Holocaust. My Grandma, unlike her cousins, aunts and uncles, survived. She and I were close. My family knows the evils of fascism painfully well. To say the least. To call me "fascist" was ludicrous beyond belief.

I've had plenty of abuse over the years. I'm a banjo player after all. But this was another level. And, owing to our association, my friends, my bandmates, were getting it too. It took me more than a moment to understand how distressing this was for them.

Despite being four individuals we were, in the eyes of the public, a unity. Furthermore it's our singer's name on the tin. That name was being dragged through some pretty ugly accusations, as a result of my tweet. The distress brought to them and their families that weekend I regret very much. I remain sincerely sorry for that. Unintentionally, I had pulled them into a divisive and totemic issue.

Emotions were high. Despite pressure to nix me they invited me to continue with the band. That took courage, particularly in the age of so called "cancel culture". I made an apology and agreed to take a temporary step back.

Rather predictably another viral mob came after me, this time for the sin of apologising. Then followed libellous articles calling me "right-wing" and such. Though there's nothing wrong with being conservative, when forced to politically label myself I flutter between "centrist", "liberal" or the more honest "bit this, bit that". Being labeled erroneously just goes to show how binary political discourse has become. I had criticised the "Left", so I must be the "Right", or so their logic goes.

Why did I apologise?

"Rub your eyes and purify your heart—and prize above all else in the world those who love you and who wish you well." —Aleksander Solzhenitsyn once wrote. In the mania of the moment I was desperate to protect my bandmates. The hornets' nest that I had unwittingly hit had unleashed a black-hearted swarm on them and their families. I didn't want them to suffer for my actions, they were my priority.

Secondly, I was sincerely open to the fact that maybe I did not know something about the author or his work. *"Courage is what it takes to stand up and speak,"* Churchill once said, *"courage is also what it takes to sit down and listen".* And so I listened.

I have spent much time reflecting, reading and listening. The truth is that my commenting on a book that documents the extreme Far-Left and their activities is in no way an endorsement of the equally repugnant Far-Right. The truth is that reporting on extremism at the great risk of endangering oneself is unquestionably brave. I also feel that my previous apology in a small way participates in the lie that such extremism does not exist, or worse, Is a force for good.

So why leave the band?

On the eve of his leaving to the West, Solzhenitsyn published an essay titled 'Live Not by Lies'. I have read it many times now since the incident at the start of March. It still profoundly stirs me.

"And he who is not sufficiently courageous to defend his soul—don't let him be proud of his 'progressive' views, and don't let him boast that he is an academician or a people's artist, a distinguished figure or a general. Let him say to himself: I am a part of the herd and a coward. It's all the same to me as long as I'm fed and kept warm."

For me to speak about what I've learnt to be such a controversial issue will inevitably bring my bandmates more trouble. My love, loyalty and accountability to them cannot permit that. I could remain and continue to self-censor but it will erode my sense of integrity. Gnaw my conscience. I've already felt that beginning.

The only way forward for me is to leave the band. I hope in distancing myself from them I am able to speak my mind without them suffering the consequences. I leave with love in my heart and I wish those three boys nothing but the best. I have no doubt that their stars will shine long into the future. I will continue my work with Hong Kong Link Up and I look forward to new creative projects as well as speaking and writing on a variety of issues, challenging as they may be.

Winston Marshall

Marshall's apology was sincerely offered to his bandmates and family for having brought this on them. They, in turn, accepted his apology and acknowledged the impact of losing him from the band. In his farewell missive explaining his decision, Marshall did not apologize to the mob for his right to think freely and offer ideas in the public square, nor did he supplicate himself to cancel vultures. Instead, he stood up to them by reaffirming his principles and denouncing theirs. No one can deny his courage and integrity, which came at a high personal cost. In the end, Marshall should be remembered not as a victim, but a hero.

The Honest Apology

We have written throughout this chapter that apologies and forgiveness are essential to a healthy society. We learned from the Chris Harrison and Winston Marshall Twitter and Medium statements that not all apologies or mea culpas are equal. The cancel culture hostage apology never works. In fact, it is counterproductive, as it offers a false sense of success and undermines the giver's credibility, so in the end nobody benefits. A cancel culture hostage apology is sought when the mob believes that the accused's fear of the mob is greater than their fear of the alternative, which is often unknown at the time of a crisis.

On the other hand, the *Honest Apology* is a potent and effective model for achieving salvation. The honest apology works when the transgressor is genuine, sincere, and knows from whom precisely he or she must ask forgiveness, if anyone. There is no undefined coalition; the individual or group considered the victim is readily identifiable. Further, the transgressor must be able to conclude that someone was actually harmed, and to acknowledge their responsibility for causing that harm. The final sine qua non for an honest apology is that the apologizer must have no expectation of forgiveness. Ideally, it is not coerced, made out of a sense of obligation, or aimed at saving the person's skin; but is a genuine attempt at atoning for a mistake.

Honest apologies are never weak; in fact, they can help establish a position of strength for moving forward. Using Winston Marshall as an example, once he summoned the courage necessary to stand up to the cancel culture mob, he communicated in a fashion that accomplished three things: reestablished and reasserted the relationship value of those who mattered most to him (family, friends, and bandmates), stood up to the cancel vultures who could no longer control him by creating fear, and freed Winston to pursue opportunities that would otherwise have remained unknown to him had these circumstances not arisen.

Admittedly, most people, including Winston, are not in the proper frame of mind to look beyond the storm when they are in the middle of it. Arriving at a point of strength by charting a course forward is rarely a singular event. When asked if his life was fulfilling now, in the aftermath of his cancel culture ordeal, Winston responded: "I'm making progress. Despite the fact that I am still at the start of a journey. . . . I'm not being too hard on myself because it was a very tempestuous and torrid experience."

We have seen numerous instances where people go through witch hunts and experience a similar reconciliation process. Consumed by a faceless mob seeking their destruction, their lives grow dark and scary, and it can feel like there is no light at the end of the tunnel. However, our experience has also shown us that most people do make it through, and when they emerge, they are met with opportunities they had never imagined would be there for them. People like Winston Marshall show that a path forward does exist. There can be life after cancel culture.

Winston Marshall, Peter Boghossian, and Ilya Shapiro all were interviewed, providing insights that helped with the writing of this book. In addition, each published well-crafted public statements that ultimately helped reset power dynamics in their favor, and it is amazing to see how quickly narratives can change when someone demonstrates the courage to stand up to the mob. There may be plenty of people who still harbor ill feelings toward these men, but the power those people once held has been neutralized by their demonstrations of equal or greater opposing strength.

SUMMARY OF KEY POINTS

- Forgiveness allows failure to occur without stigma.
- Apologies are essential to healthy societies, since they allow people to recognize their errors.
- The forgiveness-apology response maintains social order in human society.
- When an apology is offered and forgiveness granted, both parties move forward.
- In the context of cancel culture, apologies are rebuffed, and a mob decrees the apologizer irredeemable.
- Cancel vultures neither seek atonement nor offer forgiveness.
- The major religions of the world encourage atonement and celebrate forgiveness.
- Apologizing is a risky proposition in a world rife with cancel culture.
- Before apologizing in the wake of a reputational attack, identify the aggrieved party, determine the legitimacy of their claim, and issue an apology from a position of strength.
- "Hostage apologies" are ineffective and may make things worse.
- Reluctant apologies do not resolve conflict.
- The honest apology is a potent and effective model for achieving salvation.
- Key components to the effective honest apology:
  - Acknowledging the wrong
  - Taking responsibility for your words or deeds without blaming others
  - Forgoing pandering or groveling
  - Asking for absolution
  - Following through on any pledges you make
  - Avoiding repetition of the same offense

CHAPTER 10

The Cancel Culture Playbook

Legendary boxing champion Mike Tyson famously said, "Everybody has a plan until they get punched in the mouth." It's an apt description for the experience of being jabbed by a cancel culture mob looking to land a knockout punch. An increasing number of books about the phenomenon of cancel culture are hitting the shelves. That is a good thing. The more we talk about cancel culture, the better people will understand how it ruins lives and erodes the principles that have always been defining elements of America. The larger the conversation around cancel culture, the more rapidly we can move to end the practice for good, for the benefit of everyone.

In this book, we have sought to define for the first time the core elements that constitute what is and is not cancel culture. Our research and writing were based on prior analysis and efforts by respected authors, professors, intellectuals, and thinkers who have studied and defined political witch hunts and observed the shifts in American education and culture. We sincerely hope that we have succeeded in building upon their work and moving the conversation forward.

But there is an important distinction that should be made. Academics spend their days carefully considering issues from multiple perspectives, writing, analyzing, and teaching. However, the majority of our time is not spent writing books like this one, but in serving organizations and individuals in need of assistance with communications challenges. Our perspective is one formed through experience in navigating today's high-stakes, always-online world and finding ways to effectively communicate to a hyperconnected public in good times and bad.

While our trade deficit numbers may suggest otherwise, so much of what happens in the United States is eventually exported overseas. We are not talking about manufactured goods, but American culture, ideas, intellectual property, food, music, art, fashion, and so on, all of which inevitably end up far beyond our borders. Hopefully, that will not be so with cancel culture, which is fundamentally un-American. Cancel culture replaces the liberal democratic values shared by Left and Right alike with illiberalism.

While we hope that you never are forced to endure a cancel culture attack, hope is not a strategy. What will you do when the cancel vultures come for you? This chapter is meant to provide a playbook and help you answer that question. This chapter, especially, is intended to be a guide you can employ should you find yourself under fire. Before you get punched in the mouth you need a plan—one that is strong and thoughtful enough to ensure that when flurries of punches come your way, you can rely on your training and preparation to stay on your feet and persevere.

Accept Reality: It Could Happen to You

No plan can anticipate every eventuality. Predicting the future is a dangerous game, and one that typically doesn't go very well. We have many limitations, and foretelling the future is certainly one of them. And yet, a careful consideration of your life, your business, and your area of expertise can provide clues and indicators that suggest from where a cancel culture attack is most likely to emanate. The process for building a cancel culture plan is similar to developing a detailed crisis communications plan.

The very first step in creating a plan for weathering a cancel culture assault is to set aside the notion that something like this could never happen to you. That is a dangerous mentality based on wishful thinking rather than reality; pursue this course of action at your own risk. To deny the very real possibility of terrible things happening, or to avoid even considering them, is a natural psychological reaction rooted in fear. It resides in the part of the brain known as the amygdala, which triggers the fight-or-flight response. But flight is not an option for you. Cancel vultures can fly too, and they will pursue you. Attempting flight from this chapter would be an attempt to evade the possibility that bad things could happen to you. You must be willing to do the hard work and experience the discomfort of probing your own vulnerabilities; if not, you risk losing everything. Instead, our hope is that you will use these proven methods to open your mind and quell your rapidly beating heart.

A cancel culture or crisis communications plan is like insurance; no one wants to pay for it, but when you need it, you are damn sure glad that you have it. Proactive planning is a critical step for survival.

Physical Security

American psychologist Abraham Maslow outlined a hierarchy of five needs that undergird human motivation and how we make decisions. The first two categories in that pyramid are physiological needs and safety. Both are relevant categories to address when safeguarding against cancel culture. Obviously, for survival in the most literal sense of the word, you will need to meet your basic physiological needs as a human, including water, air, food, sleep, warmth, and shelter.

It may sound shocking, but cancel culture can threaten even those physiological needs. People being harassed by a group of cancel vultures often have trouble sleeping. Chemical changes are triggered in their brains that make it difficult to concentrate; often this leads to spiking anxiety levels and the triggering of depression. In the future, do not be surprised to see scientific research studies conducted that closely analyze the physiological damage suffered by those who are currently experiencing, or have experienced, a cancel culture attack.

Meeting the need for safety, which Maslow asserts is the second level of requirements, becomes even more urgent should you find yourself the target of a witch hunt by an angry mob. Many public figures employ professionals to protect their physical security. Depending on the needs and a host of factors, this can entail bodyguards or multiperson protective details. The average person, who typically does not attract widespread attention and is unlikely to face hostile visitors or threats, will more likely rely on the physical protection afforded by door and window locks, gates, and alarm systems. It is not uncommon for those being canceled to be visited at home by angry activists aiming to intimidate or even physically assault or kill them. One person we have counseled became internationally known overnight. Warned by security guards to vacate their property because security could not be guaranteed, the individual sneaked away in the middle of the night. After entering a secure garage below the building, a close friend drove the person directly to a transit station, and from there the person fled the country.

Increasingly, thanks to their low costs, easy installation, and constant connectivity, people are utilizing smart doorbells and security cameras set up around their homes. When it comes to cancel culture, these devices become critical not just for keeping people at a safe distance, but also for recording evidence should a group of cancel vultures attempt to threaten or harm you or your property. Having them fully operational is a must, and the time to become comfortable with their functionality is before you have a problem and need to rely on them.

If you think this talk of alarms sounds, well, alarmist, then think again. A tactic called "doxing" is often employed by cancel vultures. It's a term that describes seeking and publicly sharing someone's personal identifying information, such as an address or phone number of you or your employer. With these details, those who wish you ill are in a powerful position to do major harm. Once your mobile phone number is made public, you can expect a steady stream of hateful, vengeful, and in some cases shocking and frightening phone calls and texts.

Having an alternate phone at the ready from which you can make and receive calls and messages is wise. If you are not ready to go out today and buy that cheap, secondary phone—often referred to as a "burner"—then at least know of a nearby store where you can acquire and activate one quickly. One advantage to securing and setting up the phone in advance is that you can transfer your contacts to it ahead of time and even share that number with a select group of your family members and most trusted friends.

If you are a business owner or executive, then having a business continuity plan in place is obviously vital. An organization's leadership team should have a plan in place to protect the fundamental infrastructure that enables the company to function.

As the world saw during the COVID-19 pandemic, major crises can arise that grind businesses and entire societies to a halt. A good practice is to have a hard copy printout containing the names and contact details for the people most vital to preserving your livelihood. This list may include your boss, manager, direct reports, your attorney, your spouse or life partner, and any other people on whom you know you can rely completely in a time of need. Since fear is a key element of cancel culture, you need to know which members of your own "mob" will be unafraid to engage with you, speak with you, guide you, and help you should cancel culture render you radioactive. Leaders of larger organizations may want to ensure that they have the contact details for a media spokesperson, general counsel, chief communications officer, chief marketing officer, chief legal officer, COO, or some other senior person in charge of operations.

You May Feel Lost, but You Will Be Found

When you become the focus of an online mob, it is usually only a matter of time before people begin looking for you in the real world. This is especially true if your starring role as a villain spreads into the mainstream media. As we have discussed throughout this book, the press is an accelerant. Media coverage of a cancel culture situation is the equivalent of pouring a gallon of gasoline onto a campfire, instantly converting it into a blazing inferno.

People may self-select which outlets they turn to for news and information, and the declining role of newspapers may be supplanted by podcasts and Substacks. But the point is that discussions by influential outlets, of any nature, will magnify your problems instantly.

Internet sleuths can be very effective at ferreting out hard-to-find information. Crowdsourced efforts to investigate and excoriate can be incredibly effective. Meanwhile, large media outlets have investigative resources, investigative teams whose ranks are filled with experienced and ambitious reporters trained on the best ways to dig for information. These journalists are accustomed to finding ways around organizations seeking to hide activities, and they are often persistent and effective when pursuing a story. Why? Because salacious headlines and sexy stories equal money, visitors, and clicks. We know from statistics that negative news travels across the Internet seven times faster than positive stories. If a story is in the headlines, and an investigative reporter or team is intent on getting in on the action, then they will relentlessly pursue leads and information that allow them to do so. That is why you need a plan in place for handling the media when they come knocking.

Many people believe that this is an exaggeration, but it happens all the time. We know this because we have been in the middle of such situations countless times. News crews park outside people's homes or offices waiting for the opportunity to catch them entering or exiting. Reporters make calls, hoping someone will naively answer and talk. They interview friends and family members, and neighbors who live nearby. A well-constructed cancel culture prevention plan will map out expected scenarios and construct plans for handling them.

Your Trusted Team

In circumstances that create emotional distress, most people turn to family and friends. However, cancel culture often puts that support network at great risk because they become fearful of the mob's retribution should they publicly support the target. Given the choice between saying nothing and preserving your job, reputation, and ability to provide for your family, and knowingly and consciously stepping into a controversy that could render you toxic and unemployed, most people choose to remain silent. It is unfortunate but also understandable. All of this leaves the accused isolated.

An important additional resource to have at the ready in advance of a cancel culture attack is the name and phone number of an experienced guide who can be with you, counsel you, and help protect you from the oncoming avalanche of hate. Interviewing a crisis communications agency or legal expert should be done well in advance to determine that you have vetted the right partner and ensured that the firm or individual has the relevant expertise, ability, and fighting spirit that you are going to need when everything is on the line.

People in leadership positions of organizations should not overlook their colleagues when it comes to seeking out supporters if they are a cancel culture target. Those who work with them closely day to day, as well as the professionals in charge of communications, can be an important resource. In the event that an organization finds itself forced to contend with an employee under assault, then it will need to deliver a consistent and clear message to internal team members as well as the external public.

Monitoring

A helpful tool for organizations preparing for, or presently grappling with, a threat is a listening device. Not the high-tech spyware that undercover agents slip into hotel rooms and foreign embassies, but a way to monitor what is being said about you online. Cancel culture campaigns generate spikes in searches on your name, your brand, and other key terms. Manual search engine queries and scrolling through social media can help. But social media monitoring software is much more powerful and can prove to be a worthy investment. Numerous options exist in the market today, with a range of capabilities from simply alerting you to news stories to producing detailed charts and graphs with sophisticated metrics. This monitoring software tends to be expensive but can save you enormous amounts of time because it is constantly scouring major social media sites in order to better understand what conversations are taking place. One of the benefits of these software platforms is that they can be configured to score sentiment, classifying mentions as either positive, neutral, or negative. They enable you to see evolutions over time and know how online sentiment related to a topic is shifting.

At a bare minimum, organizations should set up various Google alerts related to their brand name and other keywords related to their industry. This can be easily done in Google by following a basic series of steps. Set up your Google alerts to receive automated email messages; you can determine the cadence and whether these messages come in real time, or they get batched together and sent to you in bulk at certain intervals. If you do not already have a Gmail account, then consider creating one, since it's functional and free and can be used to create your Google alerts. To preserve the account's integrity, it is best to utilize a strong password and two-factor authentication. Like most steps in the cancel culture playbook, the time to take them is before you have a problem so that you have everything in place should you need it.

Decision Time

There is a well-known truism that states there are generally three sides to every situation: what one person said happened, what the other person said happened, and what really happened. In the context of cancel culture, however, each additional person weighing in brings a perspective that could generate news, but none of these additional perspectives actually changes the truth. This is why we promote the importance of *pressing the truth*.

So, what happens if the media seizes on a story, gets the facts wrong, and the situation goes viral? Every victim of a cancel vulture attack is presented with a choice. One is to cede the battlefield and throw in the towel. If you make the decision to give up and not challenge the facts based on their merits, or provide the appropriate context, then know that you will likely be pilloried by a critical mass of mainstream media outlets with extremely large reach and influence. They will share information that may or may not be true in a way that does not advance your narrative, nor does it shed light on the situation from your point of view. The online mob will do everything in its collective power to permanently damage or destroy your future prospects for success.

The alternative to simply rolling over and being picked apart by the cancel vulture mob is to fight and defend yourself. You do this by identifying those who are willing to stand in to support you, in essence, creating your own mob. Then you must sow doubt about the accusations leveled against you, correct misinformation, and work to set the record straight. Remember, most people rarely take the time to analyze a situation. Instead, they reflexively rely on a headline or on the assumption that an article provides all available information. You must convey reasonable, articulate, and fair explanations for why your side of the story is so important to understanding the truth. Your primary goal is to help frame the narrative in a way that the public will not only understand your perspective but may even empathize with you and extend some measure of grace.

This decision point is not just for individuals, but also applies to companies or other organizations. Too often, we see examples of companies rushing in a panic to sever all ties with the specific individual under fire. This is often true whether or not the person has actually committed the alleged infraction, and before a full investigatory process has been initiated, conducted, and judged. The speed and severity of cancel culture attacks force institutions to scramble, and they often default to the most extreme option being demanded by the mob: termination and the severing of all ties with the target. Companies comply out of fear of boycotts, losing public trust, seeing their own reputations damaged, or suffering from declining sales or cratering stock prices.

In many instances, the rush to judgment proves a penny-wise, pound-foolish short-term decision with major long-term consequences. Often, these individuals file lawsuits to challenge the validity of their dismissal, and the institutions end up spending enormous sums of money on legal fees to defend the rapid dismissal of that former employee. In some cases, they also must spend money to hire specialized public relations firms focusing upon reputation repair or agencies employing search engine optimization (SEO) tactics to clean up negative search engine results and prevent the scandal of the day from permanently impacting the institution's reputation. All of this wasted effort and money could often be preserved if organizations took the time to craft detailed cancel culture plans that take into account the various decisions the organization may be tasked with making. These plans may also help the organization better withstand the onslaught of a cancel culture attack.

In short, individuals and the organizations who employ them should slow down, avoid rushing to judgment, and extend some measure of due process before concluding that the person is guilty and taking severe action. For the individual in question, the benefits of having a fair chance to make their case are obvious. And if they have done something that warrants punishment, then they can be held fully accountable.

In the twenty-first century, organizations are expected to responsibly address not only their own corporate interests, but assume some societal responsibilities, as well. Organizations serve their own interests by approaching complex cancel culture events with caution and thoughtfulness, rather than with fear and haste. Doing so also helps them avoid violating any of their corporate principles that may lead to lawsuits and litigation. If, in fact, an employee has done something that warrants punishment, then it is incumbent that their punishment be commensurate with the infraction. It is unhelpful to society writ large for organizations to mete out justice in a manner consistent with mob rule.

Damage Control: Engaging the Media and the Vultures Themselves

Since cancel culture events typically accelerate quickly and without warning, an individual or organization can become public enemy number one overnight. This makes the decision to speak with the press—to take on the mob—a terrifying prospect. For good reason. It is daunting to go up against a collective of aggressive people baying for blood and demanding the most severe forms of punishment. It therefore makes a lot of sense that the cancel culture target is hesitant to weigh in or to push back against the prevailing narrative. After all, they are already under attack and on the defensive. Why in the world would they want to provoke another round of assaults from the cancel vultures?

Consider the case of a college professor or sports coach who has said or tweeted something that generated demands that she or he be fired. In such a scenario, it is likely that hundreds, or even thousands, of communications will be sent to the university's leadership demanding action. Someone tasked with tallying communications to the provost's or president's office will see inbound communications on a certain topic go from zero to thousands overnight. And until the Twitter mob extracts its proverbial pound of flesh, they will seem committed to the cause.

One thing that institutions can do is issue a holding statement or pledge to take action, indicating that the individual or circumstances are being investigated and reviewed. In many instances, that alone will be enough to quell the outrage online, especially if the institution holds firm and under-scores that they will provide due process to that individual. What often happens next is that another day brings another news cycle, which in turn brings a new victim or topic that directs attention elsewhere. Excited with their new opportunity for online activism, the transient mob moves on to the next outrage. A holding statement demonstrating that the institution is taking the situation seriously and enacting a thorough examination to hold the person accountable is a way to score an easy victory and help reduce the likelihood that the mob will make it a primary target for its rage. It also creates space for actual due process to take place, helping to prevent orga-nizations from making the mistake of rushing to terminate an employee unfairly, sparking protracted legal issues.

Saying I'm Sorry

Elsewhere in this book, we spent some time expounding upon the compo-nents that make for an artful and effective way to say you are sorry. Now seems like a good time to reiterate that you should not apologize if you have not done what others claim. Do not accept responsibility for something you did not do in the misplaced hope of relieving your pain and inspiring the cancel vultures to fly off to harass their next prey. The opposite is most likely going to happen, and that apology will be used against you. The mob will use it as an admission that everything they said horrible about you was warranted and hold up your remorse as proof that you have sinned. It can then be wielded against you for the rest of your life.

Several cancel culture targets with whom we spoke were pressed by law-yers or (so-called) crisis PR consultants to release apologies in the hope that they would act as pressure release valves. In nearly every situation, the oppo-site was the better course. Incredibly, in interviews and multiple private and unreported conversations with some of the most famous people who have been canceled, many deeply regretted their apologies.

Both Winston Marshall and Lisa Alexander expressed remorse for their apologies under duress. (See Marshall's comment in the chapter on apolo-gies; view Alexander's statements in the affixed case study.) Cynics will no doubt question their motivations and criticize these honest self-assessments, wondering if these cancel culture targets were remorseful in retrospect only because they were caught behaving badly, and not because they have seen the errors of their ways.

Press the Truth®

Part of the reason deplatformed individuals failed to reap benefits from their hostage apologies was that these were reactive, tactical moves. In the midst of a media firestorm, and even during more sedate times, it is not enough to simply hope and pray that the truth will eventually come out. There are far too many factors that make this nearly impossible. Sitting back and doing nothing is an almost guaranteed failed strategy. A more promising path to success is to undertake a strategic approach described as *pressing the truth*. In addition to a never-ending cycle of news, websites are under pressure to constantly produce a steady stream of content. Far too many sites and sources for information are competing for attention to simply hope that your message eventually breaks through. This creates opportunities for individuals and organizations to drive messaging that conveys their narrative in the right way to the right audience, if they are committed to doing so.

Those hoping that they will get their chance to win over the public when journalists provide a fair opportunity are clinging to romantic notions of media from a bygone age. Today, many journalists will not even bother to seek comments from affected parties before racing to file a story. In other situations, websites have zero editorial process and no commitment to journalistic ethics, so they do not see it as a requirement to be balanced or to provide a genuine opportunity for response or for the airing of competing views. It may not be fair, and it may not fall within the parameters of ethical journalism taught in schools, but that is a reality. Even in a best-case scenario where a journalist does contact you before a story appears, you are likely to spend several minutes speaking with the individual only to have a sentence or two included in a story. In effect, the very nature of media gives reporters the power to deliver or shape a perspective even when creating a straight news story.

In fact, in many cases where an outlet or reporter is working on a negative piece about someone or an organization, they hold off on making the outreach to the target of their reporting until the eleventh hour, when literally the entire piece has been written save for a placeholder into which they will insert a quote if they can secure one. If they do not receive one, then they can report that they attempted to reach the organization or individual but did not hear back, or that they declined to comment. You cannot hope that a reporter acts in good faith and provides you a genuine chance to set the record straight. If you sit back and wait, you run a real risk that an article gets published with a false or misleading narrative.

Each of these scenarios illustrates the risk of being passive. Instead, a more assertive and ultimately winning strategy is to pursue a mind-set and an approach that we refer to as Press the Truth®. When you choose to Press the Truth®, you do not rely on others to drive your message. You take personal responsibility for pushing it out yourself. A general rule of thumb when it comes to effectively communicating is that *you need to tell your story on your own terms and from your own perspective, since failure to do so means that someone else is going to tell that story for you.* And you can rest assured that most of the time, they will not tell it the way that you want it told. Obviously, other parties are not going to say things in the way that you would want them said, and failure to Press the Truth® is tantamount to putting your fate into the hands of someone else who does not have your best interests at heart.

To Press the Truth® is to do the hard work of being engaged in the process and proactively producing video, written commentary, or social media posts that express your perspective. Granted, this is a formidable challenge when you are already under the microscope and the target of a cancel culture assault. But anyone under fire really has no choice. If you abdicate that responsibility and opt to say nothing, you should expect the worst. At least if you Press the Truth®, you stand a fighting chance of convincing the undecideds that you either did nothing wrong in the first place or that you did make an error but deserve to be forgiven and allowed to move forward with your life.

Press the Truth® is a philosophy that inherently demands accountability, and it encourages authenticity. Someone who is not committed to conveying facts or is hoping to push out misinformation or make false statements will be permanently undone if they Press the Truth® insincerely—because the facts will ultimately come to light. The truth eventually comes out in some fashion. Someone who does not actually regret their actions, or has no justification or case to make, runs a huge risk by employing a Press the Truth® approach. But for the vast majority of people who find themselves facing down an angry mob making much ado about a minor transgression, this is the best course of action to defend themselves.

Designated Mouthpiece and Preferred Method to Communicate

When cancel vultures gather to feast, their prey will often be faced with the choice of saying nothing or doing something. In almost every case, saying something is better. At the same time, care must be taken not to make another mistake. For those already under fire, one more blunder can be the kiss of death, compounding your misery exponentially. Anything you say in a cancel culture environment can and will be used against you in the most vicious ways possible. Assume that whatever you say or do is going to be savagely assailed by cancel vultures. Expect every word to be picked apart and assigned meanings you did not intend, as well as critiqued, criticized, mocked, twisted, and distorted. This is how the corrupt game of cancellation is played. For those reasons, actions taken to Press the Truth® must be done right.

Doing so almost always means engaging with the media and public. A core element for doing so is having a mechanism in place to formulate information and push it out into the world. In some instances, this could involve designating a spokesperson who is dedicated to you and well positioned to release information on your behalf. This could be your lawyer, but that is usually not the first choice, since it immediately raises the specter that there is a fear of legal liability, in addition to the fact that lawyers do not usually have expertise in media relations.

Relying on counsel from a PR or crisis communication professional is advisable, but often best handled with discretion in the background. Unfortunately, too many people do not fully understand that someone seeking due process and engaging consultants for help is not signaling that he or she has done anything wrong and therefore needs a "spin doctor" or "legal eagle" to cover for them. Instead, hiring professional and experienced counsel is a savvy move that indicates smart decision making and personal responsibility. A cancel culture target who engages specialized assistance is giving themselves a fighting chance at self-defense.

In instances where it is beneficial to publicly respond to the outrage of the day, statements can and should be distributed via whatever platforms are available and where they are likely to be most effective. If you are a public figure or the owner or leader of an organization, then you can draw upon all or some of the various communication channels that your company already possesses. This could involve distributing press releases, assembling press conferences, posting materials to a website, sharing materials via social media, sending out email blasts, purchasing Google ads based on search terms, circulating internal messaging or guidance to team members via an intranet, Slack, or other methods, or any number of other avenues.

There must be a plan in place for how best to disseminate information and to field media inquiries. In the event that you are embroiled in a crisis, consider sharing a singular email address across all of your social media platforms. This gives people an address and drives them to one place where you can vet their inquiries and decide whether it is in your best interest to respond in some fashion. Creating an email address and encouraging that people reach you there can be very advantageous. Consider adding it far and wide, including in your Twitter bio, Facebook or Snapchat profile, and making room for it on your Instagram or TikTok account. Expect to be bombarded with inquiries through every platform, so a singular email address can help funnel press requests (and also hate mail) into one spot, making it easier to manage. We do not recommend providing a phone number, unless you want that phone to be constantly flooded with texts, phone calls, and voicemails.

Summon Your Courage and Refuse to Be Canceled

While we have enumerated numerous concrete ways to both prevent and appropriately respond to cancel culture attacks, perhaps the most fundamentally vital element is mental fortitude. Interviews with people who lived the nightmare firsthand and survived to tell the tale shared this common message: I refused to be canceled.

It sounds simple but, in reality, it is no easy feat. When it feels like the entire world is condemning you and you are more alone than at any other point in your life, it takes a special kind of strength to prop yourself up and declare that you will not be cowed, silenced, humiliated, or defeated.

Refusing to be canceled is a self-empowering commitment born out of conviction that as bad as things may seem today, they will be better tomorrow. We can draw both inspiration and instruction from Michelle McFarland of The Wedding Shoppe, who is featured in a case study in this book. With the future of the company that she built hanging in the balance, she simply refused to back down, and instead went public with her message, setting the record straight about being unfairly targeted in a case of mistaken identity. Professor Ilya Shapiro (whose insights and experiences were featured in the chapter "A Brief History of American Liberty") chose to trade the security of his position at a top university for a new path and has since gone on to work at a prestigious think tank and start a Substack newsletter. As in so many other areas of life, the most important battle that takes place is the one that occurs between the ears, inside your mind. Win the war within your mind, and victory will follow.

For prominent people, surviving cancel culture can be easier. After all, they usually have built reputations over the years that have afforded them a platform from which they can opine on current affairs. Joe Rogan, J. K. Rowling, and Dave Chapelle are three examples of people who have faced enormous public outcries at various times but refused to be cowed. Joe Rogan chooses to press the truth, explaining himself in a way that can comes across as earnest and authentic. J. K. Rowling has shrugged off accusations of being "transphobic" and stuck to her guns when it comes to speaking without fear about her opinions on gender.

"Everything you say upsets somebody," says Dave Chapelle. Rather than operating from a position of weakness or fear, he talks specifically about cancel culture as part of his comedy routines. "If this is what being canceled is like, I love it," he declared while soaking in applause from a standing ovation.

We asked Professor Alan Dershowitz, a relentless critic of the practice who faced years of deplatforming but succeeded in court, this question: "Should public figures expect that a price they will have to pay is inevitably becoming a victim of cancel culture?"

His response was this: "No, I think it is quite the opposite. Because I'm a public figure, an intellectual who has taught for years and written fifty books, it is harder to cancel me because I can fight back. I have platforms. The real victims are these obscure professors who told a bad joke or made an unpopular reference or said one wrong word in class or were falsely accused. They have a hard time because they don't have the platform for fighting back. . . . You know, if they can do this to me, they can do it to anybody."

Which is really the point of this book. It can and it will happen to people who do not deserve it. But the key to overcoming cancel culture is making the decision that cancel vultures will not prevail. You must internalize the inordinate strength that lies in this determined mantra: "I refuse to be canceled."

SUMMARY OF KEY POINTS

- Cancel culture is a threat to everyone, not just celebrities or people living in the public eye.
- Cancel culture replaces the liberal democratic values shared by the Left and the Right alike, with illiberalism.
- Cancel culture is a threat to everyone, not just celebrities or people living in the public eye.
- Proactive planning and the creation of a plan before you need it can help you survive a cancel culture attack.

- A person's physiological and safety needs are threatened by cancel culture.
- Organizations need business continuity plans, prepared in advance of controversies.
- Doxing is a dangerous practice that is increasingly common.
- There is a benefit to assembling a team of experts to help you navigate assaults by cancel vultures.
- Monitor online conversations with alerts and social listening software.
- Deciding to defend yourself is a key factor for surviving cancel culture.
- Prepare holding statements for responding to a surge of media inquiries.
- Only apologize if warranted; and only apologize properly using the elements of an honest apology.
- Press the Truth® in order to tell your story and ensure that your messages break through.
- Select a designated method for communicating publicly when under fire.
- Refuse to be canceled.

CHAPTER 11

For Parents: Teach the Children

The reason we endeavored to write this book was to shine a bright light on the insidious dangers of cancel culture. But understanding its history, how it works, why it is presently thriving, and the devastating consequences that it can have on people's lives is only part of the equation. The next step that needs to happen is putting in place concrete measures that slow its spread. In time, our hope is that cancel culture will entirely cease to exist and will no longer be viewed as a desirable or even viable course of action. But this ultimately can only happen through education.

Obviously, the principal readers of this book are adults. Many of them have children, whose future and welfare concerns them greatly. If you have no kids and are presently reading these words, then you may be inclined to skip ahead and ignore this chapter. You should feel free to do so; but you also may want to consider sticking with us as we provide concrete recommendations for how to talk to young people about cancel culture. After all, even if you do not presently have kids, you might have them one day—and you will certainly be working with them if you are not already. Plus, it is a safe bet that you know some kids—whether they are nieces and nephews, children of your friends, strangers interacting with you in restaurants or coffee shops or at parks, or perhaps even entertaining you on airplanes. And we are 100 percent certain that at some point, you yourself were a kid. So, with that in mind, consider how we all might play a constructive part in teaching the generations to come how to make the world a better place, devoid of cancel culture.

All kids born today grow up with near-constant access to the Internet. Technology is omnipresent in their lives, and it is second nature for them to be online. Internet connectivity is probably the main differentiator between the Millennials (born 1981 to 1996) and the generations that came before. A range of software currently exists for parents looking to monitor or direct the viewing habits of their children and exert a measure of control over their access. These are particularly relevant and potentially effective when talking about younger children; but as any parent of teenagers or even preteens knows, providing 100 percent oversight over what children absorb online or with whom they are communicating is virtually impossible.

Just as quickly as we find new ways to monitor or curb our kids' access, our tech-savvy kids find workarounds. Simply trying to police them is a losing strategy. Rather than attempting to deprive kids of information, let's instead try to give them the information and tools that they can use to more effectively police themselves. Ultimately, whether we make good decisions or bad decisions sets the course for our lives. We all understand the ways bad decisions can derail and destroy lives, including instances where people attract the focus and ire of a cancel culture mob. One of the best things that we can do for our children is to teach them how to safely use the Internet. It's a topic we do not teach in schools. In fact, much of the most critically valuable information that people need to exist in the modern world is not taught in classrooms.

We do a good job of dedicating student time to abstract concepts or theoretical studies of subjects like algebra, geometry, and calculus. But what about the subjects that really matter in day-to-day life? For instance, how many classes do you remember taking in elementary, middle, or high school on effective time management? How many courses did you attend on personal finance where you received instruction on how to build a strong credit history? Did any teachers help you learn how to defuse interpersonal conflicts in a workplace?

The bulk of our life skills must be learned on the job, or through living life itself. Imagine the impact that our school systems could have if we dedicated resources to preparing the rising generation with lessons that they could start putting to use in their lives the moment they enter adulthood or the workforce. Internet education is a prime example. It is not enough to just teach kids how to access the Internet. We need to take the next step and apply it in ways that can help them in their lives.

Our schools also should make far-reaching efforts to ensure that they operate as centers of learning where inquiry and debate are encouraged.

Simply by allowing disagreement and teaching children how to formulate arguments, we can ingrain in them a mentality of acceptance that will make it less likely for them to seek to shut down others with whom they disagree. At the same time, bigotry is not an opinion, and our youth should be taught to identify and oppose it. They should feel empowered to speak out against racism, xenophobia, and discrimination in all its forms, and to value and promote tolerance and compassion. In their formative years, we must expose our kids to virtues such as humility, understanding, respect, and open-mindedness. Increasing their comfort with intellectual discourse better prepares them to be lifelong learners as opposed to dogmatic ideologues.

Kids need instruction on how to discriminate between good information that is credible, logical, and reasonable and false or less-relevant content that does not meet the same standards. Our children need to be taught about the great dangers that exist online, not as a means of scaring them, but to help protect them and to give them the information they need to choose correct paths and avoid getting into trouble in the first place.

In the realm of crisis management, the best outcomes occur when individuals take steps to prevent crises in the first place, before incurring any degree of damage, whether to reputation or your revenue. Getting yourself out of trouble is a much more costly proposition than if you had avoided controversy, conflict, or crisis in the first place. What exactly do we need to teach our kids to help them avoid becoming cancel vultures themselves, or to avoid being descended upon by an angry online mob?

Without a doubt, there are a wide range of lessons that need to be imparted. In fact, an entire book or even a series of them could be dedicated to the topic of educating the next generation. Our goal here is obviously not to address anything or everything that kids need to learn. Instead, our aim is to provide a handful of high-impact, real-life ways to spare kids the pain that comes from unnecessary, unforced errors.

Seeing Is NOT Believing

A safe rule of thumb is this: do not believe everything you see on the Internet. It seems almost ridiculous to state this, but it bears repeating. Far too many people ascribe a level of truth to information that they absorb online, when they should be far more discriminating in what they choose to believe. Do not presume that just because you see something on a credible looking news website it is based in fact. Too often, a real editorial process either does not exist, or is not followed. Children must be discriminating, questioning the veracity of what is presented to them. That means parents must work with their children to help them develop their critical thinking skills, and parents must work to develop their own critical thinking skills, as well.

Our responsibility is to talk to them about studies showing how negative content circulates at a more rapid rate than positive news. We need to underscore for them how often reporters actually do get it wrong. We need to teach them about the ways bots and artificial intelligence (AI) are utilized to create and spread misinformation and disinformation. Our kids need to understand that seeing should not be believing; they have to dig deeper. We have to instruct them how to discern between a site with an editorial process and reputation for journalistic excellence and substandard sites lacking those same guardrails.

We also need to educate our children (and probably most fellow adults) on the differences between journalism and entertainment. They need to understand the dividing line between dispassionate reporting of the facts and dramatic punditry aimed at attracting ratings and eyeballs. Flip on the channel of today's news and you will likely encounter both, but no disclaimer. People must be educated about how to spot the difference between news based in fact and content disseminated to advance an agenda or perspective.

Make Cancel Culture Part of the Bullying Conversation

For years, far-reaching efforts have been made to teach kids about the harmful impacts of bullying. At its core, cancel culture promotes a form of bullying and, therefore, should become part of that conversation. Broadly speaking, cancel culture creates an environment of intolerance where those who espouse, or even just hold, beliefs deemed malicious by a mob are bullied into submission and self-censorship. Specifically, cancel culture events rely on targeted active bullying tactics such as doxing, harassment, name-calling, and threats of violence.

We have to be up front with our children about the terrible consequences that can come from bullying, including the difficult conversation that such behavior can lead children to take their own lives. It is a horrible thing to have to talk to kids about, but it is necessary. Just as we provide guidance and warnings about the consequences that can arise from abusing drugs or making poor decisions such as engaging in risky sexual activity, we have to be willing to talk about the range of terrifying outcomes that bullying can sometimes produce. Statistics can help them understand how widespread the problem is, and that it is growing. More important than sharing numbers, we have to share the heartbreaking stories to personalize the impact. Doing so will perhaps give them pause before they participate in bullying someone else.

We also should teach kids about the options they have available to them if they find themselves the target of bullying. To whom can they turn? What are the organizations or websites that are resources? Are we as parents making ourselves available to them, helping them when they go through tough times at the hands of other children? Are we paying enough attention and being involved enough in their lives to know that there is a problem? If we sense that something is off, then do WE have the resources at our fingertips to initiate and guide potentially impactful conversations? Have we identified counselors, therapists, and other organizations available as resources to us, too? There is no shortage of in-school conversations about bullying. Now, teachers and administrators should incorporate discussions of cancel culture into those antibullying curricula to help shut it down.

Unpacking Cancel Culture

At home, we need to initiate discussions on cancel culture with our children to dispel the myth that it is an acceptable way of holding people to account for their behavior. Instead, we should consider conversations about punishments fitting crimes, and core American concepts such as due process, freedom of speech, and freedom of thought.

Kids need to be reminded that a key aspect that makes America great is our freedom to entertain a range of opinions, perspectives, and views. It is the freedom to hold noxious views that distinguishes America and the First Amendment. Yet they do not make those views less noxious.

Diversity is something that should be celebrated and encouraged. Most children care more about what their peers think of them than anything else in the entire world, and gaining that acceptance is vital to their sense of worth. To a kid, there are few things harder than feeling like you are on the outside looking in, set apart from the group because you do not look like, dress like, or think just like the others. We must find a way to get through to them and help them understand that it is not a bad thing for people to have different perspectives. On the contrary, there is value in free thinking, debating ideas, and wrestling to find solutions in cases where clear answers do not exist.

Fundamentally, we must dispel the notion that cancel culture is positive or beneficial and help kids to see that it is out of step with the most celebrated American values. Due process already exists in the legal system. In the workplace, there are other avenues by which people can report bad behavior. But we have to trust in these institutions and give them time to actually do their work. Finding out the facts is an endeavor that takes effort and time. Yes, that can be frustrating when we feel upset and want immediate action taken to curb a perceived wrong. But in order to arrive at the truth, fact-finding cannot be instantaneous.

Far too often, cancel culture mobs descend on people before they have even been given a fair opportunity to present factual information to challenge false assertions; or for a dispassionate third-party investigation to arrive at the truth. The necessity of giving due process the necessary time to produce results is something that we need to explain and discuss with our children. If we think that they are too young to understand these complex concepts, then we need to think again, because they are not. Kids today are growing up faster than ever, and these are vital issues that shape their world. In the end, we want to both prevent them from taking part in cancel culture attacks and becoming targets of them.

Real Life versus Life Online

One of the most difficult things to chip away at is the false belief that every aspect of our lives needs to be lived online. This one is a really steep challenge when it comes to kids and will take time and dedicated efforts to overcome. Our kids often find it hard to believe that there once existed a world in which people had experiences that they did not immediately share with the world via social media. A time when people saw or experienced beautiful things and recalled them later using their memories and brains, as opposed to capturing them with a camera built into a smartphone. We need to remind our children that life is meant to be lived in the real world, and not just the virtual one. Expect this to become even more of a challenge with companies such as Meta investing billions in developing and promoting a future "Metaverse" that blends real and virtual life.

In the same way we caution them not to believe everything they see on websites, they should also be taught to cast a wary eye on the things that people post on social media. Most individuals try to present the best versions of themselves on the web, focusing more on painting a picture of who they wish they were or at least how they want the world to see them. Real life doesn't come with airbrushing or filters to obscure reality and hide flaws. Kids have to be encouraged to embrace themselves and others as imperfect beings, rather than seeking or demanding perfection.

Proceed with Caution

While it is completely impractical and unrealistic to expect kids to forgo sharing their life experiences online in some fashion (whether via social media platforms or communications with family and friends), we can help them find paths for participating in online communities—but not at the expense of being present in the real world. Without employing a heavy-handed approach that leads them to employ selective hearing and totally ignoring mom and dad, we need to broach the topic of the inherent dangers of sharing too much online. Avoiding "oversharing" means discriminating about what each of us does and does not broadcast online to a limitless audience via the Internet. This can have safety implications in terms of not revealing your location to those who would do you harm or might have nefarious goals in mind.

Another aspect of this is investing more time and effort in being present in the real world than curating personal content online. While words matter, probably the best thing we can do in this arena is to lead by example. How good are we as parents at putting our own phones down and living in the moment? Have we looked at implementing important baby steps like technology-free meals that inspire substantive conversations by requiring people to show up at the table without their phones? As role models, most of us probably could do a lot better in terms of prioritizing our kids and their intellectual and emotional needs over our compulsive urges to thumb through our devices. When it comes to being dialed in and focused and actively listening and engaging, this is not a situation where we can get away with "do as I say, not as I do." Instead, we must model the right behaviors and be willing to put the phone down in exchange for real conversation and connection with our kids.

Action Items

There are several steps our children can take in order to lessen the likelihood that they will become subjects of cancel culture. Here are some specific steps that will help them avoid being canceled.

Keep It Clean and Never Take Nudes

Time and again, naked selfies prove to be the undoing of the young and the old alike. What many people fail to understand is that once a nude picture is sent, someone is literally exposed forever (pun intended). It does not matter if the image is transmitted via text, via email, or another platform. Once it leaves a device, it exists permanently and is out of your control. A major mistake that young people make all the time is presuming that nude images sent via secure chat or via platforms with disappearing messages cannot be captured. There are countless examples where individuals have sent pics via Snapchat or other similar methods presuming incorrectly that the messages would actually disappear upon receipt. There are multiple ways to get around the "disappearing" messages apps, from taking screenshots to snapping pictures or video using a second, separate device.

The bottom line is this: if you do not want the entire world to see you in your birthday suit, then do not take naked pictures of yourself or allow others to do so. And no matter what, do not circulate the pictures. Unfortunately, people sometimes get worked up and lose themselves in the moment. But time and again, this proves the undoing of everyone from public officials to (formerly) private individuals. For teenagers, it is hard to imagine anything more mortifying than having your classmates in middle or high school circulating naked pictures of you, but it happens every day.

Similarly, we need to advise our kids against using sexually explicit language in their online conversations, since those comments can be captured and shared. The only foolproof way to make sure that sexual content is not used to cause harm is not to create it in the first place. A good rule of thumb: if you are not comfortable seeing your words printed on the front page of a newspaper or trending on Twitter, then don't communicate them electronically.

Someone Is Always Watching

Many scandals are self-inflicted, but we must also remind kids that taking care of themselves is not enough. They also must remain vigilant about their surroundings, because the people around them may not have their best interests at heart. In many instances, people get into trouble when they were not doing anything wrong but were simply photographed in the vicinity of trouble or in the proverbial wrong place at the wrong time. We and our children should always assume that people around us have cameras at the ready and are sharing videos and photos online. As if they did not already have enough to worry about, kids also need to realize that if they are at parties or other places where illegal activity is happening, then they can also get into trouble.

Another serious threat that warrants situational awareness is the possibility that "friends" may be surreptitiously filming you without your consent. Revenge porn, which happens when sexual partners publicly share personal photos, has become a problem for everyday people as well as Hollywood celebrities who have also been victimized by this spiteful activity. Children today must contend with the growing risk that any sexual activity in which they engage could be secretly recorded without their knowledge or permission. It's horrifying to even think about and potentially uncomfortable for parents to discuss with their children; but it must be done to help ensure that young people do not end up in compromising positions that can lead to public humiliation.

Share with Care and Post with Purpose

In the book *Crisis Averted: PR Strategies to Protect Your Reputation and the Bottom Line*, an entire chapter was dedicated to helping people avoid social media crises. Essentially, the actions you take to avoid crises are closely linked to best practices for sidestepping cancel culture. When it comes to online activity by our kids (and us), safeguarding against a crisis and reducing the likelihood that a mob of cancel vultures will descend upon you are quite simple and come down to two things that should always remain top of mind: share with care and post with purpose.

You share with care when you choose not to broadcast your location in real time. Young people, especially girls, can set themselves up for targeting by predators if they tell them where and when they will be in a certain place. Stalkers, private investigators, or even nosy neighbors can cobble together quite a bit of information from those people who choose to share liberally online, especially in terms of when and where to find them at any point in time. We must remind our kids that posting vacation pictures while away is very risky. It broadcasts to the world that you are not home, and therefore your valuables may be accessible to people who want to gain access to them.

Posting with purpose is both a defensive and an offensive strategy for limiting your risk of cancellation. Posting with purpose means thinking about what you hope to accomplish before you do so. Before sharing images or written thoughts online, consider whether such a post puts you in the light in which you wish to be viewed. If you are not so sure, then proceed with caution. Creating a steady stream of updates without pausing to share with care and post with purpose leaves the door open for others to misinterpret or misconstrue what you have put out into the world. If you are not sharing with care or posting with a positive purpose in mind, then amend Nike's slogan by a word to protect yourself: Just *don't* do it.

Our kids must be constantly reminded that we are always being judged by the things we do and say, in real life and online. And if their posts do not place them in a positive light, then just don't do it. Because what they say and do online lives forever, they must be extremely cautious about what they put out into the world.

Too many shocking examples exist of kids ruining their lives by failing to consider the likely negative consequences of their social media posts. For example, many have generated huge backlash and horrifying consequences by posting videos of themselves singing along with rap music containing the N-word. Marcus Stokes, a top high school football prospect recruited to play quarterback at the University of Florida, had his scholarship revoked after posting a video to social media that included him rapping, "Welcome back N-." In two seconds, he blew the opportunity to receive a four-year education at a highly regarded school. In the wake of the controversy, he used the following apology:

"I was in my car listening to rap music, rapping along to the words and I posted a video of it on social media. I deeply apologize for the words in the song that I chose to say. It was hurtful and offensive to many people, and I regret that. I fully accept the consequences for my actions, and I respect the University of Florida's decision to withdraw my scholarship offer to play football. My intention was never to hurt anybody and I recognize that even when going along with a song, my words still carry a lot of weight. I will strive to be better and to become the best version of myself both on and off the field. I know that learning from my mistakes is a first important step. Marcus Stokes."

Using the N-word in a social media post is possibly the most surefire way to throw your entire future into question. The word is vile and the history of racism behind it is reprehensible, but at the same time it is widely used, especially in music. It seems patently unfair that music companies can profit from sales of music that uses the word, streaming services such as Spotify and Apple Music can distribute it, but young people who are captured singing along with the lyrics could see their entire lives upended. But that is the world in which we presently live, so we need to talk to our kids about these critically important issues and ensure that they proceed with caution.

When our kids share with care and post with purpose, they take an active role in looking after themselves and securing their own futures. While it is true that anyone can become a target of cancel culture based on the assertions or actions of others, death by your own hand is far worse. Why give your detractors or enemies the ammunition with which to kill your reputation?

Learning from Mistakes

Despite whatever efforts we make to educate our kids and guide them, it is simply inevitable that they will make mistakes. That is not just a part of childhood and growing up; it's part of life.

We owe it to our children to speak to them about the value that can come from making mistakes and then learning from them. In the context of society at large, we should decriminalize making errors or exhibiting lapses in judgment. The world used to be a far more forgiving place where people could blunder but then move on, but in the age of the Internet that guarantee does not exist.

Nobody is perfect; we are all fallible and imperfect beings, so we need to start extending to one another the freedom to make mistakes and not be punished eternally for doing so.

So many people have learned and grown by seeing the errors of their ways. Incredibly, even the most negative incidents in people's lives can ultimately prove to be positive learning experiences. In his excellent book *The Power of Regret,* author Daniel Pink reminds us that value and growth come not from having "no regrets," but from regretting past actions and using them as instructive experiences from which we can emerge as better people. Just as we teach our children to extend grace to others, we must ensure that they are willing to forgive themselves when they make mistakes. In our view, the greatest shame in life comes not from making a mistake, but from failing to learn from it.

Encouraging our kids to develop grit and articulating for them the difference between having a growth mind-set and a fixed mind-set will also go a long way toward creating confident, well-adjusted young adults. *Grit: The Power of Passion and Perseverance* is a book by academic and author Angela Duckworth that points to grittiness as a key predictor of success and accomplishment, highlighting the ability of people with grit to suffer setbacks but ultimately persevere. *Mindset: The New Psychology of Success*, by Carol S. Dweck, should also be required reading for all young people. It compares and contrasts "fixed" and "growth" mind-sets.

According to Dweck, "Although people may differ in every which way—in their initial talents and aptitudes, interests, or temperaments—everyone can change and grow through application and experience."

Kindness Matters

Another lesson our youth need to hear from us is that kindness matters, and there is a lot to be gained from surrounding ourselves with positive people. Conscientiousness and class have become harder to come by in an online world often characterized by snark and clapbacks. It is up to us to teach the next generation to surround themselves with people who give them positive energy and lift them up. Their lives will be fuller and happier filled with friends who help them along the way and are there for them and build their self-confidence, versus those who put them down and diminish their self-worth. To combat cancel culture and the atmosphere of acrimony that allows it to flourish, we must redouble our commitment to the golden rule: do unto others as you would have them do unto you.

Simply following that creed can prevent so many instances of pain, heartache, and cancel culture. People treating others in the way that they would want to be treated would fundamentally shift the tenor of all discussions in our country, political or otherwise. It is a largely universal concept that every one of us should help propagate.

SUMMARY OF KEY POINTS

- Teaching kids how to safely use the Internet will be key to ending the practice of cancel culture.
- We must provide instruction on how to discriminate between credible and false information.
- The differences between journalism and advocacy or entertainment should be highlighted.
- Cancel culture is a form of bullying and should be incorporated into antibullying curricula delivered at schools.
- Support must be provided to kids on the receiving end of bullying.
- At home we should engage kids in discussions about cancel culture and teach them that it is an unacceptable way to hold people to account for their behavior.

- Core American concepts such as due process and freedom of speech and thought should be taught and kept in mind to avoid a rush to judgment.
- We should celebrate diversity of views and free expression and make it clear that cancel culture violates American values.
- Kids should be prevented from being targets, as well as becoming cancel vultures.
- There is more to life than the virtual world alone, and part of the way to avoid being canceled is exercising restraint online and not oversharing.
- Never send nude photographs if you want to decrease the chances of being canceled.
- Someone with a camera and video recorder is always watching, so exercise caution.
- Share with care and post with purpose to avoid social media crises that can lead to cancel culture campaigns.
- Everyone makes mistakes, so we need to make the world a more forgiving place.
- Personal growth can come when you learn from errors.
- Developing grit is a way to prevent being canceled.
- Kindness matters, and we must instill self-confidence and understanding in our children.
- It is time to reinstate the golden rule: do unto others as you would have them do unto you.

Closing Thoughts

In this book, we have endeavored to define cancel culture and its central elements, point out that cancel culture stands in opposition to core democratic principles, and raise awareness about cancel vultures and the crippling effects they have on the lives of those they target. Ultimately, this book makes the case that a world without cancel culture is a better place for all.

A question we are regularly asked for which there is no simple answer: Will cancel culture be a permanent fixture in American life?

Unfortunately, this hateful and harmful practice will likely be with us for years because the trends that have fueled cancel culture continue. However, many hopeful signs have begun to emerge. Political moderates on both sides of the aisle are speaking out against the more strident partisans in their respective parties. A series of recent national elections have seen the most extreme candidates rejected in favor of more moderate options.

In the media, well-known and independent-minded journalists are leaving the confines of ideologically oriented news to contribute on a range of alternate platforms such as Substack, which boasts millions of readers and contributors. A range of news sites, podcasts, videos, and other content are reaching growing audiences, creating a more egalitarian marketplace of ideas.

In *The Cancel Culture Curse*, we draw upon research and data illustrating the vital role colleges and universities have played in facilitating cancel culture. On too many campuses, students engage primarily with those possessing similar ideological predispositions, rarely interacting with students or professors with opposing viewpoints. Free speech is shut down by banning or shouting down speakers, and the implementation of Bias Reporting Systems often leads to self-censoring, mistrust, and ideological bullying.

But there are signs of progress there, too. The University of Austin, founded by a group of high-profile intellectuals, academics, and journalists who faced cancellation, seeks to challenge the status quo of modern-day academia by introducing a disruptive education model and pledging to champion "freedom of inquiry, freedom of conscience, and civil discourse."

At the University of North Carolina at Chapel Hill, the nation's oldest public university, its trustees in 2023 voted 12 to 0 to establish the School of Civic Life and Leadership. With the stated goal of demonstrating commitment to free expression in higher education, UNC plans to hire professors from across the political spectrum to build a curriculum free of ideological constraints.

In the years to come, businesses and organizations of all sizes and across industries will inevitably be forced to grapple with the best ways to handle cancel culture attacks. Already, a growing chorus of companies are showing more resolve.

Do not be surprised to see an eventual course correction from free-thinking corporate leaders looking to move away from the rapid-fire condemnations demanded by cancel vultures. Rather than capitulating to activist demands from a vocal minority, expect to see companies choosing more measured responses to inevitable controversies. Doing so will help solidify key principles, engender employee trust, and refortify cultural acceptance of apologies and the granting of forgiveness.

We are confident that bedrock principles upon which America was founded, and which have sustained it for centuries—including freedom of thought, choice and expression, and the right to due process—will ultimately prevail over cancel culture. People are increasingly acknowledging that condemning one another is not sustainable if our collective goal is to ensure the long-term success of our democracy. None of us is infallible, nor do we deserve to have our lives destroyed by mobs of strangers citing real or imagined mistakes.

Ultimately, every one of us has a role to play in eliminating cancel culture. We should avoid defaulting to outrage, rushing to judgment, and seeking to permanently destroy those with whom we disagree. We owe it to ourselves—especially our children and generations to come—to allow people room for mistakes, and to apologize and make amends when they falter. There is much to learn by keeping open minds, asking questions, engaging in honest debate, seeking different perspectives, and having enough humility and confidence to change our minds when the facts warrant it.

We hope that this book will serve as a wake-up call and bring us one step closer to a more positive, understanding, and forgiving society. Collectively, and individually, we can and must do better. In the end, the only thing we have to cancel is cancel culture itself.

Case Study: Lisa Alexander

Situation Synopsis

Lisa Alexander is a lifelong Californian, current resident of San Francisco, and founder of the skincare company LAFACE. While walking in her neighborhood with a friend on June 9, 2020, she encountered a man using chalk to stencil onto the retaining wall outside the C.A. Belden House, a historic home owned by someone Alexander knew as her neighbor, having met him on numerous occasions while strolling the neighborhood. The Belden House, which is on the National Historic Register, is located one-half block from the building where Alexander had lived for more than 15 years.

Alexander stopped to enquire about the stenciling. Later, she learned that the man, James Juanillo, who is reportedly Filipino, is one of several rental tenants at Belden House. Juanillo recorded the conversation on his mobile phone. When he posted it online days later, on June 12, it went viral, prompting a slew of national and international media coverage aided by the efforts of a public relations firm. The crux of the stories, and the source of the outrage, was the narrative that a white woman called 911 on a person of color for using chalk to adorn his own home with the message "Black Lives Matter." After being referred to by Juanillo in the video as "Karen," Alexander quickly became known across the globe as "San Francisco Karen." The term "Karen" is a derogatory slang moniker typically applied to a white woman deemed to be entitled, intolerant, and combative.

Within hours of Juanillo posting the video and the story gathering steam on social media, a group of people triggered by the video arrived at Alexander's home with baseball bats and other weapons in hand to intimidate and threaten her. She also received hundreds of hateful messages and death threats by phone, email, and other means. Fueled by the explosive video appearing in the news, cancel vultures attacked her business with negative reviews and succeeded in intimidating her business contacts to dissociate from her, effectively driving her out of business and precluding her from earning a living.

After multiple attempts that weekend to reach out to Juanillo personally and stopping by the Belden House with a personal letter of apology that included her contact information, Alexander released a public statement in which she apologized to Juanillo. The statement read:

> I want to apologize directly to Mr. Juanillo. There are not enough words to describe how truly sorry I am for being disrespectful to him last Tuesday when I made the decision to question him about what he was doing in front of his home. I should have minded my own business.
>
> The last 48 hours has taught me that my actions were those of someone who is not aware of the damage caused by being ignorant and I to racial inequalities. When I watch the video I am shocked and sad that I behaved the way I did. It was disrespectful to Mr. Juanillo and I am deeply sorry for that. I did not realize at the time that my actions were racist and have learned a painful lesson. I am taking a hard look at the meaning behind white privilege and am committed to growing from this experience. I would love to have coffee with Mr. Juanillo in our neighborhood so I can apologize in person and share a dialogue where I can continue to learn and grow and be a better person.

The stress of the cancel culture attack induced a severe reaction that led to Alexander being hospitalized and forced to undergo emergency surgery from which she has yet to fully recover. The psychological, emotional, and physical damage she endured has never been reported because she declined numerous media requests for interviews. She says she wanted to handle it neighbor-to-neighbor and feared more onslaught from social media and other personal attacks if she engaged with the media to tell what had transpired.

For the first time ever, Alexander agreed to speak on the record with us about the incident, which completely altered the trajectory of her life. She has expressed a desire to share her story in this book as a cautionary tale, warning others about the serious, real-life, and devastating consequences of cancel culture.

Interview Highlights

Much of the criticism you have received in the wake of the encounter focuses upon your assumed wealth and privilege. How much do you think that impacted your decision to engage your neighbor?

Your question nails one of the most harmful dynamics of cancel culture: the baseless assumptions held by complete strangers who impute bad motives and intent against people they have never met, attacking them relentlessly while hiding behind anonymous identities. I was very fortunate to have come from a supportive family and to have a wonderful educational experience, but I do not understand what my background has to do with me trying to be a good neighbor. No one has handed me anything, and the building of LAFACE, which I started from the ground up, was due to my own hard work. I sacrificed everything and more to realize my dream, which was destroyed by Mr. Juanillo's video. It's amazing what you can accomplish when you have a goal and are committed to it.

But, returning to the second part of your question: despite whatever criticisms, hate, and implied motivations were spewed about me on social media, my decision to engage Mr. Juanillo was really simple: I was trying to be a good neighbor and protect my neighbor's home from being tagged.

With LAFACE what problems were you solving?

My goal out of the gate was to create a line of products that addressed skin sensitivities, and it turned out that we are a great brand for people who suffer with skin issues or have undergone chemotherapy. After going through chemo, people are so tired of having pharmaceuticals and chemicals put into their systems. Our products, which are plant stem cell-based, fill that void of effective yet clean beauty products. We were well received and in the process of a capital raise to grow to the next step. Then Mr. Juanillo happened.

I had a few self-funded ventures before, in children's clothing, couture design, a pickle company, and another in furniture design, which I did with the goal of funding the research and development needed for LAFACE. The R&D required to create skincare products is expensive, complicated, and time-consuming. However, because of my agricultural background, I understood the regulatory rules and the underlying science. But more importantly, the criticality of creating a great team because without that, you are nothing; so that's what I did. I gathered some amazing scientists, and we got very creative. It was an amazing journey, developing the brand, and I loved everything about it. But most of all, I loved my clients.

LAFACE did a tremendous amount of research to make sure that the products would be beneficial for all genders and races, and they are. Our client base was about 30–40 percent persons of color. I had never thought about our clients in terms of race, but just of the skin scientifically: how thick the epidermis is, how much oil one's complexion produces, stem cells, peptides, tetrapeptides, those sorts of things. My goal was to help people; that is how my mind works.

Tell us more about what happened that day, which we have seen on video.

I was working at my desk when my friend who lives a block away called and asked, "Hey, do you want to go for a quick walk?" We were planning to visit some friends of ours in the Marina, and I said, "Sure." He came to get me and realized he had forgotten his wallet, so we went back toward his place. As we were walking by the Belden House, I noticed the back of a person doing some sort of artwork on the wall.

I realized it wasn't the person who owned the house, John Newmeyer. I've been here in the neighborhood for 18 years—it was 15 years at the time. I had walked by the Belden House hundreds, if not thousands, of times and had years of exchanging pleasantries with Mr. Newmeyer. I mean, we did not attend each other's birthdays, but I would always say hello, as he was often sitting outside with his little dog, reading the newspaper, and drinking lemonade.

He had been your neighbor for fifteen years at that point?

Yes. I had exchanged many neighborly greetings with John throughout the years. So, when he later denied knowing of me to the press, I found it quite surprising. I still don't understand why he did that. So, while walking by the Belden House, I noticed a gentleman stenciling on the short retaining wall along the sidewalk. At that time in our neighborhood there had been dozens of car break-ins, and there are signs on streetlight poles in the neighborhood and all over the city saying, "If you see something, say something," encouraging people to call this nonemergency 415 number.

I was just trying to be nice to my neighbor, when I saw someone doing something to John Newmeyer's house, which, as I have said, is on the

National Historic Register and is one of the most beautiful homes in the neighborhood. John Newmeyer, the owner, has white hair, and I knew this was his house, as does everyone in the neighborhood. But this man had dark hair and was wearing a mask and had a different body type, so I knew it wasn't John.

I asked him politely if he lived there. Granted, when you look back at it some people wonder why I didn't mind my own business. Believe me, looking back on the reaction, I wish that I would have, but what kind of world would that be? I live in a city, not out on a ranch. I interact with people every day, and I talk to them. I ask you and your readers: if you had lived in your neighborhood for 15 years and one day you came home and saw someone you had never seen before writing on your neighbor's fence or wall, what would you do?

I stopped and I said, "Excuse me, sir. Excuse me. Pardon me, sir. Excuse me, sir. Do you live here?" because I'd never seen that person. I was not aware at the time that Mr. Newmeyer had bedrooms in his house that he rented out. This person, Mr. Juanillo, evidently, is somebody who rented one of those bedrooms, as well as living elsewhere.

You walked up and said to him multiple times "excuse me" to try to get his attention. Did he not respond right away?
I think he was wearing headphones or something. I hate to tell you this, but I can't look at the video. I've never been able to watch the video. So, this is all 100 percent from my memory. But I remember that he stood up, and I recall him having a phone out and directing it to me. And I remember thinking to myself, why is he taking pictures of me? Because I'm trying to protect someone's private property?

There was so much unrest and destruction in our country, our state, and in San Francisco at the time. What was going on socially and politically was the aftermath of the horrible and unforgivable murder of George Floyd, and there were all sorts of riots and protests happening everywhere in the States. It couldn't have been a more "perfect storm" in terms of timing. I do believe, looking back, that this opportunity was ripe for misusing. The timing was perfect, and Mr. Juanillo took it.

I believe that since we live in a civil society, we have a responsibility to look out for one another, and I don't see what's wrong with that. I grew up with elderly parents, so I'm a little sensitive to and protective of the elderly. Maybe that's part of it. I was aware that Mr. Newmeyer was a little older. But there was absolutely not one iota of racism in my reasoning for stopping

to speak with this person. The notion that my actions were in any way motivated by race or racism couldn't be further from the truth.

"Excuse me, pardon me, sir, do you live here?" He stands up, turns
around, and holds up his camera and responds, "Would it matter if I did?"

And I said, "Well, yes, because it's private property. And you're not supposed to paint on private property." And the reason why I said that was
because it is private property, and it is an historic house. I was just trying
to watch out for my neighbor. I think it's all in the video, but I'm not sure,
because I cannot watch it. But I do remember he told me to "call the police."
I remember saying "No, why?" Because I didn't understand why I would do
that. And then I left.

On our way down to the Marina, I dashed up and down quickly
from my apartment, and I was gone for about two minutes. When I came
back down, my friend was on the phone with the local 415 nonemergency
Neighborhood Watch number, saying, "It's not an emergency, but there's
someone writing on the wall outside this historical house. We asked him if
he lived there, and he wouldn't respond, which tells us he probably doesn't,
and then he called my friend a Karen," and that was pretty much the gist
of it.

Then we kept walking to the Marina and ran some errands, and then
we went to see our friends. We were waiting on their steps to go into their
home—this was an hour and a half after the encounter—and I saw someone run by. Like a "peek and then run." And I thought, "That's weird." So, I
went to look, and that's when I saw him, Mr. Juanillo. He had been following us for an hour and a half, and there he was, hiding behind the bushes of
the garage next door.

This explained why, in the beginning, a lot of Mr. Juanillo's posts online
said, "She's a nosy person, she doesn't even live in this neighborhood. She
lives in the Marina." But that clearly isn't true; I've been here in my neighborhood, half a block from the Belden House, for 18 years.

**You are waiting to go into your friend's home, look over, and see the
person with whom you had this exchange?**
I'm waiting there about three steps up from the bottom of the stairs of my
friend's house in the Marina, which is a long way from the Belden House.
As I'm looking around, this guy runs about four feet away from me. He was
checking to see where we went. He walks quickly by, sees us, runs, and hides
about 20 feet away behind some bushes next to a garage.

I thought, "that's strange," but now I now understand why, when Mr. Juanillo started talking about me in the press and social media, he said I lived in the Marina. That makes sense, given that he followed me down there.

And also, another thing that was confusing to me was his statement on one of the many TV shows he appeared on saying, "I'll never forget the look on Alexander's face when the police drove by and waved to me." Well, that never happened. We left, and he followed us down to the Marina, so I'm not sure what he's talking about. I never called 911, my friend did not either. He called the nonemergency Neighborhood Watch number posted everywhere. And I never saw the police arrive at the Belden house and wave; that is absurd.

Why do you think Mr. Juanillo didn't just say I rent a room here when you asked if he lived there?
I have no idea. To be honest with you, this should have been resolved privately and respectfully as a misunderstanding among neighbors. It should never have unfolded like this and should never have escalated past "Excuse me, sir. Pardon me. Do you live here?" Imagine if he had responded, "Yes, I actually rent a room here," or just, "Yes, I do." And I then would have said, "Hi, my name is Lisa Alexander. I live right up the street. It is very nice to meet you." As I think you can see in the video, when I finally see what he's stenciling, which is Black Lives Matter, I say to Mr Juanillo, "Your message is fine, your message is good. Just not this way, don't paint it on private property." Again, it had nothing to do with race or racism; it was all about private property and being thoughtful about Mr. Newmeyer's beautiful home.

You know, he implied in his first few interviews that he owned the Belden House, so everybody thought that was the case, which was the cause of much of the criticism directed toward me. It is amazing to me that no reporter fact-checked his assertion of being the owner, which is simply not true. He did not own the house, but whether or not he rented or owned is not the point; the point is that he had an agenda. The encounter happened on Tuesday, June 9, 2020. He found out who I was and then hired a public relations firm. They cleaned up his social media profile and got prepared before going public on Friday, June 12, 2020.

That Friday night, I received a text from one of my nieces in which she said, "Hey, Lisa, there's something going on with you on Twitter." And I was like, "Wait, what?" So, Mr. Juanillo waited from Tuesday to Friday to ensure that the PR firm could clean up his social media profile and exploit mine. Criticizing me for charitable causes, for buying tickets to fundraisers or helping to raise money for charity by donating auction items from my skincare company with the goal of portraying me as an elitist, wealthy, entitled white woman. All of this was widely circulated on social media as a negative. They wrote things like "Entitled Lisa in a pretty party dress. . ." My personal life came under fire. Those in the media—I don't understand why they did all of this, because there were so many things that were obviously not true and they could have so easily found out what was and wasn't true but chose not to.

This encounter happened on a Tuesday. It was a brief interaction.
Yes, and I didn't think anything of it until that Friday after five o'clock while driving back from Oakland to San Francisco when my niece texted and said my nephew was upset because he was receiving so many frightening calls. My phone had started ringing like mad while I was driving back, with strangers saying unimaginably horrible and threatening things to me. Someone had published my home address and phone number on social media. So, Friday night strangers started calling me and attacking me on numerous social media platforms as well as my personal numbers and emails.

Then, that Friday night after midnight a mob came to my home. They attempted to break into my building and were ringing my doorbell all night long. I have a small garden, and when I went out to peek over to see what was happening, they were there in the front of my building. People in ski masks and face coverings with baseball bats and weapons. Long guns, like shotguns. They were on the building's security camera, and that Monday someone got into the building and was banging on my front door. I was absolutely petrified. But I wasn't about to call the police. I had never called 911 when the incident with Mr. Juanillo happened, and I wasn't about to call now. I didn't get it. I knew what had happened, but I couldn't understand why anyone would take this to that level and do something like this. Why were they doing this?

The encounter occurred on Tuesday, June 9. Mr. Juanillo knew how to contact me all week before posting his video, because he found me on social media. He also had my contact information from my personal letter I had walked over to him that Sunday, June 14, and from my phone messages to him asking him to meet to discuss the matter neighbor-to-neighbor.

Why did he choose not to attempt to resolve the issue with me privately, rather than engaging a PR firm and launching a multichannel social media assault?

As the social media firestorm exploded, fanned by unfact-checked stories in the media, it quickly metastasized into me being labeled a racist. To be fair, I do not believe Mr. Juanillo ever called me that, but he lit the match by posting his video . . . and kept it lit.

The ad hominem attacks were posted, reposted, Tweeted and re-Tweeted millions of times by strangers who had never met me—who didn't know me. To call someone a racist is the ultimate lethal weapon because one cannot refute the label—you just bleed out at the knees. Having lived through this, I can now assert, without reservation, that to call someone a racist you have to know that person's entire life experience, and you should have the courage to confront the person, not this gutless hiding behind fake anonymous emails and tweets, or leaving voice messages in the middle of the night.

What were these people saying?
I don't want to repeat the language. I'll send you a small file that contains only about 2 percent of the hate mail I received. It went from the light to the very dark. People were writing things in reviews like, "I ordered face powder from Lisa Alexander, and she sent me this WHITE powder, and I broke out," but I don't sell powder. "The lipsticks she sells are disgusting," said others, but I don't produce makeup. I don't sell lipsticks. That is not something we do. There were so many lies. So many accusations untethered to reality.

With all this bombardment happening, I contacted the social media sites because as a small business I had spent many years curating my brand and reputation. I had pretty much done everything at the company and was very involved, as most founders are. Strangers were calling demanding that I be fired. They clearly had no idea that I was the founder of the company. But they were calling and telling me they wished I were dead, and they could not wait for all these horrible things to happen to me.

Then, over the next few days, I had to work on shutting down my entire online life, my website, my accounts, my social media, Nextdoor, BBB. Everything. Also, I then got inundated with people opening up fake social media accounts in my name or my business name. You know, opening a Twitter account, a Facebook account, or any of these accounts is very simple, but trying to close them down? Not easy. I wrote a letter to the attorneys at Twitter informing them I was getting death threats, that I was scared, to please, please take down my account. I told them that they had published my home address and phone number; that they had opened fake accounts. It did not matter to Twitter, or any of them.

People were attacking me because of a fabricated race issue when the situation with Mr. Juanillo had absolutely nothing to do with race at all. Later that summer, Mr Juanillo had a face mask made with the image of my face printed on it, commenting on social media that I was not even wearing a face mask that day. However, at that time there were no mask laws or mandates in place, and I wasn't wearing a mask as we were outside at the time, so it was just a way to stir up more hate. Imagine if a stranger created a mask with your daughter's image on it—or that of your wife, girlfriend, partner, husband—whatever. Is that okay?

I have been told that people sent him letters and cards, and sometimes said things in my defense regarding what he did. I don't know who these people are, but I do know that he then takes these notes and posts them on Twitter and implies that it is I who is sending them. "She could have just walked it over," I believe were his words. However, this could not be further from the truth, as I won't even walk in front of his house. Since June 2020, I intentionally walk on the opposite side of the street to avoid any possibility of interaction with him. I've heard that he has done a lot to keep this event alive. He keeps the video pinned to the top of his Twitter account and describes himself as a social justice warrior; and he has a media section celebrating all the press he got from posting the video of me. He has shared photos of himself in the masks he printed with my face on them. Clearly, he was and is proud about what he has done.

When this happened, I got so many threats I couldn't bear to read them myself, so I had to have a friend come over and place all my emails into a "hate mail" folder. I still have the really evil voicemails saved and to this day still get a lot of nasty email. One person sent eight letters in one day, the same exact letter. They spent eight times as much money on postage to send me the same hate letter eight times.

My family also got a lot of money demands. They would say things like "All you have to do is send x number of dollars to them personally, or to some 'specific organization' and they would leave me alone." They went after my family. They contacted my sisters, who are in their seventies and do not have social media at all. They contacted my nephews and everyone else they could think of, and it was very bewildering and frightening for all of them. It's terrifying. And it certainly had an impact on my relationships with my family because they were so terrified. It caused irrevocable damage. It has taken a long time for me to repair some of these relationships, with family and friends, that have always been so loving and wonderful. However, some are forever lost, which is heartbreaking to me. I'd say about 95 percent of the people who know me told me: "Lisa, if this happened to you, it could happen to anyone," and the other 5 percent were in shock and didn't know what to say to me. After about a year and a half, some of them reached out, but it will truly never be the same.

Were you getting negative reviews on Google and other sites?
Before this disaster, which should have been resolved privately as a misunderstanding between neighbors, I had a respected reputation on social media. And my brand reputation led me to partner with, among others, a great box company called Birchbox. Birchbox had reached out to me when I first started LAFACE, saying they wanted to work with my company. We had a fantastic relationship—it was awesome, nothing negative. However, we hadn't worked together for seven years when all of a sudden, after Mr. Juanillo's post and the subsequent social media toxic tsunami, Birchbox posted a statement, without the courtesy of contacting me to discuss what had actually happened, stating that they will not be working with this "racist" company. Huh? What were they talking about? We had not worked with them for years. So, they made this big misleading virtue-signaling statement at my expense. Not cool.

Did you consider fighting back against the misinformation that was being spread when the cancel culture attack began?
I never fought back against any of this, and I do want it to be known that I never once said anything negative whatsoever about Mr. Juanillo. I did not do a single interview. I've had no contact with him. I haven't contacted him since I wrote him a personal letter of apology on June 14th saying how sorry I was that I had hurt his feelings. I wrote a personal letter and walked it over there and spent about 20 minutes on the back steps of the Belden House talking to one of his roommates. Mr. Juanillo didn't want to come and talk to me or accept the apology letter. His roommate said it was because he was doing an interview with the press in another room of the house.

Over the next few days, one of the TV reporters who was going over to interview him called me and asked if I would come in for an interview. I said no but did ask that she please tell Mr. Juanillo that I had been trying to reach him personally to apologize, had walked over a letter of apology, had called to apologize, and even publicly apologized. But even with this knowledge, Mr. Juanillo kept on telling reporters he had not heard from me and that if I just apologized, then we would be fine. I tried everything I could to do so, but he didn't want anything to do with it. He also has found ways to monetize the video. I don't see how anyone has benefited from this situation except for Mr. Juanillo.

I don't believe his actions helped in the cause of fighting racism or social justice. I say this because our conversation had nothing to do with race or racism. Sadly, there are many people who are victims of real racism and discrimination, and they need compassion, guidance, suggestions, and support, but to the best of my knowledge, Mr. Juanillo's video and subsequent media appearnces did not help anyone; he just fanned a fire of hate.

Many different news agencies were contacting me for interviews. However, I was not in a state to conduct interviews or speak with anyone, because I was terrified. And all I knew was these untruths were coming out in the press and being repeated over and over.

Do you regret writing the apology letter to Mr. Juanillo?

I don't regret writing the apology letter to him, and I do hope he publishes it one day. I very sincerely cared about the fact that I thought I had really hurt his feelings and wanted to discuss that with him neighbor-to-neighbor, person-to-person. My genuine words of apology to Mr. Juanillo in my personal letters, and all the other methods to reach out to him that I had tried, did not satisfy the mob. Which is why I sometimes question my writing of the public apology—because it was written to survive. It was written under extreme intimidation, and my friends and family were being relentlessly harassed, so at the time I did not see any other option available. It was sickening. I was so scared. I just did not see any other alternative at that moment, under those circumstances.

I don't believe Mr. Juanillo's intentions were sincere. If they were sincere, why did he continue to tell reporters that I should apologize and that if I did then things would be OK, despite the fact I had apologized multiple times in my personal letter of apology to him, my phone messages to him asking to meet to apologize in person, and my public apology statement that was published in the media. You see, I had already tried to do exactly that, but he ignored all my attempts. If he were sincere, why did he hire a PR firm? Why did he sell his video? Why didn't he just respond to my attempts to talk?

Looking back, I'm not sure if I should have minded my own business or not. Bullies will take over if everyone just looks the other way, and it is important to stand up for what's right. What I did, I believe, was correct. I thought I was abiding by the law. I was paying attention to what they were telling us in our city—"If you see something, say something." I was trying to help a neighbor by asking the question when I saw someone. I did not recognize the writing on the wall of the Belden House. And I don't believe I harmed Mr. Juanillo in any way. That, most certainly, was not my intention.

The accusation that I have some sort of a problem with minorities is absurd. The majority of this city, which I love for its diversity, as well as my neighborhood, has always been made up of people from diverse backgrounds. This is San Francisco, and that is one of the most beautiful things about this city.

If I had happened to be someone of a different gender or race, I do wonder if Mr. Juanillo would have reacted the same way, engaging a PR firm and attacking me on social media like he did. Before this happened, I was never afraid of anyone, which is why I approached a person I did not know writing on my neighbor's wall and said something. That has changed, which is unfortunate, because now if someone is doing something harmful right in front of me, I'm too afraid to get involved, and because of things like this happening when you actually do or say something, and I do not believe I am alone in this fear. That's sad because that's not the kind of world we want to live in. I was raised to believe that we are part of a civil society with a responsibility to help one another. So now I'm at an impasse in many ways. Mr. Juanillo refuses to let this go. It happened almost three years ago. I am trying to rebuild my life and my health, restart my business and make a living, but I can't even maintain a social media presence without being relentlessly harassed. To this day, I continue to receive hateful emails.

How am I supposed to grow my business when I, a single woman trying to support myself, go to a beauty buyer to tell them about the excellent products LAFACE has with proven beneficial results, and when they look me up online everything since June 2020 says: "Racist, racist, racist!" People are scared.

I pray that Mr. Juanillo is able to move on with his life and let me move on with mine. I want him to move forward and to be happy. I simply would like for him and his followers to please, leave me alone.

What impact did the stress of being canceled have on your health?
I was absolutely terrified and devastated by what had happened. Being accused of racism was beyond my ability to even comprehend. What the cancel culture attack did to my health was irreparable. After the encounter, I became extremely ill. My entire body started shaking, and it would not

stop. Then I couldn't eat anything. Then I began to experience horrible pain and eventually just curled up in a ball and was taken to the hospital. At first, I refused to go to the hospital because I was too scared to go outside my door. They ended up taking me secretly to the hospital, where I underwent emergency surgery. I was on liquids for nearly a year and a half. I have since tried to add some substance back to my diet, but it has not worked well, and I'm almost completely back on liquids. This will likely persist for the rest of my life.

On top of all of this, one of our San Francisco Supervisors, Shamann Walton, then decided it was a great idea to use me as the poster child for his new bill called the CAREN Act." [Note: The bill, passed unanimously by the San Francisco Board of Supervisors, makes it illegal for people to call 911 in furtherance of racist agendas and gives the targets the ability to sue those who reported them to the police.] "I really want to emphasize that 911 is not a customer service line for someone's racist behavior," said Walton when the bill was introduced.

He [Walton] was using me as the poster child of the behavior he wanted to outlaw, so I wrote him a letter. I wrote, verbatim, "I 100 percent agree with you that people should not make unfounded or racially motivated 911 calls or reports that divert police resources from real emergencies, but that is not at all what happened in my situation." I wrote a really respectful letter and essentially said, "I think we should get the story straight because I didn't call 911 on anyone ever. I didn't file a police report. I did none of that. I didn't target anyone because of their race."

What is strange is to have people who know absolutely nothing about you making statements about who you are and what your intentions are. We live in a strange world, and people seem to be living with a lot of rage. I did nothing racist, and if people feel differently, I encourage them to explain, unemotionally and factually, what I did wrong. But that opportunity for fame and notoriety was apparently too good for Mr. Juanillo to pass up. And that was made clear when he started filming me, followed me, tracked down my information, and brought in a public relations firm to destroy me. Why not just reach out and talk to me about it like a normal neighbor? Instead, the crowd suddenly villainized me. They went after my family, who had nothing to do with this. I have wonderful friends—and they were being attacked, too.

Now I am in the process of healing, reopening and slowly relaunching LAFACE. But it's very difficult to fight or stand up to a cowardly, faceless, virtual mob that hides behind fake email addresses. You get very, very hateful mail and you think to yourself, where did this come from?

I have always tried to give back to my city because I love San Francisco. I have always participated in charity projects around the city, painting and restoring damaged storefronts, some owned by people of color, cleaning up parks and planting trees. I buy the paint, help them restore their businesses, advise them on ways to grow their businesses and create employment opportunities, and help others through internships with LAFACE. I've always been involved in various levels of community service. None of this was mentioned in all the media stories and malicious social media posts because it didn't fit their narrative.

My friends, family, and work relationships know me as a hard-working and thoughtful person. I've always tried to do the right thing. And in just a few seconds all of this was erased. That is the power of cancel culture. Nobody seems to care what has happened in your life for the past 50-plus years; they only care about what gets clicks or what the social media algorithms will drive to generate interest and advertising sales, not the truth.

It seemed like no one wanted to investigate to find out the truth. Why didn't anyone check for facts at the time, such as who actually owned the Belden House? Why weren't people looking at both sides? Why did people assume these horrible allegations about me as the truth? Why did strangers impute malevolent motives to me? You can be a good person historically, and it doesn't matter. The mob decides who you are. How do they know what I intended? How do they have any idea what I was all about? Have we ever met before? I have no knowledge of the lives of these strangers, and they have no knowledge of mine. Why were they jumping on this? Why have they made this choice to hate and hurt me?

It appears that the media accelerated and amplified the situation. Why do you think the media was so quick to demonize you, as well?
Click, click, click. I was thinking about that when Birchbox was jumping in on this. They didn't even reach out to me to discuss the matter, which would have been the professional thing to do. I had thought we had a great working relationship. If you're going to talk negatively about a person or company in public, I'd expect you to at least reach out to them to confirm the facts or ask a question.

I don't think people realize how difficult it is to stand up for the truth after people have "canceled" you. However, it's now going on three years since the encounter with Mr. Juanillo, and I am now, finally, standing up because the hate won't stop. This never should have played out as it did. In my view, this was handled incorrectly. I believe the media is heavily complicit in this regard. I believe, through what I have personally experienced, that the media of today doesn't care about the truth.

On my birthday in 2020, I watched one interview that Mr. Juanillo did. He did tons of interviews, but I only watched one, and it was on the afternoon of my birthday. It was Dr. Phil, and there was a lady that he was talking to. Mr Juanillo never let her speak. He simply jumped into "Have you ever been stopped by police because of your skin color?" And even though she was a minority, when she said, "No," he still interrupted her and would not let her finish her sentence. In that interview he said a lot of things that were factually untrue. You may ask, "Well, Lisa, if you believe that the truth was not being told, why didn't you go in for an interview?" And the answer is, "This is why."

It was never a race issue. They were determined to make it a race issue, but it wasn't. No one really seems to care about correcting this fact. The social media mob asserted it was a race issue. Period. No one ever dug into the facts to validate or disprove the premise.

Why is this incident still being talked about so many years later?
Honestly, I have no idea, but it probably helps Mr. Juanillo financially to keep the hate going because he monetized the video. Maybe I gave him a purpose. I truthfully don't know. He's had his fifteen minutes stretched into three years. When will enough be enough?

In 2022, Mr. Juanillo held this big two-year anniversary celebrating the event and invited all the press, which he has been doing each year after the encounter. He was given a "Key to the City" award from one of the San Francisco Supervisors, so understandably he feels he is in the right. [Note: Supervisor Catherine Stefani posted a photo with Juanillo on Twitter June 10, 2021, along with this message: "Yesterday I was honored to present James Juanillo with a Certificate of Honor in light of his work to hold those who perpetuate hate in our city accountable."]

Rather than minding your own business, you inserted yourself into a situation, and it had terrible consequences. You have said that you would do it differently next time. If you could go back in time, then would you change anything about how you handled the onslaught you faced in the incident's aftermath?

I believe that the approach I took to the onslaught, which was to stay quiet, was probably the best. Nobody wanted to know the truth. They wanted to hold me up as this extremely racist person. I needed to stay as quiet as possible, because I didn't stand a chance—any reaction would simply have poured gas on the fire. No matter what I would have said, it would not have mattered. It was so awful. When you see some of the emails, some of these hate letters, you'll understand.

My parents taught me that everyone has something good to offer, that no matter what, everyone has some redeeming quality. There is good out there, and everyone has a bit of good in them. Sadly, circumstances have caused many people to live on the defensive, but if you're nice and kind to them, they won't feel the need to be on the defensive, and they'll just be your friend. That's always been my approach: if you come across as nonthreatening because you are nonthreatening and don't have an ulterior motive, then everything will be fine. And that's what I was doing on that day, trying to be nice to a neighbor. I think one thing I learned, what this experience taught me, was that I was wrong in assuming everyone has good in their hearts.

Evidently, what I did was threatening to Mr. Juanillo because I questioned what he was doing and what he thought was right to do. I am truly sorry if I offended him or hurt his feelings. That was not my intention, and I repeatedly sought to apologize to him, privately and publicly. I guess people don't want to discuss things civilly anymore, and that breaks my heart. And I want to return to a couple of points. It's extremely difficult and confusing to live in a society where laws exist, but you get publicly ruined for trying to abide by them. Where do we go from here? We live in an upside-down world, and I'm not sure I understand the rules anymore. If someone has a little patch of lawn and they have a sign that says please don't let your dog do their business here and people let their dogs do their business there, I used to be the person who would say, "You might want to be respectful of that person's wishes." But not anymore; not after Mr. Juanillo. My civic engagement has been reduced to zero by the cancel culture. Unfortunately, now if I see something, I'm going to say nothing. But imagine what happens to a community when everyone looks the other way for fear of getting canceled. Things can break down pretty quickly. The book *Lord of the Flies* comes to mind.

We have spoken with many people who have been accused of things they haven't done. A video taken out of context can ruin a life, livelihood, and reputation instantly. What is your message to a stranger

out there right now on the receiving end of being doxed or attacked by cancel vultures?

First and foremost, do not speak to anyone until you have a clear understanding of what is going on. Then have someone you trust keep you away from all social media. Have a friend look, but not you. For your protection, shut down any way through which strangers can contact you. Try to figure out why that other person did it. When you truly understand why, that can sometimes help your next steps.

If you have to write an apology letter, make sure it is for something for which you are sorry, not because you are under duress. Think about your reactions carefully. Don't let the mob of strangers pressure you into it. Think before you respond. Don't let social media define you.

On the other hand, if someone is thinking about canceling someone, what would you tell them?
Number one is, why? Why are you so angry? What exactly did this person do to you? Have you ever met this person? Were you personally affected? Do you know the entirety of this person's life? There are always two sides to every story; learn both. What is your motivation for jumping on this bandwagon? I found that a huge percentage of Americans and people worldwide are on Twitter, but only a small percentage of them actively participate. So why are we allowing social media to control our lives and dictate who we are? People who you don't know at all are dictating the direction you take with your life. Do not let this happen.

The victims need to know that they are not the only ones. I was one of the early ones when it happened to me, but you don't realize until much later you're not alone in this. And I actually wondered if there could be a website where all of the canceled businesses and individuals could go and be supportive. I'm just saying, no one realizes how many people are being canceled, and the reasons behind it are really sinister and unhealthy.

Do you feel optimistic about your future?
Absolutely. But only because I know I'm capable of overcoming challenges, and I am confident in my abilities. I guess I'll just have to put on my big girl pants. And honestly, I know that when I open up in this interview about certain things, there is a chance it may trigger a fresh tidal wave of negative reactions, so I'm trying to prepare myself. I am hopeful, however, that when people learn the truth, they will move on.

This interview with you is a big deal to me. I have never talked to anybody about this, except for some family members and a couple of trusted friends. I'd like this to be in my rearview mirror. I'm an optimistic person by nature, and I want to look ahead with positivity, but I can honestly admit that I'm terrified because I don't want them to come after me again.

I want Mr. Juanillo to be happy in his life, and I want to move forward with my life and LAFACE, but I still get ugly messages on a weekly basis. I have to work hard to put them aside, as they interfere with my work, my health, my happiness, and my focus. I hope they will stop, but when?

Much of what we have found out when interviewing victims of cancel culture is that people who are attempting to cancel them believe that they are doing a good thing for society. They believe they have the moral high ground, despite the fact they are essentially bullying people and, in some cases, tearing them down and eliminating their ability to earn a living.
How is that helping society? Anonymous strangers hiding behind fake identities to tear down others to advance their cause is not constructive. And who are they to appoint themselves judge, jury, and executioner? Who elected them to the Supreme Court of Morality and Justice?

You find yourself in a position where everything you've known about yourself and accomplished throughout your life is being twisted and flipped upside down. What do you do when all of a sudden your business and ability to earn a living is gone? You all of a sudden don't matter. It makes no difference what the truth is. It's just this narrative that someone who has never met or worked with you has decided will define you. That is not okay. It is neither right, nor just.

I would advise you victims of cancel culture to stand up for yourselves if you can find the strength. I sometimes wonder if I should have said to Mr. Juanillo, "What on Earth are you talking about?" instead of being polite. But I was so startled by his reaction. In a few of the hate mails I have received, they accused me of having an "overly educated vocabulary," which the anonymous senders apparently find offensive. Huh? Well, I can't help but wonder who is being judgmental here. I have always respected and celebrated the fact that everyone is unique.

I'm moving forward with my life and LAFACE. I have a responsibility to fulfill. And I'm going to do it.

I know you thought long and hard before even agreeing to do this interview. Hopefully, sharing your story is going to contribute to eventually ending cancel culture.

I think one of the hardest things of all is that I always thought of myself as a funny person. I try to bring light to a lot of situations and make others happy, so this whole situation of ugliness is very sad and unfamiliar to me. When I was twelve years old, my father told me, "Listen, you have a choice every day to either add to the world or to take away . . . I suggest you add to the world." I love the fact that there are many different types of personalities, genders, sexual orientations, nationalities, races, religions, and points of view. Respecting and celebrating this diversity is what America is all about.

Why does anyone feel that other people's differences are a threat to them? It doesn't make sense to me. Some might say, well, obviously, the person who was stenciling on the wall never threatened you, so why did you bother him? I never claimed he threatened me, nor ever implied that. I simply couldn't figure out why a person was attempting to stencil on something that wasn't his, as it was private property and historically significant. So, in my mind, as a civically motivated neighbor, I was doing my best to do the right thing. I was just trying to be a responsible neighbor. Why did so many people impute malevolent motives?

We live in a world where people no longer communicate with one another. People are sitting across from one another at the table, not even talking, looking at their phones. It takes more effort to talk to someone nowadays, and it's not as simple as it once was, because people are afraid of getting canceled.

I want to be that person again who enjoys and feels safe in my own neighborhood and in meeting new people, and I'm not happy that Mr. Juanillo's actions took that innocence away from me. I'm not one to talk about my emotions, but that was probably the most painful.

Why can't you talk about emotions?

Well, first of all, my personal life is private. If we talk in terms of facts, then people can check up on them to verify. But when you get into emotions, people feel it is their right to start judging even without knowing the full story.

Everyone saw the video through the eyes of Mr. Juanillo, as was intended, but if they had done any research or looked at the ads on my website or taken the time to investigate my past, they would have seen that LAFACE had always worked with all kinds of people from all walks of life.

For example, I have a group on social media called LAFACEAfrica; it's like a mini fan club and has existed for many years. After this happened, one of my friends in Africa called and said, "What is going on there? What you said has nothing to do with race or racism. I have no idea what's going on there. It's ridiculous. It's all over the world. I've known you for ten years. What's the big deal?" And he was right. Nothing about this made sense. I'm not even going to argue about something that has been blatantly obvious with a lifetime of behavior to back it up. I'm disappointed that certain people didn't stand up for me a little more, but I hope that people will stand up moving forward.

Why aren't you changing your brand name?
Everyone told me I should change my brand LAFACE. It's all over the world now because of this, and my point for not changing the brand is: my name is Lisa Alexander, and I have a company that formulates face products, therefore—LAFACE. That is why it is called that. I spent years building a highly respected brand with integrity. Up until that one day, everything had been positive regarding our reputation in the industry. Right up until that moment the video went viral. All that time and money and my heart and soul, invested in this brand. Why would I throw that away?

And think about it, if I changed the name, that would be misleading, as I'm still running the company, and that would mean I'm hiding because I'm either afraid or I had something to hide. If I were, indeed, guilty, of what Mr. Juanillo and the mob accused me of, then I probably would have changed my entire career. I am not perfect. Nobody is perfect. I'm very proud of my company, and I'm very proud of my family. I have learned a lot from this. So that's where we are.

KEY TAKEAWAYS

- Lisa Alexander's experience provides a textbook example of cancel culture. All six of the CANDEM elements that define cancel culture were abundantly present in this instance.
- Alexander issued an apology in the aftermath of the attacks, but it had no impact in terms of satisfying the cancel vultures or changing the outcome for her business and brand.
- Widespread media coverage of her encounter with a neighbor dramatically accelerated the process of being canceled for Lisa Alexander.

- Alexander did not engage with the press at the time of the incident, failing to correct false information and being completely overwhelmed with a barrage of negative media coverage.
- Today, Alexander is going public with her story, in the hopes of relaunching her business, moving on from this difficult experience, and speaking out against cancel culture.

Case Study: Priya Parkash

Situation Synopsis

Priya Parkash came from humble beginnings in her native Pakistan. Through determination and hard work, she earned admission to Duke University as an international student on a full scholarship. Over the next four years at Duke, Parkash's behavior was truly exemplary—both academically and otherwise—as she comported herself with dignity, seriousness of academic purpose, and a clear talent for leadership.

She worked tremendously hard, taking an extremely heavy course load every semester to graduate with double majors in Statistical Science (highest distinction) and Economics, with a minor in Religion. She conducted extensive research throughout her undergraduate career, founded and led several student organizations, collaborated closely with university administrators to improve campus equity and STEM retention among women and diverse students, and even represented Duke on the international stage as a Rhodes scholarship finalist. Parkash accomplished all this while working two to three part-time jobs each semester to support herself and finance her younger brother's schooling in Pakistan.

As a senior, Parkash was selected by a committee composed of staff, faculty, and students to give the commencement speech at Duke's 2022 graduation—a coveted spot that required an extensive application process. Unfortunately, what was supposed to be a crowning achievement and fitting coda for an outstanding college career quickly led to the most regrettable and painful chapter in her life.

While drafting her commencement speech, Parkash sought advice from several members of the Duke international community, family, and faculty about possible themes and topics, which most people do when preparing a high-profile public address. She saw this speech as a platform to not only honor her own experience as an international student, but also give voice to her peers from abroad who experienced unique struggles but persevered to graduate, as well as foster a sense of community across borders, nations, and cultures.

However, the day after her big moment she learned that the speech— reviewed multiple times by a Duke committee and approved by them before the commencement—contained themes and even language used in a Harvard commencement speech in 2014, something Parkash had not known.

Someone she thought of as a friend recommended that Parkash work into her speech what she thought was a creative and compelling concept: "Duke Nation." This individual gave specific advice for a few passages, which later proved to be taken directly from the 2014 Harvard commencement address.

Parkash was accused of plagiarism, one of the worst possible academic transgressions, and the story exploded on campus, via social media, and then in the mainstream national and even international press. Parkash immediately began receiving threats online and by voicemail—many containing vile racist, anti-immigrant, and religious bigotry, including death threats. She was given no benefit of the doubt, regardless of her four years of hard work, academic record, and personal achievement. Every day since she has lived with deep regret that she did not do her due diligence by checking the wording that her peer had suggested.

Even though numerous Duke faculty members had voiced strong support for her character, integrity, and values, a villainous narrative of Parkash had already been painted in the media and was regurgitated by angry strangers across the Internet. Left on her own to deal with the avalanche of critical press coverage, Parkash engaged pro bono crisis management support, releasing thoughtful and regretful statements about her mistake. She apologized to the Harvard student who had initially used the themes and passages and provided a detailed account of what had transpired to Duke as part of their investigation.

After graduation, Duke completed an internal investigation and found, among other things, that Parkash did not knowingly plagiarize from the Harvard speech, something she had always maintained.

In the end, Parkash was able to escape being permanently canceled because she told the truth and refused to let others frame the narrative.

She confronted the situation head-on, engaging with the media with the assistance of experts. Addressing the mistake honestly, combined with her own spirited defense of herself and emotional and mental resilience, enabled Parkash to overcome this trying time.

Interview Highlights

What actually happened in terms of the timeline of events?

In the spring of 2022, a speech I had written was chosen to be featured at Duke University's commencement. Both thrilled and nervous at this opportunity to speak to the graduating class and their families, I worried about whether I would be able to fully represent all of my fellow students. Given my desire for my speech to reflect not just my own experiences, but also those of my peers, I reached out to several friends and acquaintances at Duke to get their perspective on the topics and concepts I should address in my speech.

One of the people I trusted lifted a number of compelling phrases and themes directly from a Harvard commencement address from several years before and presented the words as their own, giving me explicit verbal approval to use them in my speech. After I delivered the speech at graduation, the similarities were discovered and widely reported nationally and internationally. I went from a student whose speech's theme of unity across national and international boundaries was widely applauded to a global laughingstock and pariah.

Although I take full responsibility for not doing my due diligence, for not researching every suggestion offered to me by others before incorporating them into my speech, and for not ensuring carefully enough that the language used was uniquely my own, the backlash I received was improperly generalized and disproportionate to my mistake. I was canceled overnight for trusting the wrong person.

In February 2022, Duke put out a university-wide announcement inviting all graduating students who wished to be considered for the position of commencement speaker to submit a brief outline of the themes and ideas their speeches would discuss, as the first step in the selection process. I had spent my undergraduate career advocating for international students, who tend to be an overlooked minority, and promoting international awareness and cultural responsiveness on Duke's campus. Naturally, I saw this speech as a great platform to mark the end of my time at Duke by voicing and celebrating the international student experience. So I submitted a brief outline detailing how, if selected as the commencement speaker, I would emphasize the diversity of perspectives at Duke and our ability to come together as "one"—the class of 2022—despite varying countries of origin and backgrounds.

About two weeks after I submitted my outline, I received an email inviting me to the second phase of the commencement speaker selection process. In order to move forward I was required to submit a draft of the speech and choose a time to deliver it aloud to the selection committee, composed of faculty, administrators, and students.

I was thrilled at this opportunity, and since there were no rules against collaboration, I reached out to several of my fellow international students, asking them to contribute their thoughts and ideas. I wanted to solicit ideas because, while Duke is an American institution, I saw my speech as a chance to reach a far broader and inclusive audience, given my own foreign background and as a campus champion for my fellow international students. Within five days, I compiled over a dozen pages of detailed notes and exciting ideas for my class's commencement speech, incorporating my friends' input as inspirations and developing around the common themes that resonated most with me.

Given how important it was to me to foster a sense of internationalism and cross-border unity among our diverse student body, the concept of a "Duke Nation" as shared with me by a college peer really caught my attention. This individual was someone I interacted with frequently and trusted as a friend. As a fellow international student, I appreciated their contribution and deeply valued the message of bringing voices, nations, and tribes together to be a greater sum than their constituent parts: a Duke nation.

A few days after submitting my written speech and reading it at an audition for the role of commencement speaker, I received a university email informing me that, at the selection committee's recommendation, Duke University's President Price had chosen me as the commencement speaker. I was ecstatic! Over the next two weeks I would have to meet with several administrators to further vet and refine my commencement address.

Leading up to commencement, I met with several groups of administrators four or five times, for an hour each, to revise and rehearse the speech. The University's Communications team also did an extensive profile about me and the upcoming speech for *Duke Today*, the official university news hub, that would later be deleted. When the big day finally came, commencement itself was a blur of excitement, joy, and good-byes—whenever someone stopped to congratulate me and ask me how I had come up with the ideas in my speech, I honestly and proudly shared that it was a team effort by several members of Duke's international community.

The Monday following commencement, when I had just finished packing my college apartment and was driving up to meet my parents, who were visiting from Pakistan, my phone started blowing up, with messages that I didn't fully understand at the time. Then someone texted me a link to the *Duke Chronicle* article alleging plagiarism as I sat there confused and stunned, with tears rolling down my cheeks. Over the next few days, I would become a public figure as the media painted an out-of-proportion, villainous, half-baked, and poorly researched narrative that undermined and questioned all my undergraduate work and my integrity, opening the gates to what would become the most traumatic and regrettable chapter of my life.

What was the psychological impact of being a target of cancel culture?
The summer after graduation is supposed to be a period of rejuvenation, reflection, and celebration, but instead it became one of the darkest periods of my life. At barely twenty-two, I became a national spectacle with millions of strangers trying to tear me down without knowing anything about me or the full story behind this embarrassing incident. Almost immediately, I began experiencing panic attacks and anxiety from all the hate directed at me.

Feeling already isolated and publicly shamed, I felt unsafe being a part of social events for many months afterward. Trauma has a way of manifesting itself even in the most mundane of life experiences. For instance, just going on a walk by myself would trigger internal panic and paranoia that random strangers on the street were staring, pointing fingers, and talking about me. This made me want to hide behind closed doors.

However, as much as I wanted to isolate myself, I realized that the only way I was going to make it through was by continuing to exhibit strength of character, tenacity, and determination, so I decided to focus on the learnings from this experience instead of all the negativity. I also started meeting with a trauma therapist in the fall, who has since helped me make significant progress in processing the incident and moving forward.

Describe the types of things that people said to you when you were in the midst of the crisis.
An army of keyboard warriors threatened me, sent me hate messages, and called me names. Here is a small sample of the hate I received:

- "Go back to where you came from."
- "From rags to riches and now back to rags."
- "She probably cheated her way through college."
- "Duke should run all her undergrad work through a plagiarism checker." (Every assignment/paper at Duke is actually already run through a plagiarism checker.)
- "Such an embarrassment for Duke."
- "All these elite institutions should stop bringing these broke international motherfuckers from poor countries to the US."
- "Duke should revoke her degree."
- "Make sure she never works again and lives a life of oblivion."
- "Pakistan should have burnt all the Hindus when it had a chance."
- "I am sure she plagiarized her college essay that got her into Duke."
- "All international students are plagiarists."

The stunning extent to which people who had never met me would so gratuitously take to painting me in such vile and hurtful terms continues to deeply wound me. I sought to unify our diverse campus across borders and ethnicities in my commencement address. Instead, I was now a caricature and someone to be pointed at as a reason why international students shouldn't even be allowed into the country, and this continues to haunt me.

How did you know what to do in terms of handling media inquiries?
When it became clear that Duke University was not going to offer any help or guidance in navigating the situation, a university spokesperson suggested that I hire a public relations firm. One of my remaining friends put together a spreadsheet of top crisis PR firms in the country for me to call. As a low-income international student, I did not have the means to afford the hefty fees, but I maxed out all my credit cards to pay a discounted retainer to Red Banyan. Over the next few months, as the firm had the opportunity to know me as a person and the reality of my situation, they refunded me my retainer in full—without my ever requesting it—and offered me their services pro bono throughout the entire summer following graduation.

Red Banyan's crisis team was a godsend. Overwhelmed with the negative media that was corroding not only my reputation, but also my self-image and sense of self-worth, they gave me critical guidance in the weeks and months to follow, helping me survive the turmoil.

How did you have to adapt your life as a result of going viral?

How does one adapt to suddenly going viral for an unwanted reason? Can someone adapt? I had to delete all my social media accounts to distance myself from what became a never-ending barrage of vitriol, threats, and insults hurled at me by people who had never met me and automatically assumed that I had knowingly plagiarized.

Over the next few weeks, I witnessed a steady stream of friends and mentors distancing themselves from me in order to avoid being associated with someone who had received significant public backlash. The impact this had on me was devastating, as I felt increasingly alone in an hour of need.

However, a number of Duke classmates, faculty and staff, and friends further afield did not turn their backs on me and offered a shoulder to cry on, letters of reference, encouragement, and advice. One lesson I've learned from this ordeal is the importance of having a strong network of real friends, who are the people who have helped me process and start to heal from this trauma.

While threats and insults still trickle their way into my life from the digital world, I focus on repairing my life by quietly remembering who I am, what my values are, and focusing on the learnings from this mistake and its aftermath.

You refer to your values and being true to yourself. What do you see as your identity?

Growing up as a member of a minority faith in Pakistan and coming to the Old South to attend Duke University for college made me a minority within a minority. I was always conscious of this and sought to make the best of my unique vantage point by being a global connector, a bridge builder between communities, races, and creeds. That was exactly what I strove for in my commencement address: *E Pluribus Unum,* out of many [we are] one.

I try to remain true to my immigrant values: honesty, hard work, true grit, and slow and steady wins at the game of life. But to say that this experience hasn't jaded me or undermined my ability to trust others' intentions would be untrue—it will probably be a long time until I feel whole again.

What was the impact of being canceled on your loved ones? Was your family concerned for you?

My family was very concerned for me, and the impact of my experience on my loved ones cannot be summed up easily. My parents' first visit to the United States became shrouded in confusion, frustration, and concern for me as a result of this event. While they were disappointed and stunned by how everyone reacted, they continued to be my rock and support me throughout the summer and beyond.

Perhaps what's most disheartening is that the trauma of this experience extends far beyond my immediate family and me and will trickle into the wider international community at Duke and beyond, many of whom will think twice before channeling their voice publicly after witnessing my dehumanizing experience enveloped in xenophobia and racism at the hands of keyboard warriors.

Did the media report the truth or a totally false picture of what took place?

While I acknowledge and accept responsibility that the inclusion of those words in my speech was a regrettable error on my part, there was little, if any, immediate effort by anyone to pause and determine whether the accusations made fit the circumstances. Instead, quick reporting with little real news value dominated the headlines, as a media agenda to go after a perceived scandal at an elite institution overshadowed the ethical duty to investigate, verify, and run an accurate story about the situation. For example, the reporters did not investigate or even shed light on the fact that my commencement speech was vetted and reviewed several times by university administrators well before I came on stage. The spectacle seemed to matter more than quality journalism.

What is your message to those who have been targets of cancel culture?

My message to those who have been targets of cancel culture is: this too shall pass. In the moment, your world might very well be ending. Friendships, relationships, and even employment might come to an end. It's certainly easier said than done, but remain calm, collected, and try to utilize your analytical skills and come up with a rational approach to get you through one day at a time. Recall and protect your side of the story, write it down, and refuse to engage with trolls and hecklers in the crowd. And never lie. The truth will set you free, eventually. The frenzy will pass, and, if you are lucky, you might have a moment to be heard along the way. Eventually, one way or another, the light at the end of the tunnel will be there.

And finally: never let your detractors succeed in devaluing your humanity. We are all worth a saving grace, and a kind word or two, on our worst days. Even a smile is charity.

What is your message to someone considering trying to cancel someone else?

Bullying someone online while using an alias or posting anonymously is still bullying. Knee-jerk reactions to half-baked fake news online cheapens your existence because it shows how easily someone can be conned for shock value. If you were to put yourself in the shoes of someone being canceled, wouldn't you want others to hear your side of the story before you were presumed guilty? Don't fall prey to groupthink—your integrity and self-worth should count more than the cheap thrill of scoring a well-liked comment on a social media site.

KEY TAKEAWAYS

- Despite humble beginning in Pakistan, Priya Parkash earned a full scholarship to Duke University, where she worked multiple jobs while she double-majored in Statistical Science and Economics.
- Following a highly competitive process, she was selected by a committee to give a commencement speech at Duke's 2022 graduation.
- Language used in Parkash's speech, which was suggested to her by a friend asked to provide input, was taken directly from a Harvard commencement speech years earlier.
- Despite apologies and a Duke investigation concluding that she did not knowingly plagiarize the speech, Parkash became a victim of cancel culture.
- Parkash experienced panic attacks and anxiety after receiving death threats and being publicly shamed in leading US media outlets.
- She grew increasingly alone and isolated as friends distanced themselves due to the public backlash.
- With pro-bono assistance from crisis management and communications professionals, Parkash opted to press the truth and share her side of the story in public statements and comments given to reporters.
- She refused to be canceled and has since moved forward with her career and life.

Case Study: Ilya Shapiro

Former Executive Director of the Center for the Constitution, Georgetown University Law Center, and Senior Fellow and Director of Constitutional Studies, The Manhattan Institute

Situation Synopsis

During his campaign, Joe Biden announced that, if given the opportunity, he would nominate a Black woman for the US Supreme Court. On January 28, 2022, President Biden got that opportunity when he announced the retirement of Justice Stephen Breyer and recommitted himself to naming the first-ever Black woman to replace him.

On January 26, 2022, with foreknowledge of Biden's announcement, Constitutional scholar Ilya Shapiro engaged in an ill-advised activity: late-night tweeting following a long week of travel. Ilya sent the following response to President Biden's upcoming announcement: "Objectively best pick for Biden is Sri Srinivasan, who is solid prog & v smart. Even has identity politics benefit of being first Asian (Indian) American...But alas doesn't fit into the latest intersectionality hierarchy so we'll get lesser black woman."

Upon waking the next morning and seeing a number of outraged responses, Shapiro tweeted, "I apologize, I meant no offense, but it was an inartful tweet. I have taken it down." A day later, Georgetown Law School's Black Students Association demanded Shapiro be fired, claiming his tweets were "offensive, racist, sexist, misogynistic, inflammatory, deplorable, insensitive, and unprofessional." Within days after that, Georgetown placed him on paid leave pending the results of an internal review.

The investigation by Georgetown University's Office of Institutional Diversity, Equity, and Affirmative Action took several months to complete, finding grounds to maintain Shapiro's employment based on a technicality: that he tweeted prior to his actual employment. Despite retaining his position, Shapiro sent a resignation letter to Georgetown making the case that he could not work in that environment with a sword of Damocles hanging above his head.

The ordeal affected his family and future, but Shapiro found a way to take control early, and his actions in this regard proved invaluable.

Interview Highlights

What elements do you think define cancel culture?
I don't have a good working definition. Perhaps by the time I finish reading your book and write my next book, which will most likely be about illiberal trends in academia, particularly legal academia, I'll polish it up. Actions have consequences, and I don't think anyone could disagree with that. We are talking about actions, not speech, and the consequences must be proportionate to the crime. So, my working theory about cancel culture is that there are presently personal or professional consequences for politically incorrect speech.

And obviously, the devil is in the details with how you define politically incorrect, how you define consequences, what is considered disproportionate. All of that is fair game to discuss. But, in general, it [cancel culture] has risen with social media because it has facilitated outrage mobs, as well as willful misconstruing and spreading.

It doesn't always have to be the Left against the Right, MAGA types canceling insufficiently MAGA or Never Trumpers or RINOs and such. But, given that the Left controls the commanding heights of culture, education, and technology, that is cancel culture-focused. You say something that isn't in line with the Progressive orthodox zeitgeist, and all of a sudden, your job, your livelihood, is threatened. And there's a difference between celebrities and people like me who have their own platforms, and then, normal people who get boycotted, doxed, or fired for donating to a politically incorrect cause. That is, perhaps, even more concerning than high-profile events that make national news, like mine.

So as far as I'm concerned, one defining feature appears to be a disproportionate response to the action. It's an iconic type of mobbing function in that it is not simply saying to your employer, "Hey, I really didn't like that tweet; it doesn't reflect well on us." It's more like, someone on Twitter says,

"Hey, *New York Times*, go get your boy here who tweeted this thing," and it's kind of trying to foment going after your job.

There is absolutely cancel culture on the Right and Left, but the media appears hesitant to expose this more.
It's probably more important for the media to simply maintain the narrative that there is no such thing as cancel culture than it is to police or shine a spotlight on intra-Conservative cancellations.

But what about Right-wing cancel culture aimed at the Left, especially on campus?
I suppose that's happening at some Christian colleges or something along those lines, but FIRE, of course, has been ecumenical. And they don't care what the content is; they've been completely content neutral. And in that regard, it appears, given the cultural dominance of the Left, I don't know if it serves their interests to point out counter examples, because that might lead to movement cleaning up this dynamic. And, because it is disproportionately to the Right, those who want to use cultural influence to affect political change on the Left would not want the dynamic to be cleaned up.

Other than social media, are there specific events that took place in the US that you believe served as paradigm shifts?
I haven't studied the history of cancel culture in depth. So, once you've finished talking to everyone and compiling all of your research, I'm looking forward to reading your book.

I mean, there's the classic early example of the executive who boarded a flight to South Africa and tweeted a bad joke, which went viral on Twitter by the time she landed, something about, "I'm going to Africa, but I can't get AIDS because I'm white or something." It was a bad joke. And it was turned into this entire thing. [Note: The canceling of Justine Sacco is a powerful example of cancel culture.]

That was one example that I can think of in terms of social media. I do think the pandemic accelerated this because we were all literally locked down. As someone put it, there exists a laptop class: those who make a living from ideas, who can work anywhere, who are not interacting physically with people, and it became easier just to foment mobs and go on cancellation campaigns. And I believe that some illiberal trends have just sprouted in various ways. Things that were already there were accelerated, just like Trump's illiberalism, which I don't think he created, but he accelerated existing views and perspectives that were already there. Which is a separate debate, but I believe the pandemic and George Floyd were pivotal, which is hard to say given that this happened only a little more than two years ago. But it appears to me that there has been a significant increase in cancellations in recent years.

Cancellation occurs in a relatively small universe. When that person is canceled in their universe, and they exit, their life continues. What are some of the life lessons that you learned from going through it? What feelings did you have?

Well, I thought I was savvy about academia and law schools, but apparently not enough about Georgetown. I'm not sure if the same thing would have happened to me in every institution, but I don't think so. I guess I learned the basics of crisis management. And I was fortunate in that I had friends in the PR, political, and journalism worlds who knew other people with big platforms and megaphones on whom I could rely. I knew the guys at FIRE, who quickly helped me out with everything, including facilitating my legal representation. I got to know Bari Weiss within about 24 hours or so.

I was just grateful to find out how many friends I had, those I interacted with on a regular basis, those I hadn't talked to in a long time, and those who just kind of stood up for me on their own volition, which was a very reassuring part of the whole process. I would have preferred not to have had the opportunity to learn as much as I did, but that was a good thing.

Refusing to be canceled, I think, is important. I would say that the first four days were hell, and then when the dean announced that I'd be suspended, that began four months of purgatory.

What was going through your mind at that stage?

The first day I woke up, looked at my phone, and saw that the last thing I tweeted before going to bed was blowing up because a couple of instigators have manufactured outrage. So I deleted it and apologized, saying, "I phrased this poorly; sorry about that." But it was too late at the time. And it was the second worst day of my life, after the death of my mother when I was in college. And I was thinking about my decades of hard work to establish my reputation, making a living for my family. I mean, everything was just in jeopardy. And it all felt like a nightmare. It was a horror.

I was trying to respond. And for four days, I was navigating the inside game with Randy Barnett, my boss at Georgetown, figuring out how to put out a couple of statements that were narrowly apologetic in order to avoid being fired immediately. So, it served that limited purpose. When I was invited to apologize again during the purgatory phase, I declined because I had said everything I needed to say and there was nothing else I could do about it. But, yes, I couldn't sleep for four days because of physical manifestations. It was just trying to survive.

Who was your first phone call—your lifeline call to a friend?
I was in touch with Randy right away, my boss, to discuss how to navigate this. I called my wife and a couple of friends in public relations and the political world. I was quickly put in touch with FIRE, whom I knew and had on my contact list. And they quickly started an email thread with seven or eight of their top people. I think we had something like 100 messages that day, and it went on like that. Kmele Foster was incredibly helpful. He's on their board. And he's a friend of mine; not a close friend, but we have known each other since our days in DC about fifteen years ago. And he's just got a good head on his shoulders for things like this. And he advised me.

Then, I believe by Friday afternoon, which was day two of the scandal, I learned that no action would be taken. In fact, there's an email from the associate dean for Centers and Institutes at Georgetown Law, who emailed saying no action would be taken that day, which I believed was a good sign because if I wasn't fired in the first two days, they're clearly trying to do something else. Then we had a Zoom meeting with the dean on Sunday, and he was as weak as a deer in headlights. And I definitely learned that most university officials are not woke radicals, but rather weak, spineless bureaucrats. And he was, in effect, looking for my advice on how to extricate himself from this situation.

He wanted his talking points from you, is that it?
Yes, he wanted any further statement from me, and I was like, "Look, I put out a lot of statements. I've said everything I've said, and I've worked on it. Randy advised me to distribute it via the faculty listserv, which I did. And there is nothing else I can say." I knew he was getting heat because I was helping to orchestrate some of it, both publicly and privately, whether it was donors or high-ranking alumni or something like that. Finally, the next morning, he decided that I would be immediately placed on paid leave. So, it was Monday when he said that because the next day, Tuesday, February 1st, was when I was supposed to start work.

Then I listened to my counsel's advice on how to conduct this type of investigation, prepared for my interview, and three weeks later, I was interviewed by HR and the diversity office for about an hour via Zoom. And it was a kind of evil banality. They didn't start attacking me; instead, they kept asking, "Tell us what you meant by this tweet. What was the context of this tweet?" And they expected me to grovel or apologize or something. I responded, "Look, I phrased it poorly, but in essence what I was saying was what various senators were saying, and what 76 percent of the American "people agreed with, and I by no means back away from that." And they were like, "Well, what if people don't want to take your class?" and I said, "Well, it's a free country. I'm not teaching any mandatory classes." And they eventually said that because some didn't want to take my class that constituted a lack of access and contributed to the toxic educational environment that I was creating.

Anyway, that Zoom lasted an hour, then nothing happened for weeks upon weeks. And after a while, my counsel said, "All right, this is a sham, as we expected, so go forth and be public and show your expertise on Supreme Court cases, free speech, judicial politics, and all that." So, right around the time I was supposed to give a talk at Hastings, my event was shut down. It is still the only time in over 1,000 public speaking appearances that I have been protested.

That made national news again, but then Yale happened in March of this year, which was pretty stressful for law schools, obstruction, and other such things.

[Note: Shapiro is referring to a March 10 law school event hosted by the Yale Federalist Society at which dozens of protestors interrupted the introduction of a conversation between Monica Miller of the American Humanist Association and Kristen Waggoner of the Alliance Defending Freedom, before walking out in protest and then disrupting the meeting by carrying on their protest in the hallway outside.]

Then Ketanji Brown Jackson was nominated, the confirmation was going on during the big Supreme Court term with the leak [related to overturning *Roe v. Wade*] and everything. And, as I was commenting, I think I published eight op-eds during purgatory, and I started doing media and joining briefs and sort of trying to get back into the regular swing of things while this sham investigation was going on. Everyone was telling me the conventional wisdom, which ultimately proved to be correct, that Georgetown was simply waiting out the semester, waiting for the students to get off campus, in order to try to reinstate me in some way.

And so, the purgatory time was a personal and professional emotional roller coaster. I had some offers, people asking, "What are you going to do?" I felt it was too soon and just wanted to keep this job. I had come to Georgetown to have a different kind of impact, to shift my career in a slightly different direction, to take on new challenges, to build something. On the one hand, it was productive in terms of writing; I updated my book, which came out in paperback in early July, did a lot of speeches, I think I did thirty speeches or something like that.

But it was simply purgatory. It was during this strange period. It was disturbing. It wasn't hell, but purgatory. The checks were clearing from Georgetown, so I was okay in that regard. I was just kind of sitting there. And my counsel advised me to do whatever I wanted as long as I didn't explicitly criticize the Georgetown administration.

How long did it take you to write your letter of resignation? What led to it?

There were four days in hell and four months in purgatory. I haven't given the last four days a name. The dean scheduled a Zoom on Thursday, June 2, I believe, and said I was being reinstated on the technicality that I wasn't an employee when I sent the tweet. And then he issued this condemnatory statement. Nevertheless, once the Zoom was scheduled, as it had been the night before, I tipped off the *Wall Street Journal* and other journalistic friends who had been favorable throughout my travails, and the *Journal* responded, "Yes, we'll take another piece from you." And then everything happened. I got the notice from the dean, accepted, and celebrated the technical victory in the *Wall Street Journal*.

And then, around dinnertime or later that afternoon, I got the report from the diversity office. As I was reading through it that night, I sort of skimmed it. The next morning, I started reading it thoroughly, as did my counsel and my wife, who is probably a better lawyer than all of us. I did a little media that day, but not too much, because it would have been a bigger story had I been fired or completely vindicated. And I realized, late Friday evening or early Saturday morning, that there was no way forward and that they were setting me up to fail. As I put it in my resignation letter, this was a slow-motion firing in which I would not take part.

I started writing that letter on Saturday, around midmorning, and contacted the Manhattan Institute, which I'd known for a long time, with the idea that at Georgetown, I'd be an adjunct of theirs or something. But I called them and said, "There might be an opportunity to have a deeper relationship." And to their credit, they had put together an offer for me within 36 hours. So, when I actually submitted my resignation letter on Monday morning, I already had the Manhattan job in hand, although again, I didn't start planning that until I decided to resign on Saturday morning. But I'm proud of my four-page resignation letter, as a piece of lawyering, as a piece of public relations.

And then I condensed that into yet another *Wall Street Journal* piece to go out something like 45 minutes after I sent the letter to the dean. I thought they wouldn't take another one, it might be some sort of record to have two *Journal* pieces published in four days, but they say, "We're covering the story. This is good and we're going to run this." I announced my move to the Manhattan Institute on Tucker [Carlson] the next night, Tuesday night, as one does. That started two weeks of interesting and fun media in which I was completely in charge of the narrative for the first time. And it was gratifying to put that platform to use at the time. I didn't want to be there, but I was going to play the cards that were dealt to me in order to shine a light on the rot in academia in general, and Georgetown, specifically.

Receiving the first notification that you were found not guilty on a technicality was a Pyrrhic victory. But taking the time to think about it further got you to where you are, which is empowered. What would you say to a person under attack by cancel vultures?
Well, I imagine it is what you advise your clients; you have to be strategic, and you have to think. What are the possibilities? I had this conversation again and again with my counsel as time went on. What are they likely to do? What are the possibilities? I had producers for various shows contact me and say, "As soon as there is a resolution, we want you on." I did Megyn Kelly's podcast on Friday, I think, the day after I was reinstated just before my resignation. In fact, she asked me that question, which now appears to be prophetic. She asked, "Why do you want to do this job? Do you really believe you can succeed given this situation?" That conversation was certainly in my head as I was coming to a decision.

Those first four days in a crisis situation, I went through the same kinds of considerations. Which media outlets should I prioritize? What is the message I'm going to leave them with, and what are the legal ramifications? How can I protect my legal rights? What legal options do I have? What effect do the media or another component have on all of this? What is my goal? You have to be goal focused. If I had said from the beginning: "Okay, this isn't going to work, I'm just going to become a media darling," then I would have behaved differently the first four days or become a cancel culture martyr.

I learned about crisis strategy since the first four days were acute crisis strategy. But then it was just like, this will end at some point. We eventually realize that it will end when the students leave campus, and we must be prepared for that, as well. It's unlikely that they'll simply say no problem at all. They could have said that at the start. If they wanted to fire me, they could have done so immediately. What happened was exactly what we expected, especially since my counsel contacted the university's counsel and had an increasing dialogue in the last couple of weeks or so before the final announcement. We had a pretty good idea of what to expect, without obviously the details of the report, that made things untenable. I've always thought about: when this ends, what do I do? How do I position myself to be effective as a professor and as a communicator?

That weekend, when I decided to resign, was another type of acute crisis planning. But in a more positive sense in that it was still a shock that I was going to resign. But now that I had the other job, I could say, "OK, now I'm going to jiujitsu this; I'm going to turn the tables on Georgetown and put them in a tough position." And how exactly do I do that? Then, very early on, Substack approached me. So, I launched a Substack. During that two-week period, I accomplished a lot of things that I planned and things that came to me as a result of what my counsel and my wife and I were thinking about. And I'm still in that phase, even though I have been at Manhattan for a month. I've had publishers approach me about my next book, and I'm thinking about how I can't just do cancel culture, even free speech and First Amendment stuff, because I have other things that I do that I want to get back to. But I still have this platform and this heightened profile. So, how do I take advantage of that to get what I want rather than what whoever else wants to use me as the next icon for pursuing whatever agenda? And how do I use this moment to get it?

To boil it down to a core element, it appears that you had a plan at every stage of this process. And that strategic plan helped guide you, while also giving you a sense of comfort and control that you would somehow get through this tumult.
Yes, definitely. It was a constantly shifting plan that would be adjusted as circumstances required.

To what extent did this impact your family and friends?

My wife was in tears for the first few days, and it was rough. She kept yelling at me, "Fix this, fix this. I warned you about this, that you had to be more careful about race and sex when you went into academia. When you enter academia, you are viewed through a different lens." And then I stepped right into what my wife had warned me about. I was informed by the dean that I would be on paid leave. That was okay because I was in a vulnerable situation; it was a period of transition. My Cato Institute salary was about to end. And I wouldn't be allowed to stay or return to Cato for reasons that are a separate discussion. So, for God's sake, I needed that income, and I needed my family's health insurance. So that made it very real that I needed to figure this out now. I knew that I had friends and that I am marketable and that I would get a job. But there is a difference between knowing that and actually having the security of a job offer or a steady paycheck.

Judge James Ho offered a genuine, full-throated endorsement of you in the wake of this controversy. Did you read his remarks about you?
I did. I have known Jim for about twenty years, but I didn't cross paths with him. He probably finished law school in Chicago a year or two before I did. But we were in the same circles, through the Federalist Society and elsewhere. But I had no idea he was going to do what he did. In fact, I was on a plane when he gave that speech at Georgetown, and when I landed, I was bombarded with media questions. What are your thoughts on Judge Ho and what the judge has said about you? And I'm like, "Okay, let me see what he said." And I don't think we had a complete transcript at the time. But, based on how that was reported, I got the gist and issued a brief press statement essentially saying, "I'm grateful that Judge Ho supports me; he's a mensch." That's all I said, and he liked that. I got in touch with him later that evening. In addition, he is active in the Federalist Society in Dallas, where he currently lives. So, he arranged for me to come out and speak there. And I joked with him that I would just rip up my prepared remarks and start loading his jurisprudence at that point.

But I thought it was a significant moment. Because I had my media supporters, like Rich Lowry at *National Review*, who was just phenomenal. He even said once that if I needed a place to hang my shingle, you know, while I figured out job options, they would have me. I have written for them fairly regularly in the past. The *Journal* publisher checked in with me every other day and stuff like that. So, I had media supporters and Bari Weiss, but having a federal judge at Georgetown say these things was significant.

Contrast Judge Ho's take with a scathing article that was published by Elie Mystal.

He believes that everyone who disagrees with him, every nonprogressive, is a racist.

He has a law degree from Harvard. How do we square the circle when Jim Ho and Elie Mystal are both competing for people's minds?

There will always be people whom you simply cannot convince, who will not accept what you say in good faith. . . . Typically, I do not engage with those people, since it is a waste of my time. I either mute or block them on Twitter depending on the level of what they say to me or about me. But no, I don't engage with that because there's nothing to gain from engaging with someone who doesn't approach in good faith.

While cancel culture appears here to stay, do you see an alternative system developing as a market force response to cancel culture?

I have seen green shoots in society writ large. Whether it's Netflix saying, "If you are not comfortable with what we put out, maybe we're not the right place for you." Some say it was like State Farm withdrawing some of their more extreme DEI programs in the wake of the abortion decision. There wasn't a flood of companies, but some were announcing that they would pay for employees to travel to other states. They were not, however, roundly condemning the Supreme Court as they had in the past in response to other news developments. And there are other things I think, normal people, not political activists, not people who spend their time reading political magazines and listening to these sorts of podcasts all the time, who are just concerned about their families, their livelihoods, when they see just kind of ridiculous things. There have been "emperor has no clothes" kinds of moments in society writ large.

With regard to academia, I am much less sanguine. It is possible that we've reached the point of no return. That there is simply insufficient critical mass to stem the tide. And, to be clear, what's going on in academia with cancel culture or illiberal trends isn't the decades-old complaint: well, liberals have taken it over. It's not that—it's that the illiberal have control; not because they are the majority, but because they have cowed everyone else into submission. As I have said, administrators, deans, presidents, and department chairs are generally not woke radicals; they are bureaucrats who simply do not want to be involved in controversy because they know that the radical Left will hit them harder than anyone else in that context. So, they just kowtow and placate, creating a dynamic in which the Overton window of permissible policy and values, expressions and views, is narrowing and shifting.

I just don't know if that dynamic can be reversed, even though it could be simply by having more administrators come from the outset and enforce an ethic, a culture, of civil discourse. Most institutions of higher education have free speech and free expression policies; Georgetown certainly does on paper. However, university officials who are willing to do so are few and far between.

Are you optimistic about the next ten years?
On America, writ large, I'm with Justice Kavanaugh on the sunrise side of the mountain. I'm generally optimistic because I believe this country has a lot going for it, especially when compared to other countries. In academia, I'm pessimistic for the reasons that I just went into. We're still not completely out of the pandemic, and certainly not out of the pandemic mind-set for many elites in various parts of the country. When we are more fully out of that, will it be a reprise of what we had in the 1920s? Forget that irregular period and move to an economic boom and flourishing of different kinds. Is it going to morph, or will it remain the same? I'm not sure, it's difficult to make predictions, especially about the future, as Yogi Berra once said.

One other dynamic I should note. Part of the issue is a loss of a sense of grace in our society, being able to forgive foibles and slip-ups. And also, and I think this comes out of the secularization of America, there is still a craving for some spiritual sustenance. And politics provides that to a lot of people. In that context, someone who disagrees with you politically is a heretic, and not worth your time. And so, therefore, we no longer treat our political enemies as merely wrong. They're just evil. And that's not a healthy thing.

I have two little kids and twins on the way. Our little cancellation babies are due around Thanksgiving, a boy and a girl. [Note: Professor Shapiro's wife gave birth to two healthy babies in 2022.] I'm looking after my little platoon. And I want to live an impactful life, to set a good example. I want to contribute to the advancement of liberty in this country that I freely chose and for which my parents sacrificed to get me out of the Soviet Union. So I can enjoy the life, liberty, and pursuit of happiness that this country has to offer. And I hope that I can continue to provide my children and their generation with the same opportunities that I have.

KEY TAKEAWAYS

- Shapiro recognized his mistake immediately and sought to correct it by deleting the offensive tweet and offering a succinct apology explaining his error.
- Refusing to be "canceled" is an essential mind-set for anyone being attacked by cancel vultures. Knowing your limits steels the mind and helps with pressing the truth.
- Shapiro knew exactly what he was apologizing for, and he refused to grovel for acceptance.
- Knowing the right people to call in the face of a crisis is critical to gaining some sense of control. Thankfully, Shapiro had Greg Lukianoff (FIRE) and Kmele Foster, both of whom are well versed in these situations; but most people don't know to whom they can turn.
- Having a strategic action plan helps:
  - o Create control over the narrative, and your future
  - o Provide empowerment during a period of time that could otherwise leave you feeling hopeless
  - o Focus your effort and mind on those things that you can control, and that can make a difference
  - o Establish opportunities to pursue, regardless of various outcomes
- Political opponents are not heretics or enemies.

Case Study: Michelle McFarland

President, National Bridal Retailers Association and
Owner of The Wedding Shoppe

Situation Synopsis

Following the 2020 presidential election and the subsequent charges of voter fraud by now-former President Donald Trump, two Republican members of Michigan's Wayne County Election Board said that they would not certify the results of the contest. In the wake of widespread and extreme public pressure, they ultimately reversed their positions and voted in favor of confirming the outcome. Before changing her mind, one of the two, Monica Palmer, had proposed that the Board "certify the results in the communities other than the city of Detroit." This produced huge public outcry accusing Palmer and other Republicans of racism and trying to disenfranchise voters in the predominantly Black city.

Angry political activists began scouring the Internet for previous posts by the controversial election commissioner and discovered a Tweet that Palmer had sent: "Enter to win a private dress fitting party for a bride and 10 loved ones at The Wedding Shoppe in Berkley, MI, today!"[70]

A mob of cancel vultures concluded, incorrectly, that Palmer owned The Wedding Shoppe or was somehow connected to the store. Within hours they began bombarding the local business founded and operated by Michelle McFarland with negative reviews, delivering threats to employees by phone and email, and encouraging a complete boycott of The Wedding Shoppe. One social media influencer latched onto the story, further expanding the reach of the controversy.

Wisely, The Wedding Shoppe aggressively countered the misinformation, convincing the influencer to remove the post that was generating threats. The store issued and widely disseminated a press release that clearly articulated the facts. McFarland even took the extra step, again wisely, of engaging local media to let them know about this case of mistaken identity, going on-camera to decry the targeting of her business and ensuring the truth reached a critical mass of people and potential customers in her community.

Those efforts worked, and the cancel culture attack ceased nearly immediately. The Wedding Shoppe was able to survive and to this day continues to thrive, focusing on its mission of serving brides.

Interview Excerpts

Give us a little background on your business.
I started my business over twenty-two years ago and didn't have any experience in bridal. I just knew I wanted to run my own business someday, and the opportunity kind of presented itself and I went for it.

I started it from the ground up at a time when I had my eye on a specific retail space and just kept imagining, what can I do in there? And at the time, I had been married for a few months. It seemed like everyone in my friend circle was getting married, and I thought, maybe there's something to this wedding thing. And so, I started researching and opened my business as an accessories-only bridal boutique. But then I went into doing alterations because brides were asking where they could get their dress altered; and then we evolved into carrying wedding dresses. And the rest is history.
We have twenty-eight people on payroll right now. At the start, it was just my sister and me. She is still my general manager today.

What was your reputation like before you experienced a cancel culture attack?
We have always had such an amazing reputation. That was probably our saving grace—how well-thought-of we are in the community. I think a lot of people saw stories about us [during the cancel culture episode] and said, "Oh, that's just a bunch of rubbish. That is not who they are." And so, I was very thankful for that, because had I been on shaky ground, then this could have toppled the entire store.

What was the impact of the COVID-19 pandemic on you and your business?
As a retail business that is nonessential, we had to close for two months, which was very stressful. Wondering about what would happen to my employees and customers, as well as how long we would be closed and what it would be like when things reopened. Because there was so much uncertainty, we didn't know if society was going to just dissolve into anarchy, which is what I kind of prepared for, because I was worried there would be a food shortage and looting on the streets and I would come back to a building that had been firebombed. The brides were under a lot of stress. They weren't sure if they would be able to have their weddings. They were making changes to their plans, and all their stress just trickled down to us, because we tried to be there for them in any way we could. Listening to their sad stories every day was extremely taxing on everyone who worked here.

Do you remember the timeline of the situation you experienced?
Yes, very vividly. My husband and I were on our first post-COVID vacation. We had flown to Las Vegas, which has always been one of our favorite places, and had intentionally booked our flight to return home later in the day so that we could get up in the morning and just enjoy ourselves for a few more hours before getting on the plane and returning to reality. And when I woke up that morning, I started looking at my phone and saw a lot more Instagram and Facebook messages than normal. I started reading through these comments. The first one you just play it off like somebody's crazy and has the wrong business. Then, I had to try really hard to wrap my head around what was happening.

It was a very confusing situation, since they were saying in these messages that someone else owned my store and what a horrible person she was and that no one should come to my business because of it. I had been unplugged for a few days enjoying a vacation with my husband and wasn't paying attention to the local media. So I had to educate myself on what was going on back home. It was only a week and a half to two weeks since the elections, and some Republican canvassers were not certifying the vote in the city of Detroit. They were accused of being racist and of wanting to suppress the Black vote so that their votes wouldn't matter. All of that is neither here nor there, because I am not involved in politics. I don't work in politics; I sell wedding dresses.

One person was communicating with me, and I said, "I'm so sorry, I have no idea what you're talking about. Could you tell me where you got this information? What is being said? Because, that person does not own this business, I do and my name is Michelle, not Monica," and she said that this person, Monica Palmer, was the Republican canvasser for Wayne County, and that she was being targeted right now because she would not certify the vote, and someone had gone into her Twitter account and discovered that, over six months ago, in March of 2020, before the world shut down, she had shared a tweet from my page about a contest we were holding to give one bride a free VIP experience in my store. So, all of this came from one shared tweet, not even an original tweet. It was assumed that she was the owner of my store, The Wedding Shoppe, and that the store should therefore be canceled.

I didn't know who to turn to. I happen to be a part of a very helpful and robust business community. I posted on this Facebook community that I needed immediate help from a PR firm that knows how to handle this. One of my friends saw it and said, I know Evan Nierman from Red Banyan and you need to call his company. And I thought to myself, "Well, this is perfect because I'm on the West Coast right now, and I need someone who's awake." You guys were on the phone with me within twenty minutes, and my stress level was already decreasing because I knew that if I had to respond to all of this without help, it would never come off right. It would have blown up even more if I threw gasoline on a fire. The team immediately got down to business and started writing a response to these shared Facebook posts.

What had happened was a very influential woman in Detroit had written a post under the mistaken assumption that Monica Palmer was the owner of my business, and it had been shared over eighty times in just a few hours. And so, if we hadn't been able to get something up within hours to refute that claim that this person owned my business, I'm not sure how that would have kept snowballing over the next few hours and days. By the end of that day, we were able to post, saying, "Wait, hold on. You've got this all wrong. That is not what is happening. And that's not what this business stands for. And please don't destroy a hard-working, long-standing business in this community over a false assumption."

Since going through this experience, I've talked to a lot of other bridal store owners who were going through other situations that were blowing up on them, and I always tell them, "Listen, I know that right now it may feel as if your world is literally ending and that your business will never recover, but I want you to know that it will, and it will recover even faster than you could possibly imagine. So, let's just focus on solving the problems right now so they don't worsen, but it's going to be okay."

You moved quickly, and your approach to the social media influencer was made in a very respectful, courteous tone. You set the record straight and asked her to take down the erroneous post and share your public statement with her followers. Correct?

We were able to speak with her personally, but she responded to a direct message, saying: "If I made a mistake, I'm very, very sorry," before pledging to remove the post. But it took her 24 hours to remove it, and the team and I said, you know what she's doing? She is trying her hardest to prove that somehow, I know this woman and that I am guilty by association. She's trying to prove that I have some sort of connection to Monica Palmer, but there was none. I had never heard of this woman in my entire life. I've never met her. How do you prove that you don't know someone? It is nearly impossible to prove a negative. That's what we were up against. And lucky for me, I did not know her. But what if I had? That was what scares me the most . . . what if I had worked with her twenty years ago at a previous job, or if we went to college or high school together, or she was my husband's cousin twice removed, or any other crazy connection? Then I would have been guilty by association. That made me sick to my stomach, because it's not fair to do that to people. Even if they know someone, it is not acceptable to attack them.

One of the things that you also did, which was a very bold and smart move, was proactively reaching out to local media to tell your story. Talk us through how that happened.

Well, it's funny because what happened was that I immediately began sharing our first public statement on the local Facebook groups to which I belong in my city. There are some reporters who live in the city who are always looking for stories, and they contacted me and wanted to come out and speak with me, which I welcomed because I wanted to clear the air and assure everyone that racist or discriminating is not who we are.

Within 48 hours of everything happening, the press came out, and their story ran. That was really nice because I could then share that link on our social media pages to show everyone that we were the ones who were truly being victimized. But you know, and I know, that everybody's first inclination, as it was mine, was, "I'm going to hire a lawyer and sue them." But you can't do that because, as the lawyer explained to me, it means that I'm now turning around and victimizing them, which could backfire on me. So, I couldn't. I felt I had no recourse but to make a statement.

What was the tone of the messages you were receiving in the midst of the cancel culture experience?
After reading the first few, I stopped because I knew that I wasn't going to be productive in resolving this issue. If I got caught up in that, then I would be personally upset and feel personally attacked. I'll tell you, though, my sister, who is my general manager, did read them, and she was so upset that I thought, okay, I can't do that to myself because I need to be working on this, so she can read the messages and she can take screenshots of them in case we need to do anything later. Being attacked in that manner was terrible, and all I could think about was how far I was from my team, and how much they needed me right now. Because I had no idea if people would start showing up outside of my business or swamping us with phone calls harassing us all day long. Did my employees need to be worried walking out to their cars when they left the store? Were customers coming in going to be harassed? I had no idea because the situation surrounding the election was so intense and people were so raw from the entire year. I had no idea how out of control it could get.

Were the people who were reaching out angry and accusatory?
They were saying never go to the store, they're racists, they're suppressing the Black vote in Detroit, and none of that was true. What I do is completely unrelated to politics. Our culture in my store is that we embrace everyone and accept love in any form it may take. And, if you want to wear a wedding dress, you come on in because I will assist you no matter what, and I don't care who you are or how you identify. We love everybody, and my entire team feels the same way. So to witness them [my team] having to deal with being accused was really hard.

What were some of the other emotions that you and your team were feeling?
I know they work as hard as I do every day for the brides who visit us and purchase wedding dresses. And even those who don't, since we care about their lives, weddings, and future. I was thinking that they might lose the jobs that they love and cherish and the connections that they have with these brides; or that the brides might think differently about us or stop coming. When this happened, I was thinking, "This is going to be the end of us, and the things they are saying aren't even true."

I was concerned about my family, my extended family, which is my team. And that was my main concern: Will there be a drop in appointments, affecting their paychecks? Will I have to lay off anyone? They enjoy what they do and would be devastated.

We had done nothing wrong. We were being attacked for no apparent reason. So, it felt like I'd never get any justice because people could just say and do whatever they wanted and destroy the business that I'd worked for over twenty years to build and employ close to thirty people. I thought I'd lose everything, which broke my heart because we are a beloved company and business in our area. And all through no fault of my own, or anybody that worked for me.

You have obviously had a very firsthand brush with cancel culture. Share your overall thoughts.

I believe that in life, people frequently feel helpless. So, when they see something that they perceive to be an injustice, they can go online as a keyboard warrior and make a statement that they would not even make verbally in person to anyone. And it's so much easier to attack when no one is in front of you. And they don't even ask what happened or what the story is; they just assume right away that you did something wrong and deserve to be punished for it.

I equate it to the bullies in junior high or high school who, as you walk down the hallway, just push you into the locker because they can and get a power trip out of it. In reality, they're just online bullies. And the next day they're off to bully someone else. They don't even truly believe in it or stick to it. Everything blew over in a matter of days for me. These people who are bullying and attempting to shut down businesses do not have a true conviction. They don't believe in it enough to stick with it. So, it is truly tragic. It's a sad state of the world that we're living in right now.

What was the personal impact of these people you have described as keyboard warriors? Do you really believe they could have ended your business?

Yes, I believe it could have been a lot worse if these women hadn't just been on Facebook. One thing I had going for me is that if they had been savvier and used TikTok or even Instagram, this could have been a million times worse. But because it was only on Facebook, it really did keep it from blowing up and getting bigger, because if they had been on a national level instead of just within their little Facebook community, then I could have been attacked from all over the country, which is what I've seen happen to other people. If she had been a little savvier and posted her false assumptions on TikTok or Instagram, things would have been much, much worse for us.

What kind of feedback did you get from loyal shop customers and people you knew in the community after you were able to clear the air?
It was so heartfelt. It was such an emotional day because it started in panic and ended in, "I'm so glad we've built the community that we have because people know who we are—and they love us." The statement we issued received hundreds and hundreds of likes and shares from our customers, new and old. It got out into the world, and that's how the reporter picked up on the story and came out the next day to talk with me. By that evening, the story had made the news. So, it really was a flash in the pan, but the cancel attack was terrible while it was happening.

What did you learn from the experience?
I learned that you must have a plan. I am also the president of the National Bridal Retailers Association, and because of what happened to me personally, the following February we did a webinar for all of the bridal stores in the country. We talked with three stores that had been victims of cancel culture, mine being one of them. The silver lining was that I was able to use my platform to go out and educate other stores on how to have a plan. And with the help of your company, we put together checklists for bridal store owners on what to do when cancel culture happens to you and how to contact the support you need and minimize the impacts of the incident. Not if, but when, because I do believe that everyone has the potential to have it happen to them at some point.

My own daughter, Noa, who is thirteen, recently had a healthy father-daughter debate with me about cancel culture. She said that she thinks it is an important way to hold bad people or companies accountable. You have a unique vantage point as someone who was targeted, but not ultimately canceled. Do you have a message to young people like her, or others, who may have participated in cancel culture in some form?
I would say that there are always two sides to every story, and that the truth lies somewhere in between. And in most cases, when these situations arise, it is due to a misunderstanding or someone's perception of what happened.

You should try to figure out what actually happened. Talk to both sides. Find out, because these things often grow out of misunderstandings and hurt feelings, and they're not real. The person you're attacking is a real person with a life, a family, and potentially a business, and they're trying to pay other people. Why are you trying to put people on unemployment because you want to destroy a business over something that probably didn't happen?

Two stores who were on that webinar with us did nothing wrong. In one case, an upset customer went on TikTok with a three-minute rant, and none of what she said happened was actually true. It was just her reaction to what was said. In the other instance, an influencer visited a bridal store in California. They misinterpreted not being able to take them immediately for an appointment due to COVID restrictions and only being allowed to have ten people in the store. But they saw it as the store not wanting to help them because they were a mixed couple or thought they didn't have any money. The truth was that they needed to make an appointment. They were shown around the store and the situation was explained to them, but when they walked out, they were still upset because they couldn't get in when they wanted to. Keep in mind that just because someone says something happened to them does not mean it is true.

Any other closing thoughts?

This situation is something I've put behind me. I try not to think about it; it's in the past. To be honest, it was a ridiculous, comical situation. I mean, how can anyone make that assumption about my company based on one shared tweet on someone's Twitter account that they never even use?

At the time when this crazy thing happened, it truly felt like the end of my world when I realized what was going on. I thought: we're in Detroit, where this is a hot topic. People are dissatisfied. And they were feeling unheard, and that they would not be allowed to take part in a national election. The only good thing that came of it in the end was putting out the fire as quick as possible and me being able to assist other stores with having a blueprint for saving themselves.

And if I end up featured in this book, explaining how cancel culture hurts good people when mistakes happen, then that could be the best thing.

KEY TAKEAWAYS

- Owner Michelle McFarland moved quickly when cancel vultures descended on her business in a case of mistaken identity.

- The Wedding Shoppe quickly engaged a firm specializing in crisis management and with prior experience handling cancel culture incidents.
- McFarland released a statement publicly via press release, which her team also circulated widely online and via social media.
- The store directly engaged an influencer stoking the fires of controversy, providing her with evidence of their innocence and requesting a specific action to remedy the situation: taking down the social media post that was prompting activists to demand a boycott.
- The business engaged local media as a means of amplifying their messages and conveying the facts to a large audience of potential customers.
- A good reputation within the community built over years helped bolster the company when it came under fire and embroiled in the controversy.

Acknowledgments

As anyone who has ever written a book knows, the effort is rarely an individual one. *The Cancel Culture Curse* is no different. Family, friends, fellow authors, and subject matter experts from a variety of backgrounds all played large parts in the creation and publication of this book.

Though they are public figures who need no additional recognition, we would be remiss not to thank Peter Boghossian, Alan Dershowitz, Winston Marshall, and Ilya Shapiro for sharing their stories and reflections with us, and for playing key roles in thwarting the curse of cancel culture.

Important research is drawn from the work of Zach Greenberg and Komi Frey at the Foundation for Individual Rights and Expression (FIRE), who spent their valuable time helping us identify and understand the trends taking place on college campuses.

Lisa Alexander steeled herself to speak openly and candidly about her experiences. We are thankful for her trust in our ability to convey her story to the public for the first time. Lisa's courage to persevere, despite what she continues to endure, will hopefully provide inspiration to others suffering similar fates at the hands of cancel vultures.

Numerous people spoke with us on the condition that we not reveal their names, while others were still so fearful that they insisted that our conversations be entirely off-the-record. We have fully honored all such requests.

We would like to thank all our colleagues at Red Banyan. Their research, insights, and experience operating in today's media environment have been invaluable, while their professionalism and poise enabled us to redirect some of our own focus and time to writing this book.

Many thanks to our diligent editor, Hector Carosso, who guided us expertly through the process and made this book better. Also, appreciation is due to Skyhorse Publisher Tony Lyons for having the courage to tackle difficult subjects and his steely commitment to free speech and ensuring an open marketplace of ideas.

Mark would like to thank his wife, Tracy, who typically sees things a bit differently, and often much better, than he does, especially when it comes to their three daughters, Emma, Maya, and Lyla. The writing of this book, in part, is to better their futures by giving them some tools to think more critically and with more complexity about difficult subjects.

Evan wishes to express his deep and abiding love for his children, Gabe and Noa, and his prayer that they will always do their part to make the world better. He is grateful to the numerous family members, colleagues, and friends who sustain and inspire him. You know who you are, and your belief in me elevates my life.

And to our readers, thank you for taking the time to read this book and for considering the ideas we present. We look forward to your input, and to continuing the conversation with you.

With deepest appreciation,
Mark and Evan

Notes

Chapter 2

1. Merriam-Webster, "cancel," https://www.merriam-webster.com/dictionary/cancel#h1.
2. Dan Kovalik, *Cancel This Book* (New York: Skyhorse, 2021), 40.
3. Levi Parsons, "Piers Morgan unleashes on Harry and Meghan and the woke brigade 'marching around like they're Kim Jong-un with a dash of Vladimir Putin' in fiery interview on 60 Minutes—and warns 'cancel culture' is threatening to destroy society," *Daily Mail*, June 6, 2021, https://www.dailymail.co.uk/news/article-9657157/Piers -Morgan-unleashes-Meghan-Markle-fiery-interview-Karl-Stefanovic-60-Minutes.html.
4. "Why Piers Morgan refuses to be 'cancelled' in explosive interview | 60 Minutes Australia," YouTube video, "60 Minutes Australia," June 6, 2021, https://www.youtube.com /watch?v=UoELLyeibj4.
5. Parsons, "Piers Morgan unleashes on Harry and Meghan," *Daily Mail*, June 6, 2021.
6. Piers Morgan, Twitter post, March 10, 2021, 1:11 a.m., https://twitter.com/piersmorgan /status/1369531295794085889?lang=en.
7. Alan Dershowitz, *Cancel Culture* (New York: Skyhorse, 2021), 124.
8. Albert James Bergesen, "A Durkheimian Theory of 'Witch-Hunts' with the Chinese Cultural Revolution of 1966–1969 as an Example," *Journal for the Scientific Study of Religion* 17, no. 1 (1978): 19–29, https://doi.org/10.2307/1385424.
9. Emile Durkheim, *The Division of Labor in Society*, edited by Steven Lukes (New York: Macmillan, 1984), 64.
10. Ibid.
11. Greg Lukianoff and Jonathan Haidt, *The Coddling of the American Mind: How Good Intentions and Bad Ideas are Setting Up a Generation for Failure* (New York: Penguin Random House, 2018), 100–102.
12. Kovalik, *Cancel This Book*, 14.
13. Kovalik, *Cancel This Book*, 92.
14. Emily Burack, "Salman Rushdie Remains in Critical Condition Following Attack," *Town & Country*, August 15, 2022, https://www.townandcountrymag.com/society /politics/a40897713/salman-rushdie-attack-health-update/.

Chapter 3

15 The Federalist Papers: No. 17, The Avalon Project, Yale Law School, https://avalon .law.yale.edu/18th_century/fed17.asp.

16 The Federalist Papers: No. 17, The Avalon Project, Yale Law School.

17 Thomas Hobbes, *Leviathan*, The Project Gutenberg, part I, chapter XI, (1651), https:// www.gutenberg.org/files/3207/3207-h/3207-h.htm#link2HCH0011.

18 Hobbes, *Leviathan*, part I, chapter XIII.

19 Hobbes, *Leviathan*, part II, chapter XVII.

20 David Antonini, "Social Contract Theory," 1000-Word Philosophy, October 3, 2018, https://1000wordphilosophy.com/2018/10/03/social-contract-theory/#_ftn6.

21 John Locke, Second Treatise of Government, The Project Gutenberg, chapter VIII, (1690), https://www.gutenberg.org/files/7370/7370-h/7370-h.htm.

22 John Locke, *Two Treatises of Government,* 3rd ed. (New York: Cambridge University Press, 1988), Book 1, Sec. 30.

23 John Stuart Mill, *On Liberty*, edited by Kathy Casey (Minoela, NY: Dover Publications, 2002), 10.

24 Mill, *On Liberty*, edited by Kathy Casey, 10.

25 David French, "Against the Demolition of the American Spirit," *The Dispatch*, October 23, 2022, https://thedispatch.com/newsletter/frenchpress/against-the-demolition-of-the -american-spirit/.

26 French, "Against the Demolition of the American Spirit," *The Dispatch*.

27 https://dailystoic.com/seneca-quotes/.

28 Martin E. Seligman, PhD, *Learned Optimism: How to Change Your Mind and Your Life* (New York: Vintage, 2006).

Chapter 4

29 Rachel Kleinfeld, *Journal of Democracy*, 32, 4, (October 2021): 160–176.

30 ADL, Backgrounder QANON, https://www.adl.org/resources/backgrounder/qanon.

31 George Orwell, "Politics and the English Language," The Orwell Foundation (1946), https://www.orwellfoundation.com/the-orwell-foundation/orwell/essays-and-other- works/politics-and-the-english-language/.

32 Lukianoff and Haidt, *The Coddling of the American Mind*, 32.

33 Ibid.

34 Lukianoff and Haidt, *The Coddling of the American Mind,* 86.

35 Peter Baghossian, "'Idea Laundering' in Academia," WSJ Opinion, November 24, 2019, https://www.wsj.com/articles/idea-laundering-in-academia-11574634492.

36 Intelligent Higher Education Team, "Students Surveyed Fear Expressing Their Ideas in Classrooms," January 2, 2023, https://www.intelligent.com/college-students-fear- expressing-ideas-in-classroom/.

37 Merriam-Webster, "equitable," https://www.merriam-webster.com/dictionary/equitable.

38 Damian Fisher, "Rising Dem Star Was Kicked Out of Dartmouth Dems Over Sexual Abuse Allegations," *Inside Sources*, August 14, 2022, https://insidesources.com/rising -dem-star-was-kicked-out-of-dartmouth-dems-over-sexual-abuse-allegations/.

39 Collin Anderson, "Top DeSantis Challenger Paid Thousands to Gen Z Liberal Activist Facing 'Campus-Wide Allegations of Sexual Assault,'" Washington Free Beacon, August

9, 2022, https://freebeacon.com/democrats/top-desantis-challenger-paid-thousands-to-gen-z-liberal-activist-facing-campus-wide-allegations-of-sexual-assault/.

40 "Student v. Student: Cocchiarella v. Kim," *The Dartmouth Review*, September 27, 2022, https://dartreview.com/student-v-student-cocchiarella-v-kim/.

41 K. German and S. T. Stevens, (2022), "Scholars Under Fire: 2021 Year in Review," FIRE, 2022, https://www.thefire.org/research/publications/miscellaneous-publications/scholars-under-fire/scholars-under-fire-2021-year-in-review-full-text/.

42 Lukianoff and Haidt, *The Coddling of the American Mind*, 111.

43 Cass R. Sunstein, "The Law of Group Polarization" (John M. Olin Program in Law and Economics Working Paper No. 91, 1999), 8, https://chicagounbound.uchicago.edu/cgi/viewcontent.cgi?article=1541&context=law_and_economics.

44 Lukianoff and Haidt, *The Coddling of the American Mind*, 109.

45 Speech First, "2022 Free Speech in the Crosshairs: Bias Reporting on College Campuses," http://speechfirst.org/wp-content/uploads/2022/07/SF-2022-Bias-Response-team-and-Reporting-System-Report.pdf.

46 Peter Boghossian, "My Resignation Letter," https://peterboghossian.com/my-resignation-letter.

47 Arthur Brooks, PhD, "The Science of Happiness," Apple Podcasts, https://podcasts.apple.com/us/podcast/the-science-of-happiness-arthur-brooks-ph-d/id1400828889?i=1000582124893.

48 Lukianoff and Haidt, *The Coddling of the American Mind*, xx.

49 Conor Friedersdorf, "The Perils of Writing a Provocative Email at Yale," *The Atlantic*, May 26, 2016, https://www.theatlantic.com/politics/archive/2016/05/the-peril-of-writing-a-provocative-email-at-yale/484418/.

Chapter 5

50 Gary Fields and Christina A. Cassidy, "Many remain critical of state of US democracy: AP-NORC poll," AP News, October 19, 2019, https://apnews.com/article/2022-midterm-elections-presidential-election-2020-democracy-33823de7f22a601a192fc82-eeb88e630?eType=EmailBlastContent&eId=612c0ae1-0a36-45fd-a641-6ece8900150e.

51 John Tooby, "2017: What Scientific Term or Concept Ought to Be More Widely Known?" *Edge*, https://www.edge.org/response-detail/27168?utm_source=ActiveCampaign&utm_medium=email&utm_content=Hypocrisy+and+the+Real+World&utm_campaign=Hypocrisy+and+the+Real+World.

52 Christopher Seneca, "How to Break Out of Your Social Media Echo Chamber," *WIRED*, September 17, 2020, https://www.wired.com/story/facebook-twitter-echo-chamber-confirmation-bias/.

53 Alan Dershowitz, *Guilt by Accusation* (New York: Skyhorse, 2019), 81–82.

Chapter 6

54 Ani Petrosyan, "Number of internet and social media users in the United States as of January 2022," Statista, September 20, 2022, https://www.statista.com/statistics/1044012/usa-digital-platform-audience/#statisticContainer.

55 "108 Internet Statistics & Facts (2022)," FirstSiteGuide, September 20, 2022, https://firstsiteguide.com/internet-stats/.

56   Black Lives Matter, https://blacklivesmatter.com/about/.

57   Larry Buchanan et al., "Black Lives Matter May Be the Largest Movement in U.S. History," *New York Times*, July 3, 2020, https://www.nytimes.com/interactive/2020/07/03/us/george-floyd-protests-crowd-size.html.

58   Rich Moran et al., "Police Views, Public Views," Pew Research Center, January 11, 2017, https://www.pewresearch.org/social-trends/2017/01/11/police-views-public-views/.

59   Matt Vasilogambros, "The Feds Are Investigating Local Police Departments Again. Here's What to Expect," Pew, May 3, 2021, https://www.pewtrusts.org/en/research-and-analysis/blogs/stateline/2021/05/03/the-feds-are-investigating-local-police-departments-again-heres-what-to-expect.

60   Rashawn Ray, *Ethnic and Racial Studies*, 40, 11 (2017), https://www.tandfonline.com/toc/rers20/40/11.

61   Rashawn Ray, "Black Lives Matter at 10 Years: 8 ways the movement has been highly effective," Brookings, October 12, 2022, https://www.brookings.edu/blog/how-we-rise/2022/10/12/black-lives-matter-at-10-years-what-impact-has-it-had-on-policing/.

62   Kim Parker et al., "Generation Z Looks a Lot Like Millennials on Key Social and Political Issues," Pew Research Center, January 17, 2019, https://www.pewresearch.org/social-trends/2019/01/17/generation-z-looks-a-lot-like-millennials-on-key-social-and-political-issues/.

Chapter 7

63   Larry Greenemeier, "False news travels 6 times faster on Twitter than truthful news," PBS News Hour, March 9, 2018, https://www.pbs.org/newshour/science/false-news-travels-6-times-faster-on-twitter-than-truthful-news.

Chapter 8

64   Federal Election Commission, "Political Action Committees (PACs)," https://www.fec.gov/press/resources-journalists/political-action-committees-pacs/.

65   Federal Election Commission, "Political Action Committees (PACs)."

66   Jane Mayer, "The Case of Al Franken," *New Yorker*, July 22, 2019, https://www.newyorker.com/magazine/2019/07/29/the-case-of-al-franken.

Chapter 9

67   Matthew Syed, *Black Box Thinking: Why Most People Never Learn from Their Mistakes—But Some Do* (New York: Portfolio, 2015).

68   Alex Young, "Winston Marshall to Take Leave of Absence from Mumford and Sons Following Andy Ngo Tweet," Consequence Sound, March 9, 2021, https://consequence.net/2021/03/winston-marshall-apology-andy-ngo/.

69   https://mrwinstonmarshall.medium.com/why-im-leaving-mumford-sons-e6e73-1bbc255.

Case Study: Michelle McFarland

[70] Monica Palmer, Twitter post, March 8, 2020, 12:54 p.m., https://twitter.com/monicaspalmer/status/1236696859604811776.

Index